[illegible] biogra[illegible]
Hitler and *The Monks of War.*

'What a good book this makes; one of the best published in 1993 in my opinion. It is honest, well-informed and beautifully written.'

JOHN MARTIN ROBINSON,
Evening Standard

OTHER BOOKS BY DESMOND SEWARD

The Monks of War: the military religious orders
The Hundred Years War: the English in France 1337-1453
Monks and Wine
Richard III: England's Black Legend
Henry V as Warlord
Naples, a travellers' companion
Byzantium: a journey and a guide (*with Susan Mountgarret*)
Napoleon and Hitler: a Comparative Biography
Metternich: the first European

THE DANCING SUN

JOURNEYS TO THE MIRACLE SHRINES

DESMOND SEWARD

Fount
An Imprint of HarperCollins*Publishers*

Fount Paperbacks is an Imprint of
HarperCollins*Religious*
Part of HarperCollins*Publishers*
77–85 Fulham Palace Road,
Hammersmith, London W6 8JB

First published in 1993 by Macmillan London

This edition published in Great Britain
in 1994 by Fount Paperbacks
1 3 5 7 9 10 8 6 4 2

A catalogue record for this book is
available from the British Library

ISBN 0 00 627821 3

Printed and bound in Great Britain by
HarperCollinsManufacturing Glasgow

IN MEMORY OF E

But I am also the fiery life of the divine essence – I flame above the beauty of the fields; I shine in the waters; in the sun, the moon and the stars, I burn.

HILDEGARD OF BINGEN, *Liber divinorum operum*

ACKNOWLEDGEMENTS

My first debt is to Julian Allason – who has seen the sun dance – for unfailing encouragement, for inspired suggestions at every stage and, above all, for otherwise unobtainable information about Medjugorje.

Among others whom I must thank are:

Count and Countess Josef Czernin de Chudenic; Dr Andrzej Ciechanowiecki; HE Dr Tadeusz de Virion; the late Dr Karl Eibenschütz; Fr Richard Foley, SJ; Mr Mark Fudakowski; Monsignor A. N. Gilbey; Archpriest Sergei Hackel; Miss Sonya Hlutkowsky; Mrs Anita Tyszkiewicz Hooper; Miss Zofia Korzeniowska; Mr Hubert Kos; Fr Stanislaw Kowałski; Bishop Michael Kuchmiak; Prince Franz Lobkowicz; Mr Michal z Lobkowicz; Mrs Macdonald of Clanranald; Miss Kate Macdonald; Lady Moncreiffe of that Ilk; Fr Zinovi Stepanovich Mykut; Count Juliusz Ostrowski; Professor Dr Jan Ostrowski; Mme Karoline Poupova; Prince Mikołaj Radziwiłł; Dom Julian Rochford, OSB; Dr Anatoly Vassilievich Shevel; Fr Simon Stefanowicz; Dr Max Thurnauer; Major David Trappes-Lomax; Mr Piers Wauchope; Mr Constantine Zelenko; and Fr Jan Zemanek.

The author and publishers would like to thank the following who have kindly given permission for use of copyright material:

Cambridge University Press for permission to quote from *The Medieval Manichee* by Sir Steven Runciman

Darton, Longman & Todd for permission to quote from *Walk to Jerusalem* by Gerard Hughes

Eyre Methuen for permission to quote from *Brideshead Revisited* and *Officers and Gentlemen* by Evelyn Waugh

Everyman for permission to quote from the introduction by T. S. Eliot to *Pascal's Pensées*

Faith Press for permission to quote from *Witness to Apparitions and Persecution in the USSR* by Joseph Terelya

Fowler Wright for permission to quote from *Medjugorje Retreat* by Robert Faricy

William Heinemann Ltd for permission to quote from 'A Visit to Morel' by Graham Greene

John Murray for permission to quote from *A Time to Keep Silence* by Patrick Leigh-Fermor

John Murray for permission to quote from *The Polish Way* by Adam Zamoyski

Penguin Books for permission to quote from Roy Campbell's translation of the poems of St John of the Cross

Viking for permission to quote from *Powers of Darkness, Powers of Light* by John Cornwell

Weidenfeld & Nicolson for permission to quote from *Alone of All Her Sex* by Marina Warner

Every effort has been made to trace all the copyright holders but if any has been inadvertently overlooked, the author and publishers will be pleased to make the necessary arrangement at the first opportunity.

CONTENTS

PROLOGUE

Doubts

I falter where I firmly trod,
  And falling with my weight of cares
  Upon the world's great altar-stairs
That slope thro' darkness up to God,

I stretch lame hands of faith, and grope . . .

TENNYSON, IN MEMORIAM

Seventy-five years ago, the Virgin appeared at Fatima, the sun dancing in the sky over a terrified crowd. This book looks for links between Fatima and other places where the sun has danced and the Mother of God has warned of disasters which threaten the entire world. It is also an account of someone rediscovering his faith – perhaps.

I was an increasingly sceptical Catholic, whose faith was not so much a state of mind as a series of affirmations of belief in the face of growing doubt. If a sense of sustainment by a God who was supposed to listen (but who didn't say much in reply) might be lost, so too might my fear of damnation. I knew many Catholics who seemed happier for abandoning their religion, despite that other spectre, personal extinction. One of them asked me, 'Who wants to live for ever?'

As T. S. Eliot put it, 'Every man who thinks and lives by thought must have his own scepticism, that which stops at the question, that which ends in denial, or that which leads to faith.'

In my case the question would be asked during an investigation of the paranormal, at shrines where the Virgin was supposed to have appeared. If the sun really had danced at these shrines, then the solar system would surely have collapsed, destroying the Earth. Or so I thought at first.

All my background made me want to believe in a miraculous explanation. I had pleasant memories of Ampleforth and its Benedictines. A spoilt, only child who had never been away to school before and who loathed games, nervous, distrustful and bookish – my hobby was 'incunables', books printed before 1500 – in theory I should have been miserable at such a place. It had a name for being tough and Spartan; I had heard of a boy who broke down under the regime and had to be taken away. Yet I came to love it.

I cannot exaggerate how romantic mid-twentieth-century Ampleforth seemed to my young eyes. If the grey limestone buildings were ugly, they were impressive and in a beautiful setting – I shall never forget that marvellous valley. There were ruined abbeys within walking distance, Byland and Rievaulx, whose ghosts came alive in the monastery church, where the old Latin liturgy was celebrated with great splendour and the Gregorian chant had an almost hypnotic effect. The last enchantments of the Middle Ages kept all their magic amid the Yorkshire moors.

It was a very self-contained world. Most of the monks had been through the school themselves, and some of the lay masters too; even the village doctor was an Amplefordian. It was said – I don't know how accurately – that the monastery lands were fifteen miles in circumference. The abbot's banner flew from the College Tower while across the valley Gilling Castle, half-Tudor, half-Palladian, housed the prep-school. The place resembled some princely abbey of the Holy Roman Empire. (There was still a prayer for the Holy Roman Emperor in our Missals, with the note 'This prayer is not now said, the Holy Roman Empire being vacant.') Yet at the same time it was very English indeed.

The romantic atmosphere was enhanced by the recusant tradition, much in evidence. The recusants were those old land-owning families whose loyalty to Rome had ensured the survival of Catholicism in England. For generations they had paid for their fidelity with the loss of all political and professional advancement; until 1829 no Papist could stand for Parliament or hold a commission in the army or the navy; till the 1890s they were unable to go to the universities. The names of the great recusant cousinhood rang out like a litany in the books we were given to read about their sufferings during the Elizabethan and seventeenth-century persecutions or as Jacobites: Scrope, Dormer, Weld, Stourton, Throckmorton, Hornyold, Tempest, de Hoghton, Stonor, Clifford, Howard, Eyston, Charlton, Fitzherbert, Riddell, Plowden, Trafford, Blount, Nevill and the rest.

A man of recusant ancestry himself, Dom Paul Nevill, the headmaster from the 1920s to the 1950s, was inspired by their memory. His ideal was the recusant gentleman. If a boy did not possess the blood, at least he could acquire the outlook; this included a fierce tribal loyalty, together with stubborn resistance to change and an indifference to the rest of the world's disapproval, even to its hostility – which may explain why the recusants have numbered so many eccentrics. Key books for producing such paragons were Robert Hugh Benson's *Come Rack, Come Rope*, Chambers's *Life of St Thomas More* and Evelyn Waugh's life of Edmund Campion, a Jesuit hero martyred under Elizabeth. We never had fireworks on Guy Fawkes' Night – 'too dangerous' – but we had them if the school won a football match. On the very rare occasions when we penetrated into the monastery, we saw that its walls were hung with proclamations for the arrest of recusant priests, or broadsheets recounting how they had been hanged, drawn and quartered.

Evelyn Waugh's novels cannot be understood without some knowledge of the recusant world. His heroes, the Crouchback family, are recusants. (Mr Crouchback senior was modelled on a Scrope.) The Flytes aren't. Bridie admits, 'it's not as though we were old Catholics with everyone on the estate coming to Mass.' However, Lady Marchmain is: her family 'was typical of the

Catholic squires of England; from Elizabeth's reign till Victoria's they lived sequestered lives, among their tenantry and their kinsmen, sending their sons to school abroad, often marrying there, if not with a score of families like themselves, debarred from all preferment'.

Recusants pride themselves on being English of the English, descendants of men and women who resisted a new, foreign, religion (and a foreign dynasty), people of the English countryside. No one's origins could have been less recusant than mine. An Anglo-Irishman who claimed to be descended from a cornet of horse in Cromwell's Army of Ireland, my great-grandfather James Seward became a Catholic on his marriage in 1841. His sons were partners in a firm of Bordeaux wine merchants while the zenith of my father's career was as an industrialist in France with a factory at Asnières. I was born in Paris, in a White Russian nursing home. We lived in the rue de Longchamps and then in the Boulevard Pérèire – opposite Rudolf Sieber and his wife Marlene Dietrich who, I'm proud to say, admired me in my pram. Then we moved to Bucharest, to '*Opt, Strada Vasile Conte*' (8, Count Vasile Street) so that my first words were Romanian, learnt from Anuska, my Hungarian nanny. But for the war, I would probably have made my life in France. At Ampleforth I was reticent about this background and sang with fervour the recusant anthem 'Faith of our Fathers':

> 'Our Fathers, chained in prisons dark,
> Were still in heart and conscience free . . .

The monks fascinated me. At first I found them alarming. On my second night I ran into the headmaster, walking up the hill in the mist towards my house, a tall brooding figure with a black hood drawn over his head. He told me to come to his study on Wednesday at midday, when a half-holiday began. I expected to be beaten for some crime which I had unknowingly committed. On presenting myself, without a word he marched me along long passages into the monastery, down into a basement room where another monk was waiting. 'This is Father Barnabas,' said the headmaster. 'He will show you our incunables.' For an hour I handled books printed just before or just after the discovery of America; Aldines and Wynkyn de Wordes, a Nuremberg Chronicle (with its blank last pages on which to record the final age of the world). I heard the tragic tale of the stolen Richard Pynson. Ampleforth was sympathetic to oddities such as myself, even if I found it difficult to make friends.

Far from being repressive, the monks were astonishingly broad minded. I disliked my housemaster intensely, a dislike which was reciprocated, but I had to respect him. An exquisite water-colourist whose hobby was Aristotle, he was an advocate of legalized brothels while, I hasten to add, in no way suggesting that we patronize them; I can still hear the tones in which he cautioned us to beware of 'The painted ladies of Piccadilly'.

I hunted over the moors with the school beagles (they met at places with names like Fangdale Beck), followed the local foxhounds on foot, bicycled to inspect tumuli and monastic remains. The atmosphere suited my preferred reading very well; Helen Waddell's *Wandering Scholars* and Johan Huizinga's *Waning of the Middle Ages* are still among my favourite books. The first introduced me to medieval Latin verse and the *Carmina Burana*; the second re-created a wonderful world in which terrible cruelty and devouring pessimism went hand-in-hand with brilliant colour and total belief. The painting which I admired most in all art was the Isenheim altarpiece of Mathis Grünewald, with its tortured Christ (disliked by the water-colourist as 'a monstrosity'). I fear that my beliefs were alarmingly Gothic; hell-fire, devils and most of us damned.

And yet, perhaps surprisingly, although a miserably solemn boy when I arrived, I had learnt to laugh. I don't think I have ever laughed so much in my life. Some of my laughter was a little cruel, as when my new housemaster (who had replaced the old water-colourist) was rumoured to have been caught poaching by

Lord Faversham's keeper, red handed, with a brace of pheasants in each hand.

This housemaster, Dom Jerome Lambert, was very likable. A true countryman, a keen fisherman as well as a fine shot, he and a friend once provided enough brown trout for the entire house's breakfast. I remember with less pleasure how he took me out at two o'clock in the morning to catch poachers who had set 300 snares for rabbits. (Those were the days before myxamatosis.) 'Here's a whistle – if you blow it, they *might* think the police were coming.' Luckily, they had already removed their snares. He diagnosed my depression, telling me how to deal with it. 'When you're up, remember that you're going to come down; when you're down that you'll go up.' He instilled a conviction that the Catholic religion was the most natural thing in the world, 'common sense'.

I don't want to give the impression that life at Ampleforth was some sort of pious idyll. One could not go home at the end of a bad day; a term was an interminable three months. Tensions built up, occasionally leading to combats of real ferocity – the young male can be a very savage animal. I remember opening the door of what I thought was an empty classroom, to find two boys slamming away at each other, panting and covered in blood. Once I challenged someone who was tormenting me to a fight of this sort but he backed down, to my infinite relief.

Even so, there was a strong emphasis on our existence here being a mere preparation for the next. When the headmaster of Manchester Grammar School asked Fr Paul if he thought he was educating his boys for the modern world, he replied, 'We educate our boys for death.' By the time I was sixteen I hoped to become a monk. Then, suddenly, all the zest went out of my religion; I still believed but all the emotion had gone. (I gather this is not uncommon among boys of that age.) My convictions settled into a pattern which I afterwards realized was very like Jansenism; not only did I think that very few could be saved but I was inclined to believe that men were more or less predestined to heaven or hell –

though I didn't know where I was going myself. Some of my 'Jansenism' may have been due to my tendency to depression. I remained distrustful, with very few friends.

Despite the plainchant and the incunables, in those days the school's intellectual climate tended to be a little Philistine; inevitably, since it was trying to produce all-rounders – the games master was also the art master. A boy in my house read Auden and Day-Lewis, but he was a rarity. Belloc or Chesterton, those were the poets, even if I was taught to appreciate Herrick and Andrew Marvell. We were encouraged to enjoy Evelyn Waugh though I suspect this was largely because he was a 'Catholic novelist'. (Fr Paul made everyone going up to the universities read *Brideshead Revisited*, presumably to prepare them for the temptations which lay ahead.) Yet a history master of genius, Tom Charles-Edwardes, told me to try the satirical, cerebral, Regency novels of Thomas Love Peacock – 'makes you think a bit, especially the footnotes' – besides encouraging me to write.

When I was about seventeen I received a sound vaccination against Marxism by a monk who I think must have been a party member at some stage. It was based around *Das Kapital*, with some potted Engels and Lenin; I was given an explanation of how the dialectic was supposed to work. Even at that tender age Marx's Law of Increasing Misery struck me as unconvincing. I decided that the dialectic was never going to achieve self-realization and that the system was about as up-to-date as a horsehair sofa, an impression which never left me.

Socially I had had closer contact, of a sort, with Communists than most boys. Between the wars my parents acquired many Russian friends in Paris and Bucharest. Among them, and very close, was Katya Krasina. Her father was the Old Bolshevik L. B. Krasin, who had worked closely with Lenin from as early as 1905; (it was Krasin who suggested that Lenin should be embalmed). Later he was Commissar for Trade until, if the rumours are true, he was poisoned by Stalin. He had prudently sent his wife and children to Stockholm in 1916, just before what modern Russians call the 'Bolshevik Putsch'; a director of Siemens-Schuckert, he had no wish for them to suffer with the rest of the bourgeoisie. But most of our Russian friends – such as Nina and Mikhail from Odessa in the basement at Strada Vasile Conte or old Mme Anding from Moscow next door – were Whites, so that my early childhood was full of horror stories about the Revolution.

My tendency to depression grew worse at Cambridge, following the usual manic pattern of alternating gloom and wild high spirits. At first my Jansenism was fuelled by my discovery of François Mauriac's novels. Since my cousins were Bordeaux wine merchants (at one point my father and I were almost the only male Sewards who spoke English without a French accent), the background was far from alien, though if would be unfair to say that *Nœud de Vipères* in any way described my relations. I had a marvellous university chaplain (and family friend) in Monsignor Alfred Gilbey, and also an impressive Catholic tutor in the historian Oliver Macdonagh who warned us constantly that Marxism was infiltrating every aspect of intellectual life. Fatuously I didn't believe him; I know better now. Meanwhile, young women and whisky began to tempt me. I found I was gregarious, although still very suspicious of strangers. For a time I grew much less interested in religion.

I did not work nearly hard enough at the history I was supposed to be reading. I was a rather wild undergraduate who drank far too much, went to as many parties as possible and had a first love affair with a clever, very pretty girl at Newnham, who introduced me to Blake, Kafka and James Joyce. I read lots of novels, especially American novels: Theodore Dreiser, Scott Fitzgerald and above all William Faulkner. I read English novelists too; E. M. Forster (to be seen sitting cloth-capped in King's Fellows' Garden) and Virginia Woolf. For a short time I was impressed by the priorities of the Bloomsbury Group (consciousness of beauty and human relationships) until a Catholic friend commented, 'Yes, but what else?' I was non-political, if vaguely traditionalist and an admirer of the romantic though reasoned conservatism of Edmund Burke. But it was a period of great mental stimulation, more than I could take.

While I am proud of having been to Cambridge, only less than of being born in Paris, my fits of depression there were worse than any I can remember. However wonderful the setting, however gilded the days, youthful intensity and fenland mist proved a venomous brew. I felt much better after going down. The next decade was spent in trying to find a way of life which would let me do what I wanted; to write about what interested me. Neither employers nor publishers were sympathetic. Throughout, I retained my almost cosmic pessimism, never expecting to live till I was fifty; both my grandfathers had died at forty-two while my father's career had foundered when he was in his forties.

Over the years my faith waxed and waned. A revival in my late twenties nearly landed me in a monastery – 'Think of the poor abbot!' said a friend – but there was also a period in my thirties when I stayed away from the Sacraments, though I went on going to church. Another revival followed.

Although I remained a practising Catholic, I read very little theology – no von Hugel, let alone Küng or Schillebeeckx. Later I tried the last two; the first analyses religion away, the other reduces it to mere symbolism. I agree with Graham Greene when he says that such theologians may be Christians but they are scarcely Catholics, whose faith is belief in the inexplicable, not the credible.

On the other hand I went through the medieval English mystics: Walter Hilton, Julian of Norwich and the *Cloud*. I dipped into Meister Eckhardt, tried unsuccessfully to like Thomas à

Kempis's *Imitation of Christ*, for a time found helpful Brother Lawrence – the seventeenth-century Carmelite – and was impressed by his contemporary, the Carthusian Innocent le Masson. I read a good deal of Thomas Merton; the early books before he went crazy. Mysticism and contemplation have always appealed to me more than active Christianity which, since I am neither a mystic nor a contemplative, is of course a damning admission.

For a time mysticism had a very strong appeal indeed. I remember reading, bewildered, the verse of St John of the Cross:

> I entered in, I know not where,
> And I remained, though knowing naught,
> Transcending knowledge with my thought . . .
>
> So borne aloft, so drunken-reeling,
> So rapt was I, so swept away . . .

Teresa of Avila disturbed me, however much I admired her; I didn't care for her entrails being pierced with a burning lance and the pain causing 'intense sweetness'. I very much liked the sound of Nicholas Love, the fifteenth-century Carthusian of Mount Grace in Yorkshire, who assured his fellow monks that contemplative prayer could make the soul sing like 'an throstle-cock'. But I never truly fathomed what any of these writers were trying to convey. Once I experienced what I *hoped* might have been a mystical experience. When about twenty-nine and going through the most fervently religious phase of my life – attending Mass every day and even trying to help other people – I was praying in Southwark Cathedral when suddenly I had a sense of time having stopped, of everything being in suspense. It never occurred again. Shortly after, I began a disastrous affair with a very odd woman which turned me into a lapsed Catholic for two or three years. Ironically, I was brought back to the path by a Carthusian.

I sometimes stay at monasteries, though not so often as in the past when I had to hold down uncongenial jobs in order to support my writing habit, and needed an escape to reduce the pressure. After a week of going to bed at nine p.m. (with sleeping pills) and rising at four thirty a.m., of silence, simple food and no alcohol, I would emerge a new man. Sometimes I dreamt of becoming a monk, dreams which I soon dismissed; I don't enjoy the exclusive company of my own sex and am miserable without female friendship. After I started writing full time, I realized that my monastic fantasies had been the purest escapism.

Yet I suspect there is something of a monk in a surprising number of men, if only they knew it. In *A Time to Keep Silence* Patrick Leigh-Fermor has written of the 'healing and mysterious enchantment' of religious houses. Although not a Catholic, he is well aware of the value of monastic sojourns:

> For, in the seclusion of a cell – an existence whose quietness is only varied by the silent meals, the solemnity of ritual and long solitary walks in the woods – the troubled waters of the mind grow still and clear, and much that is hidden away and all that clouds it floats away to the surface and can be skimmed away; and after a time one reaches a state of peace that is unthought of in the ordinary world.

That has been my experience too.

My faith was once so strong that I could never have given way to despair, whatever the circumstances. Save for one thing. I had a terrible fear of going insane, of losing my reason. There had been a certain amount of insanity in my paternal grandmother's family and I retained a dread of this until early middle age. Anyone who said to me, after some piece of erratic behaviour, 'Desmond, you're mad!' made an enemy for life.

My religious reading was far from exclusively Catholic. As a very young man Dostoevsky was my favourite author. I had been put on to him when I was about seventeen by a monk, the water-colourist, who said truly enough that he was 'powerful stuff'. From him I gained an inkling of the nearness of good and evil – how a murderer or a whore may also be a saint. During my early twenties a Jesuit warned me that if I went on 'living my life like a Russian novel' I must accept the consequences, though I don't think my sins were in quite the same league as those of Raskolnikov or a member of the Karamozov family. But Prince Myshkin in *The Idiot* fascinated me, as did Stavroguin in *The Devils*. Dostoevsky led me to the ex-Marxist Nikolai Berdyaev, with his conviction that a fight against God may be an affirmation of him if it is against an unworthy concept of God, and with his understanding of the human face as the greatest triumph of spirit over material chaos.

Through Dostoevsky and Berdyaev I encountered the Orthodox Church. I read Gregory Palamas and Nicholas Cabasilas, dipped into the *Philokalia*, besides reading the writers of the amazing Russian religious renaissance in exile of the twentieth century – Soloviev, Bulgakov, Elchaninov, Zornov. I learnt to admire the 'apophatic' tradition (that all we can say about God is what we don't know about him), and the approach to God through beauty. I acquired a lasting interest in Orthodoxy, with a conviction that the greatest disaster which has befallen mankind is the schism between Catholics and Orthodox. I even contemplated joining the Orthodox Church, though this was partly in order to marry a divorced girl. (Orthodoxy allows three marriages.) A Russian priest dissuaded me, pointing out that I was 'too much a man of the West'.

I also developed an interest in Martin Luther, the 'seven-fold devil' of my school days, trying to learn German in order to read his hymns and *Table Talk*. I was intrigued by his conquest of the fear of damnation, impressed on being told that the only person who had ever understood Luther's soul was J. S. Bach, and moved by the tragedy of the man and his career. While heartened by his doctrine of justification by faith, and by Paul Tillich's rephrasing of it ('man cannot accept himself, therefore God accepts him'), I doubt if I ever grasped what either was talking about.

Save for its seventeenth-century poets and divines, and its beautiful Bible and Prayer Book – which it has now thrown away – Anglicanism never appealed to me very much, although it is the religion of some of my closest friends. If I'm to have Catholicism, I want the real thing; if Protestantism, then Luther and Bach. I am cautious about ecumenism, save for reconciliation with Orthodoxy. I do not admire prelates who trumpet their disbelief in basic doctrines, regardless of the anguish this may cause simpler members of their flock. What does one make of pastors who tolerate sleeping with one's neighbour but not with one's neighbour's wife? In any case, for me a form of Christianity without the Madonna is an emotional impossibility.

No novelist moves me more than Graham Greene. I like his very personal Catholicism; before the 1960s he was scarcely considered a Catholic by his Church, though outsiders knew more about Papists, and the way their minds worked, from his books than from any other source. Some things I don't like, such as his dismissal of Hell or Satan. But I am fascinated by the way in which he emphasizes the place of *doubt* in a Catholic's life. Years ago, just after coming down from Cambridge, a Dominican told me that it was better to live with one's faith on a knife-edge. Reading Greene helped me to see what he meant.

What Greene found hardest to believe in, initially, was God Himself. When convinced of the existence of 'something we call God' (he disliked the word's anthropomorphic tinge) he was able to believe. Much later, he acquired a taste for miracles. 'If we are to believe in some power infinitely above us in capacity and knowledge, magic does inevitably form part of our belief – or rather magic is the term we use for the mysterious and the inexplicable,' he wrote in *Ways of Escape*. He felt a need to accept miracles.

Born a Catholic, I find my own experience has been quite different. I was emotionally convinced long before I had a mature intellect. Yet only recently have I made myself confront miracles. I avoided them, refusing to go on pilgrimage to Lourdes.

*

This was not easy after I joined the Order of Malta, whose knights go to Lourdes annually as part of their hospitaller tradition. They defended the Holy Land during the Crusades, continuing the war on the infidel from Rhodes and then Malta, until Napoleon evicted them. Since 1834 their headquarters have been the Palazzo Malta at Rome; the smallest sovereign state in the world, the Order exchanges ambassadors with over fifty countries and issues its own passports. Membership is largely restricted to Catholics who can show proofs of nobility, though not so many are needed as in the past – only one of a hundred years in the male line being sufficient for the lowest noble grade. (In Britain the Order considers 'nobility' to be possession of a coat of arms on record at the College of Arms or the Lyon Court of Chivalry.)

I was invited to join after writing *The Monks of War*, a book on military orders – Hospitallers, Templars, Teutonic Knights, and so on. Luckily my family had had their arms confirmed in 1844. My proposer was an impeccably recusant friend, with ancestors who had been hanged, drawn and quartered for plotting to replace Elizabeth I with the Catholic Mary Queen of Scots. (Once I asked him if his family had been in the Gunpowder Plot. 'No,' he said, with a grin. 'We had our own.')

It is hard for a Knight of Malta not to be fascinated by his Order's history, and by its trust in help from God and His Mother. Every September the knights celebrate the relief of Malta in 1565 with a Mass of thanksgiving, the 'Vittoria' Mass. Until the loss of their island the *Capitana* (the general of the galley's flagship) went into action flying the Order's great banner, red with a white cross, which bore the legend *Vias tuas Domine demonstra mihi* – 'Show unto me thy ways O Lord'. A banner of the Virgin flew from every mainmast, banners of St John the Baptist from the masts fore and aft. Mass was said daily at sunrise on the poop, while the knights prepared for battle by confessing to the ship's chaplain and taking communion. Every day the Little Office of the Dead was said by men who, whether in the desert or at sea, were generally outnumbered and anticipated death as much as faced it, whose only hope was God's direct intervention.

Though a shadow of when it ruled in Malta, let alone when it defended Jerusalem, the 'Sovereign Military Order' remains an inspiration to its members. The company of so many cheerful, like-minded believers, several of whom I had known at school – even the Grand Master is an Amplefordian – was to be a great support, while I acquired friends all over the world.

Looking back, I can see why Catholicism became so central to my life. As a boy and as a young man, I was only too ready to accept the identity which it offered, while it attracted me as a still point, emotionally and intellectually; if reason could not explain the human condition, then a God above reason made sense. Much more important, however, was the conviction that all men are flawed by nature. Time and again I have felt that I was saved, not only from disaster but from doing very real evil, by what the priests call grace. Beyond that, I needed an insurance against infinity, the terrifying endlessness of eternity – '*Le silence éternel de ces espaces infinis m'effraie.*'

I welcomed the Second Vatican Council. If the first had been divinely inspired, so must be the second. General acceptance by the Church was, in Newman's words, 'the ultimate guarantee of revealed truth'. Nor did I question its decrees, the directives for reform and renewal, for new roads to God. 'The ideas of the French Revolution have at last penetrated the Church,' an ancient monsignor said to me gloomily. Well, not all of them were so bad.

What I questioned was the way in which the decrees were interpreted. The old Christian Europe, the entire heritage of Rome, the Middle Ages, the Renaissance and the Baroque went by the board, jettisoning the 'blessed mutter of the Mass' together with Gregorian chant, Palestrina and Mozart. Catholic

England no longer had any time for the recusant tradition which I had been taught to revere during my youth.

At some French seminaries the real presence of Christ in the Host was compared to Wagner attending the Bayreuth Festival in spirit – 'he died long ago, but you know he's there'. Hell and the Devil disappeared from sermons. Devotion to the saints was discouraged, even devotion to the Virgin; the Rosary was said less and less. The bad old days before the Council were condemned again and again. A 'wider perspective' was everything – meaning humanism or a crude form of Marxism.

The Church was attacked from within by theologians who claimed to reflect the spirit of the Second Vatican Council while rejecting its decrees. They set human reason above faith and put this world before the next, saw Christ as man instead of God. 'Our Christianity is at best neo-capitalism', was a phrase often heard. They banished the idea of the holy, turning the Mass into 'a celebration of the People by and for the People'. Private prayer was condemned as a contemptible obsession with personal problems. They wanted a Church which was little more than a social-work agency for agnostics. They reflected the mortal sickness of Western civilization.

Once most Catholics would have agreed with Tennyson:

> Hold thou the good: define it well:
>   For fear divine Philosophy
>   Should push beyond her mark, and be
> Procuress to the Lords of Hell.

That sort of wisdom became anathema. Dr Faustus might have found a place among the new theologians without too much difficulty. What was happening all seemed uncomfortably like Newman's description of Antichrist preparing the way for the 'general Apostasy', offering illumination, science and enlargement of mind. 'He scoffs at times gone by,' wrote the Cardinal. 'He scoffs at every institution which reveres them.'

Needless to say, the overwhelming majority of Catholics did not at first share these new views, which at the start were restricted to a tiny if noisy 'élite' of opinionated intellectuals. But soon there was confusion everywhere; the old order and certainty, which had been such a feature of the Catholic religion, was destroyed. Bewildered priests, monks and nuns left in droves, while ominously recruitment to the priesthood plummeted as did church-going. Monasteries were shut down, religious orders died out, seminaries were closed. All that the remaining clergy could do was to mutter lamely, 'It was so easy to be a Catholic before the Council', implying that for nearly 2000 years most of us had believed from mental and spiritual inadequacy.

For a long time I kept my nerve and remained undismayed. Not only was I temperamentally averse to change but I was also equipped to resist it. I had always been a natural conservative, looking to the past and not the future for inspiration. The earliest book from which I could remember deriving any sort of opinion of my own was Fenimore Cooper's *Last of the Mohicans*, given to me for my ninth or tenth birthday. The two Red Indian heroes who were the last of their tribe awoke in me a deep fascination with dying breeds and lost causes which has never left me. I find glamour in species harried to extinction (wolves, bears, pine-martens), doomed tongues such as Irish or Basque, and hopeless loyalties like Jacobitism. I was never frightened of becoming an anachronism; anachronisms don't date. Even so, every time I went to church and attended the new services I felt an increasing sense of melancholy which began to verge on despair.

At about this time I came across a group of French cousins whom I had not previously met. They turned out to be kindred spirits, with just the right dash of Irish blood. Among them was a writer whose work I admired enormously. A painter and film producer blinded during a mugging attack in New York – sulphuric acid was thrown into his eyes – Hugues de Montalembert wrote semi-autobiographical novels. He shared my passion for the exotic, for black humour and for Middle Europe. As for religion, he was 'feeling his way back' to Christianity. His great-great-grandfather once told the French Chamber of Peers, '*Nous sommes les fils des croisés et jamais nous ne recoulons devant les fils de Voltaire*' – we are the sons of the crusaders and we shall never retreat before the sons of Voltaire. But today Catholicism is everywhere in full retreat.

French Catholicism has spiritual traditions and practices which can be very different from those of English Catholicism. One is a belief in the 'Sacrifice' – offering one's life for somebody else. I was told of a father with a son hooked on drugs who did this; within a year the father was dead and his son had become a Carthusian novice. My cousins disliked the changes intensely though they resisted the blandishments of Archbishop Lefebvre and the '*Intégristes*' (who rejected the decrees of the Second Vatican Council and insisted on keeping the old Tridentine Mass).

During the mid-1980s I began to find the liturgy intolerable – the clumsy tax-form English, banal music and fabricated new ceremonies. Now I knew what was meant by the word 'kitsch'. I could accept the end of Latin, though I mourned it, but not the departure of beauty and dignity. In the old days a priest saying Mass was distanced from the congregation; now he was thrust at them, so that it was disastrous if he had a less than pleasing personality. Nor, like Graham Greene, did I care for the freedom given to priests to introduce endless extempore prayers and turn the Mass into one long sermon. I also detested the emphasis on group worship – 'an on-going community event'.

Above all, I deplored the banishment of the numinous. (The word comes from the Latin *numen* and means a cloud veiling the Divine.) No longer did I feel a sense of awe. The emphasis, so it seemed to me at any rate, was no longer on God but on the priest and the congregation. My attitude was not some aesthete's revulsion at the destruction of an ancient work of art, nor an 'elitist' shudder at popularization. It was the gut reaction of an ordinary, reasonably well-educated man to the demythologizing of a mystery – *the* mystery. More and more, though not invariably, I felt that God was absent from these new Masses. If I was in a minority, I knew a surprising number of Catholics who had stopped going to church because of the changes and I suspected that many others had done so too. Occasionally I found myself sneaking off to the Liturgy at the Russian Orthodox cathedral, especially when it was in English.

I told a chaplain of the Order of Malta about my unhappiness. He quoted St Peter's response when Christ asked the Twelve if they meant to desert him, 'Lord, to whom else shall we go?' Yet having once been completely at home within the Catholic Church, I felt that I had become an outsider.

My alienation was due to more than change in the Church, probably to some form of mid-life crisis. Increasingly severe bouts of depression may have had something to do with it. Self-pity at never having married and being childless? As Belloc puts it:

> A lost thing could I never find,
> Nor a broken thing mend:
> And I fear I shall be all alone
> When I get towards the end.
> Who will there be to comfort me
> Or who will be my friend?

I had had a reasonably happy and rewarding life, but separation from the companion of a decade, followed by her death, had shaken me. She haunts many pages in this book.

I was suffering from doubts about almost every aspect of Catholicism. I wanted to go on believing – disbelief was a far from easy option – and to whom else could I go?

> The Bat that flits at close of Eve
> Has left the Brain that won't Believe.

But the Bat of William Blake would not leave my brain because it still believed, after a fashion. That arch-heretic Paul Tillich suggests that religion is a sense akin to visual sense or to a sense of music in not being given to all. Well, it had been given to me, though often showing signs of trying to flit at close of Eve. This conflict between belief and disbelief was frequently painful, occasionally anguished. I suspect that it is a conflict experienced by many modern Catholics. ' "Why, it is one of the most common confessions of all for a priest to hear – almost as common as adultery," ' Graham Greene makes one of his characters say. ' "Father, I have lost my faith." The priest, you may be sure, makes it himself often enough at the altar before he receives the Host." ' And Greene was writing long before the Council.

As so often, I went to my copy of Pascal's *Pensées*, the Everyman edition. In his introduction T. S. Eliot observes, 'I can think of no Christian writer, not Newman even, more to be commended than Pascal to those who doubt, but who have the mind to conceive, and the sensibility to feel, the disorder, the futility, the meaninglessness, the mystery of life and suffering, and who can only find peace through a satisfaction of the whole being.'

I re-read the passages in which Pascal argues that the Apostles were either the twelve biggest mugs or the twelve biggest conmen the world has ever seen, or that they were telling the truth when they said Christ rose from the dead. Yet even this had lost its power to calm. I didn't want to end up an agnostic, a 'don't know'. (I could remember reading, in the 1950s, Jung's advice that it was healthier to be an atheist than an agnostic.)

Pascal imagines a man who foreshadows many of my unbelieving friends. This man says, 'I only know that when I leave this world I shall either be annihilated or fall into the hands of an angry God, so I've decided to spend every day of my life without bothering to investigate what's going to happen to me.' Pascal then asks, 'Who has most reason to fear hell? The man who doesn't know whether there's a hell but will certainly be damned if there is one; or the man who's sure there's a hell and hopes to be saved?'

He admits that we can't be certain about religion; it may be true, it may not. But his 'wager' made me even more anxious to go on believing. It runs like this: 'We accept that mathematical infinity exists, if aware we can never hope to grasp what it means. We should accept God in the same way. It's too risky not to. Betting on his existence, living a Christian life, we may go to heaven; if we don't, we end up in hell.'

It's a bet we can't refuse. 'You haven't any choice,' Pascal tells us. 'You're already committed.' May we see the back of the cards? Yes, read the Bible, he answers. 'What harm can choosing this way do you? You'll be a faithful man, honest, humble, grateful, generous, a sincere friend.' The wager can be criticized for reducing salvation to a gamble. Nor does it prove anything. Yet undoubtedly it has persuaded many men and women to search for the hidden God and to go on searching.

I needed a new approach. Pascal's '*Vous êtes déjà embarqués*' seemed to indicate a journey, a pilgrimage. To where?

I had heard of Medjugorje from an old friend, who had watched the sun 'dancing' there some years before. A painter, she depicted water and clouds with a haunting luminosity which conveyed mystery and even holiness. She painted Virgins and angels which, although they were not paintings of visions, gave that impression. What she had seen, beyond question, was the sun at Medjugorje. She described it as spinning like a catherine-wheel, emitting rays of prismatic light, with a black rim as if there was a disk behind it.

I read a lot about Medjugorje. I learnt that the sun had danced at other Marian shrines, or that a silver light had shone, that wherever this occurred the Virgin appeared to warn of the danger of Communism. It first happened at Fatima in 1917, the sun spinning like a catherine-wheel over a crowd of 50,000, her message being that catastrophe threatened the world. She gave the same message in a forest near Turzovka in Slovakia during the 1950s, when hundreds of pilgrims were enveloped in a cone of prismatic light. She appeared at Garabandal, a remote mountain hamlet in northern Spain, in 1961, amid blinding flashes. Similar apparitions and solar phenomena, with the same message, had been taking place at Medjugorje in Herzegovina since 1981. She was seen by half a million witnesses at Hriushiw (pronounced hrooshoo) in the Ukraine in 1987, in flaming robes, floating within a bright orb which rested on a beam of silver light 200 metres high.

Though the sun had not danced at Częstochowa, Poland's national shrine, there appeared to be recordings of phenomena there down the centuries. The 'Black Virgin on the Hill of Light' changed many lives. So too did the Virgin of Svatá Hora, the 'Holy Mountain' in Bohemia.

Oddly enough, till my late thirties I had only a lukewarm devotion to the Virgin, even when at Ampleforth. An Anglican friend assured me pityingly that the Madonna was a goddess taken over from paganism, just as temples had been converted into churches, a substitute earth mother whose cult had been developed to satisfy psychological needs. While disagreeing with her, I had to accept that what she called 'mariolatry' was the biggest of all the many barriers to any real sympathy, let alone unity, between the Church of Rome and the Church of England.

During the 1970s Marina Warner's *Alone of All Her Sex* stressed superficial resemblances between the Mother of God and the Babylonian sky deity Ishtar, who changed one of her lovers into a mole because he told her that she could not give him what he wanted. If for a while Mary's love 'can seem a fortress against frosts, it is only a reed for the sinner who feels the frost-swollen wind of Christ's justice blowing down from heaven, while to the non-believer it seems a wretched placebo'. Marina Warner concluded that 'like Ishtar, the Virgin will recede into legend'. But her identification of the Madonna with Ishtar and with Isis loses most of its credibility when one realizes their cults' association with promiscuity – temples of Isis were little better than brothels. They share one or two very minor features which are coincidental. '"These things are in heathenism, therefore they are not Christian"; we, on the contrary, prefer to say, "these things are in Christianity, therefore they are not heathen",' as Cardinal Newman wrote. Far from declining, the cult of the Virgin Mary thrives.

I do not worship the Virgin. Nor do I see her as 'the fourth Person of the Trinity'. On the other hand I venerate her as God Bearer, the most perfect human being after Christ, with the second most awesome role in history. I believe she is an intercessor, who intercedes with her Son. It has been said that praying to the Mother of God is to insinuate that she is more merciful than her Son. Well, women *are* gentler than men.

What particularly interested me was that the Virgin offered such a challenge to belief. Visionaries were making amazing claims, to have seen her recently and to be continuing to see her. Could I really accept the truth of the apparitions? Here, surely, I would put my faith to the ultimate question.

Some might object that if my pilgrimages were inspired by Pascal's wager, his wager was about belief in God, not about miracles when the Virgin appears and the sun dances. But Pascal was wagering that the whole body of Catholic doctrine is true. And while the Church does not insist that her members believe in miracles, she has recognized as genuine what took place at Fatima in 1917; apparitions, messages, warnings and 'solar miracles'. One day Rome may also accept as genuine what happened at other shrines, above all at Medjugorje.

In the modern world most Christians, including Catholics, distrust the very idea of miracles. They have done so for a long time. 'Give me but a little leave, and I will set before your eyes in brief a stupend, vast, infinite Ocean of incredible madness and folly' wrote Robert Burton in the seventeenth century, beginning his angry account of Religious Melancholy; among such madness and folly he included devotions at Marian shrines and praying for miracles. Yet the real miracles which I wanted to encounter on my journey would be the strengthening of my faith. Nor was I in search of 'blind faith'. I remember reading about a nun in a Bavarian orphanage who lit a 'holy candle' in a crêche; the curtains caught fire and every baby was burnt to death.

I was encouraged during my pilgrimage by the knowledge that other doubting Catholics like me, unsettled by changes in the Church, had been reassured by the shrines. So I was intrigued to find them gently criticized by Gerard Hughes in his *Walk to Jerusalem*, clearly a book of considerable appeal to those who share the author's opinions (though I was puzzled by his being able to travel to Medjugorje on foot and then pass through Greece without, apparently, meeting a single Orthodox priest or layman). He writes:

> Apparition piety has a special appeal to people of rigid views, usually those on the far right politically and theologically, because such a spirituality does not challenge their thinking, but confirms them in their mental idleness and their unwillingness to face change . . .

It is a piety which enables people 'to benefit materially from the unjust social and political structures in which they are living', the author tells us.' Furthermore, 'clergy, who are noted for their devotion to Mary, are often noted for their chauvinist attitude to women.' Quite.

No doubt with the best intentions, and obviously fearing for my sanity, a non-believing friend sent me three quotations. 'Miracles occur only in times and countries where miracles are believed in, and in the presence of those ready to believe in them' (Renan, *Vie de Jésus*). 'Whatever a man prays for, he prays for a miracle. Every prayer reduces itself to this: "Great God, grant that two and two be not four" (Turgenyev). 'The happy do not believe in miracles' (Goethe).

However, neither contempt for 'apparition piety' nor the combined wisdom of Renan, Turgenyev and Goethe could deter me.

— 1 —
Medjugorje

Yes, but you must wager. It is not optional. You are embarked.

PASCAL, *Pensées*

This wondrous Sun begun to comfort earth.

DANTE, *Paradiso*

Flying into the then beautiful city of Mostar in autumn 1990, in a small party, I was suddenly angry with myself for being there at all. Although I was with three other Knights of Malta, I felt even more distrustful than usual. A suspicion that the trip was going to be a waste of time was lulled briefly by the spectacle of the majestic River Neretva, then by a long drive through wild hills, but it revived on reaching Medjugorje with its cheap new hotels, some only half built. The streets were lined with shops selling plaster statuettes, fancy jewellery and gaudy carpets. An English girl told me how the place had changed since she was there in the spring – it would be unrecognizable within five years. Exploring, I at once encountered greed; a glass of the local white wine cost me £2. By the time I went to my bed, which was short and narrow, to be tormented by mosquitoes, I was thoroughly hostile.

Thirty miles west of Mostar, the Herzegovinan capital, Medjugorje is really two villages: Medjugorje proper and Bijakovići. In the Brotjno valley (famous for its wine) up in the mountains, they and the adjoining hamlets were inhabited by a community of about 2000 Croats when the visions began in 1981. The area had been conquered by the Turks in the fifteenth century and freed only in 1878, to be ruled by the Habsburgs till 1918. Throughout the long period of Moslem domination, Catholicism was kept alive by Franciscan friars from the coast, who went on serving Medjugorje's Christians under the Communist regime.

On Wednesday 24 June 1981, midsummer evening, three girls and a boy were walking on the lower slopes of the Crnica mountains near the hamlet of Podbrdo ('Under Hill') – to the south of Medjugorje though in the parish. Ivanka Ivanković, aged fifteen who came from Mostar, and Mirjana Dragičević, aged sixteen, from Sarajevo, were staying at Medjugorje with their grandparents. Vicka Ivanković, fifteen, and the boy Ivan Dragičević, sixteen, were locals. Suddenly the four saw a strange light on the mountainside, then, within the light, a young woman, holding a child. She called to them but, terrified, they ran home.

Next day, led by Ivanka and accompanied by two young people – Marija Pavlović, sixteen, and a ten-year-old boy, Jakov Čolo – they returned, despite the mockery of their parents. Climbing the mountainside, they found themselves confronted by an apparently impenetrable wall of light, so bright that they feared the mountain might melt beneath them. Again they fled. Turning to look back as they ran, they saw that the light had moved on to the hillside opposite, Mount Križevac. The young woman emerged from it, a woman of amazing beauty, in a glow so dazzling that she seemed as if 'clothed with the sun'. Once more she called to them but, panic-stricken, they did not stop until they reached Podbrdo.

On 26 June the six came to the mountain again, accompanied by as many as 5000 people. Seven times they recited the *Oče Naš*, the *Zdravo Marijo* and the *Slava Ocu* (Pater, Ave and Gloria – a local devotion in honour of the Seven Sorrows of the Virgin). They had just followed it with the Creed when, shortly after six p.m., many in the crowd saw three great rays of light pass overhead, and then realized that the children were seeing something very strange indeed. She was so near that the six might have touched her had they dared. Looking about twenty years old, slender and dark-haired with blue eyes, in a grey dress she seemed human enough, though she had what appeared to be a crown of stars upon her head and was standing on a white cloud just above the ground.

'If you are Satan, go away,' said Vicka, who was clutching a jar of holy water for protection. 'Don't be afraid,' came the reply. 'I am the Virgin Mary.' 'Why have you come?' asked Vicka. 'I have come because there are so many good believers here,' answered the Virgin, smiling. 'I want to be among you, to convert and to reconcile.' On their way down the mountain, Marija Pavlović saw the Lady standing in a cross of rainbow-coloured light, her blue eyes full of tears, repeating over and over again, 'Peace. Peace. Be reconciled.'

On Sunday, a multitude flocked from all the Catholic lands of what was then Yugoslavia to what was becoming known as 'The Hill of Apparitions'. For the next few years, the Lady appeared to the six young people once a week, always at about six p.m. The crowds grew bigger and bigger.

The authorities soon intervened. This was still a 'Socialist' country, aggressively hostile to religion, especially to Catholicism. The young people were taken to a doctor, to see if they had been using drugs, after which they were examined by a neuro-psychiatrist. Neither could find anything abnormal. On the day when the Lady was expected to appear, a social worker took the visionaries for a long drive, to keep them away from the Hill. However at six p.m. they saw the Hill in the distance, and began to pray and sing. Blinded by a sudden light, the social worker had to stop the car. The six jumped out and ran away, the Lady appearing to them in a field.

Cures took place, and there were mysterious phenomena. In August 150 people saw the sun become a white disc emitting multi-coloured rays, and then spin around a cloudless sky, pulsating, expanding and contracting, till a white cloud settled on the Hill and the orb grew red again, reverting to its normal self. A fire broke out on the Hill; there was no sign of it when the fire-brigade arrived. There were rainbows when there had been no rain. The Croat word for peace, '*Mir*', was emblazoned in letters of white light over Mount Križevac, where it could be seen by everyone in Medjugorje. A great stone cross, thirty feet tall, erected on the mountain in 1933, spun round and round. Angels were seen in the sky, and the silhouette of a tall, slender woman standing upright against a flat luminous globe.

On 2 July Jozo Zovko, the Franciscan friar who was parish priest of Medjugorje, took spiritual charge of the six. He had heard a voice telling him to protect them. At first he feared it might be Satan's voice, but when he opened the Bible his eye fell on the passage where Moses finds water in the desert. Having interrogated them, he decided they were telling the truth.

More and more pilgrims arrived every day, some by car or lorry, others on bicycles or on foot. Each evening crowds came to the parish church of St James to hear Mass. Fr Jozo told them that the visionaries were saying that the '*Gospa*' (the Croatian for Lady) urged everyone to fast on bread and water on Wednesdays and Fridays, and to say the Creed daily, followed by the Pater, Ave and Gloria seven times, then the Rosary. Many who had not confessed their sins for years now did so, 100,000 people receiving communion between the beginning of July and the end of October. The villagers were transformed, attending Mass daily. Land disputes which had dragged on for centuries were settled in a few days.

The authorities reacted with fury. On 12 August pilgrims were forbidden to visit the Hill of Apparitions because 'the terrain is too dangerous for large numbers'. No cars were allowed in the late afternoon or early evening, the time of the apparitions. No religious meetings might take place in the parish church. Confined to their parents' houses, the six were examined by teams of psychiatrists; the leader of one team, a woman doctor, told them, 'You six little children are trying to destroy a system built on our blood.' 'We aren't trying to destroy anything,' they protested. 'We're only repeating what the *Gospa* said.'

A media campaign heaped scorn on the apparitions and on anyone who believed in them. There was even a cartoon of the Virgin as a terrorist, appearing to the six with a dagger clenched between her teeth – 'The true face of the Blessed Mother'. All the churches were locked, their doors barred with heavy beams, and cut off by road blocks. The villagers were terrorized by militia, who threatened them with rifles. Nuns at the local convent were made to strip to their underclothes. Pilgrims were beaten up. But the apparitions went on while, despite every obstacle, Fr Jozo managed to keep in touch with the visionaries.

Early in August Fr Jozo was arrested by the secret police. His church and presbytery were wrecked, books, papers and money seized. The monstrance was thrown into the river; a large metal object for displaying the Host, it is said to have been found floating on the surface a few days later. He was put on trial at Mostar and sent to a maximum security prison as a 'public enemy'. He was tortured savagely – though his gaolers are reported to have grown nervous when mysterious rays of light shone out from his cell. By the end of 1987 fifty people had been arrested, two more friars going to prison for publishing an article favourable to the apparitions.

This reaction was partly due to fear of Croat nationalism. To be a Croat is to be a Catholic, and Medjugorje forms a Croat enclave within predominantly Orthodox or Moslem Herzegovina. There had been massacres of Serbs here during the Second World War; fifty men, women and children were made to jump from a mountaintop while at the Orthodox monastery of Zitomislić nearby every monk was buried alive by the Croat militia.

Yet almost from the beginning the Serbian Orthodox hierarchy accepted the apparitions as genuine. There have been many Orthodox pilgrims to Medjugorje, for the East venerates Mary no less than the West, as 'Mother of God, Ever Virgin and All Holy'. She symbolizes how much Catholicism and Orthodoxy have in common.

Moslem pilgrims came too, often praying for children or for a safe delivery in childbirth. In Herzegovina members of their faith have always been more tolerant of Christianity than elsewhere; till the seventeenth century the Gospels were read side by side with the Koran in many mosques. Christians who read the Holy Koran must be struck by the tender way in which the Prophet speaks of 'Mariam the Virgin'. Islam reveres her as a saint, if not as the Mother of God, venerating any place associated with her.

In January 1983, during a conversation tape-recorded by the Franciscan Tomo Vlasić, a visionary said that the Virgin insists that no one can be a true Catholic who does not respect other religions; too many people at Medjugorje were mocking Moslems and even Orthodox Christians. (For Orthodox she used the word 'Serb'.) Critics of the apparitions have distorted this message, taking it out of context and claiming that it means all religions are equal.

While Fr Jozo was in prison his curate, Zrinko Čuvalić, looked after the parish. The six went on seeing the *Gospa* and pilgrims kept on coming. In October the cross on Mount Križevac became a pillar of light; the figure of a woman could be seen at its foot, looking towards the church. The authorities did their best to discourage pilgrims, but the villagers put them up in their own houses, feeding them from their own inadequate larders, the mother of the family blessing the scanty meals.

As Marxist Socialism waned, life became easier. Fr Jozo was

released in 1988, returning to a hamlet near Medjugorje. Hostels were built for the hordes who now arrived daily, among them journalists and television crews. Pilgrims came from all over the Catholic world, many returning again and again – not less than ten million between 1981 and 1990.

There have been more tests on the visionaries by medical men, who found them to be oblivious of noise, light or even pain during the apparitions. Further psychiatric investigation confirmed that they were perfectly normal. Two, Mirjana and Ivanka, are no longer visited by the *Gospa*, after receiving ten secret prophecies. So far the other four visionaries have received only nine of these secrets. Eventually Mirjana will reveal them, at a time to be appointed by the Lady herself, through the priest Petar Ljubicić. One of the secrets concerns a great sign on the hillside, permanent, indestructible and beautiful, which will be sent to convince the unbelieving. There are also monthly messages (at first weekly) in which Christians are chided for not responding and are warned that Satan is toying with their souls.

The secrets are apocalyptic in content and speak of events leading up to the last days of this world. They involve terrible 'chastisements'. Many people will have died in them by the time the sign on the hillside occurs and those who remain alive will have little time for conversion before the next disaster overtakes them. Only prayer and fasting can avert the punishments.

According to the visionaries, the Virgin has said that the world is passing through a period of unparalleled darkness. Never before has Satan had such power over humanity as during the twentieth century. He is waging a great battle for souls with the Mother of God, who has been sent by the Eternal Father to warn and to hearten them – for, as God told the serpent in Genesis, the woman 'shall crush thy head'.

The local bishop remained incredulous and questioned the reality of the visions. He had his supporters. In 1988 a fierce attack on Medjugorje appeared in *Fidelity*, a North American journal which caters for conservative Catholic intellectuals, in the form of an article written by its editor, Michael Jones, who began by quoting seemingly unanswerable texts: 'It is an evil and unfaithful generation which asks for a sign' (St Matthew) and 'The Devil rejoices greatly when a person desires to receive revelations' (St John of the Cross). He even detected resemblances to the seventeenth-century witches of Salem. 'Unlike the Portuguese nun [at Fatima] who saw the Virgin 71 years ago, relayed the message, and slipped quietly away from the scene, the seers at Medjugorje have decided to become part of the tourist industry,' he observed. However, Fatima undermines Jones's entire argument – there *were* signs and revelations there, signs and revelations which the Church has accepted as genuine.

In 1987 the Holy See appointed an official commission of enquiry, though everyone realized that a decade would elapse at the very least before it reached a conclusion. A similar commission of enquiry at Fatima had taken thirteen years to do so.

My forebodings on that first night seemed more than justified during my first full day at Medjugorje. I felt that I had made a bad mistake in coming. Morning Mass in English was concelebrated at the parish church by a priest from Kentucky with a hundred other clerics. (I recall a dignified old monsignor telling me that these sort of Masses reminded him of the Nuremberg Rally.) The Kentuckian's interminable sermon included a moving account of his agonies in giving up Coca-Cola, after he had responded to the Virgin's call to do penance. If soul-stirring for some, to me the liturgy was the purest kitsch. I did not stay till the end, walking out in a fury.

I wandered gloomily through vineyards and tobacco fields, past the whining beggars squatting by the path and the small grey Balkan cattle, to the hamlet of Podbrdo for an audience with a seer, Ivan Dragičević. Outside a comfortable-looking villa, next to an old stone house, a crowd, mainly American and Philippino, was waiting eagerly. Ivan appeared half-way up a concrete staircase, about twenty-five, slight, dark-haired, sallow and nondescript, self-conscious, perhaps a little sullen. He was wearing a tie and a brown suit, both expensive by local standards. For a quarter of an hour he waited silently, until everyone had arrived, flanked by two interpreters ready to translate into English and Tegalog. He looked a very ordinary young man, indistinguishable from the waiters in the cafés. Apparently he had twice tried to become a priest but each time left the seminary after only a few weeks. Cameras clicked incessantly. Written petitions to the Virgin were handed in; I was told that they asked her intercession in problems which ranged from medical to financial, from amatory to professional. When these had been gathered up (the *Gospa* is not expected to read them – they are merely brought in a satchel to where she is appearing), the questions began in earnest.

Ivan was non-committal about political enquiries such as the Gulf War, simply urging prayers for a peaceful solution, but responded at length to questions about the dangers facing young people – drugs and drink, materialism, education which emphasized the rewards of success rather than religion. When asked if the Virgin had said anything about the conversion of Russia, he answered she had been praying hard for Russia's conversion and renewal, adding that the West needed conversion too.

How did the visions manifest themselves? This question was greeted by a general murmur of approval. Ivan said that the apparitions always took place during the saying of the Rosary in the parish church from six p.m. to seven twenty-five p.m., at about six forty between the recitation of two 'mysteries' (prayer sequences). Sometimes they occurred at home, especially if one of the visionaries was ill. She came in indescribable light, announcing herself with the words, 'Praised be Jesus Christ, my other children.' She spent five minutes to half an hour with them and they prayed together. She explained how she suffered because of humanity's sinfulness, sometimes sobbing though never shedding tears. Once a month she gave five basic messages – peace, conversion, prayer, penance and fasting – urging everyone to pray for not less than half an hour each evening. Occasionally she showed them visions of heaven, purgatory and hell. Again and again she returned to the need for constant prayer if the world was not to be overwhelmed by catastrophe because of its neglect of God and his commandments.

Asked to describe heaven, Ivan laughed, retorting, 'Go there yourselves.' Would he accept the findings of the Vatican commission? 'Yes, as a loyal son of the Church.' What did the *Gospa* mean for those Christians who did not believe in the Blessed Virgin? 'She is the mother of us all.'

What did she look like? He saw her three-dimensionally, as any other human being. She had dark hair, blue eyes and rosy cheeks, but her feet rested on a cloud and did not touch the ground. Usually she wore a grey dress and a white veil but at Christmas and Easter she wore gold, carrying the Child in her arms at Christmas. Ivan said he could talk to her in the same way that he was talking to the crowd. He could even touch her.

I walked back gloomily. Ivan looked too prosperous for a mystic. (Later I learnt he had been dressed for a wedding.) A small crowd stood on the steps of the parish church, shouting and pointing. A campanile of a sort one associates with Italy rather than Yugoslavia could be seen on the horizon about a mile away; on and off it could *not* be seen. There were cries of 'Apparition!' An Italian priest grew very angry when I said, '*Questo, é miragio*!' '*Non é miragio, é vero*!' he yelled. But I had heard of mirages of this sort before, in southern Italy.

In the afternoon I took a coach to Tihaljin, where Fr Jozo had been parish priest since his release from prison. Pilgrims flock there to hear his account of the apparitions. The hamlet is near Ljubski on the road to Banja Luka amid the usual vineyards and tobacco fields, beneath lowering mountains. It was a beautiful drive and I was sorry to arrive. Buses stood outside a gleaming new church, disgorging crowds who seemed to be mainly American or Australian – a fair proportion were Croat emigrants or the children of emigrants.

In his brown habit, the bespectacled Fr Jozo looked to be in his early forties. He had a winning smile, speaking Croat in a soft, pleasant voice. A pretty black-haired girl in a red shirt and dark skirt, Hollywood's ideal of a Slav beauty, interpreted for him. She too had an attractive voice, almost hypnotic. Apparently she was a former party official. (I was told that an ex-secret policeman was among the priests on the altar.)

Fr Jozo described the first apparitions, how the people of Medjugorje had been locked out of the church and threatened, and then as if by a miracle an order had come, 'Let them go to church.' Yet the authorities had been enraged by the Virgin appearing in a Communist country. He recalled the doctor who accused the children of trying to destroy the Communist system. 'That was nine years ago. Since then the Virgin has destroyed the system throughout the world. Fatima is coming true at Medjugorje. The liberation of Eastern Europe is not due to Reagan or to Bush but to the *Gospa*.'

He begged his hearers to obey her – say the Rosary daily, fast, read the Bible and confess once a month. Pictures of the *Gospa*'s statue in the church at Medjugorje were handed out, the congregation responding with basketfuls of dollar bills. A lengthy service of healing began. After the laying on of hands people started to embrace each other, many weeping – some fainted when hands were laid on them.

I went outside to wait until the bus could take me back. I derived more comfort from the sun setting – normally – over the mountains than from what was going on inside.

At the *pansion* that evening my misery was compounded by

wild tales about 'miracles'. The crossbar of the cross on Mount Križevac, I was told, disappeared from sight during the elevation of the Host at Mass in the parish church. The Host had been seen in the sky, as had a dove, and even Christ himself. A photographer had taken a snap of the Virgin. A Manchester woman claimed that her rosary had turned into gold, whereupon someone else recounted how *her* rosary had also changed into gold, 24 carat gold. I contemplated bringing a suitcase of rosaries.

Why had I come to this madhouse? Despite admitting to myself that was what the pilgrims wanted, that perhaps I was a shade too fastidious or sophisticated or both, the atmosphere was beginning to induce something like nausea. I felt that by the time I left I wouldn't believe in anything at all. I went to bed with a bottle of šlivovica – the measure of my desperation since I was aware of the murderous hangover which it could give me.

Next morning I awoke a different man. I have a fairly mercurial temperament but I have never experienced so swift a change of mood, and it wasn't the šlivovica. My whole attitude to life had altered; all depression, all worries, had gone. I felt greater peace of mind than I could ever remember. At breakfast a man spoke of the famous 'Medjugorje effect', which often took place after an initial period of hostility. The woman with the golden rosary (who taught maths at a Manchester comprehensive) explained that whatever happened *something* would change in my life; if Medjugorje did not solve problems, it showed people how to handle them. But they warned that the effect lasted for a few weeks at most.

I was in a state of euphoria. My doubts vanished. It was Sunday so I went to the Italian Mass at the parish church, full of noisy, weeping charismatics. I did not find them irritating and they sang beautifully. I prayed for guidance about something in my personal life; I expected to be told to give it up but, to my surprise, the answer was to continue. Afterwards there was a Croat Mass and I admired the deep Slavonic voices.

People had come from all around for the Croat Mass. Yugoslavia is the last part of Europe where folk costume is worn every day as a matter of course and not as mere fancy dress. Some women were in long black narrow-waisted dresses, trimmed in maroon or yellow, with a black or yellow bobble at the breast, and Dutch-looking mitre-like caps. Others wore white serge bloomers with black aprons and headscarves piped in red. I beamed at them – until I realized that my smiles were being taken for leers.

I went to see another visionary, Vicka Ivanković. She too lived at Podbrdo in a small modern villa. A slightly built, pleasant faced girl with a mass of thick black hair, she wore a yellow shirt and blue jeans. Because of bad health she had to live at home, where the *Gospa* came to her. Speaking in Italian, she began by emphasizing the need for prayer and fasting, warning that Satan is very strong; one should always carry a blessed object, such as a rosary, a crucifix or a holy medal. Her description of the *Gospa* was similar to Ivan's. There were always three flashes of light before she appeared. At Christmas she came holding the Infant Jesus, at Easter accompanied by the crucified Christ with his five wounds and crown of thorns.

Unlike Ivan, she described heaven, purgatory and hell. Heaven was remarkable for a beautiful light in which people in grey, pink and yellow robes walked, prayed and sang. Angels flew above. In purgatory, hidden by mist, there was a sound of hammering at prison-bars. In hell men and women emerged from a vast fire unrecognizable as human beings; the more they hated God, the deeper into the fire they went. Vicka commented that they were in hell only because they wanted to be; those who fight against God in this world go on doing so in the next – their worst mistake is thinking they will cease to exist when they die.

*

I believe in hell. Sometimes I think about it in the night, sweating. That is when I would prefer not to have faith. Teresa of Avila saw hell as being pushed down a muddy passage into a cupboard in the wall, a vision even more frightening than Vicka's. Loneliness of the self-centred sort must be an intimation of hell. 'The heart of men is the place Devils dwell in' observed Sir Thomas Browne in *Religio Medici*:

> I sometimes feel a Hell within myself; Lucifer keeps his Court in my breast . . . every Devil is an Hell unto himself; he holds enough of torture . . . and thus a distracted Conscience here, is a shadow or introduction to Hell hereafter. Who can but pity the merciful intentions of those that do destroy themselves? The Devil, were it in his power, would do the like.

A Catholic, surely, has to believe in hell.

Yet Graham Greene did not. He found fear of hell meaningless, because he could not believe in the mortal sin which incurs damnation; in his view that was sin committed in deliberate defiance of God. 'I doubt whether a man making love to a woman ever does so with the intention of defying God,' he argued. I only hope he's right.

Climbing Mount Križevac, the Hill of the Cross (with the spinning shaft), I met boys and girls in Beneton T-shirts climbing barefoot, trainers tied round their necks. It is 448 metres high, and the steep twisting path studded with knife-edged rocks makes it a painful ascent even for those wearing shoes, but worth it. From the summit the Dinarić mountains stretch north as far as the eye can see, very different to the flat plateau to the west on which lies Medjugorje. The Virgin's great sign will appear here, so the mountain is also known as the Hill of the Sign.

*

On Monday, still euphoric, I went to see a third visionary, Marija Pavlović. A small mousy person in jeans and a pink shirt, she too lived at Podbrdo, in a concrete house rendered grey; it had an orange tiled roof and a pretty balcony covered in geraniums. She spoke good Italian, in a whisper. She looked shy; when the visions cease, she hopes to enter a convent.

Marija stressed prayer and self-denial more than the others. Mass takes precedence over social work; an hour should be spent in prayer before it and an hour after. Wordless prayer is of great value. One ought to fast on bread and water every Wednesday and Friday, giving up alcohol, cigarettes and television. During the nine days before any important feast one should renounce what one likes most, e.g. coffee. The Bible must be read throughout the day. If anything weighs heavily on one's soul, it is vital to find a spiritual adviser and confess to him regularly. Despite my euphoria, my heart sank at all this.

Leaving Marija I climbed the Hill of the Apparitions, just outside Podbrdo, on which stand the Stations of the Cross, an easy ascent compared to Mount Križevac. Along the muddy path and on the flat plateau at the top, the stations were weirdly decorated. I saw roses and carnations with plastic flowers; a potted palm and a Yugoslav flag; ties, scarves, handkerchiefs and towels; a woolly toy and a camp stove. Yet the hill had an extraordinary feeling of peace. There were always people on it, standing or sitting in silence. Many visit it at night, lighting their way with candles.

I was sorry to miss a fourth visionary, Mirjana, because she had seen the Devil. (I retain an unfashionable belief in a personalized devil.) She told a friar in 1983 that the Devil was blackish and altogether horrifying. Laughing, he had said that she was beautiful but must give up the Lady who brought only trouble. He vanished when she refused. She was sure that he was very active today, taking possession of people who lacked balance or were confused. He also entered the lives of those with deep religious convictions since he would rather seduce believers than unbelievers. The *Gospa* had told Mirjana that God had permitted the Devil to choose one century in which to rule the world and he had chosen the twentieth.

This echoes a popular legend, the 'Vision of Leo XIII', which claims that during the 1880s Pope Leo was warned by God that Satan would rule the world for a hundred years. He undoubtedly ordered a prayer for protection against the Devil to be recited after every Mass: 'Holy Michael, Archangel, defend us in the day of battle; be our safeguard against the wickedness and snares of the Devil. May God rebuke him, we humbly pray; and do thou, prince of the heavenly host, by the power of God thrust down to hell Satan and all wicked spirits who wander through the world for the ruin of souls.' In 1930 Pius XI gave instructions for the prayer to be said specifically for the conversion of Russia, but after the Council it was a casualty at the hands of liturgical demolition experts.

I began to enjoy Medjugorje. The white Žilavka wine was excellent and so was the red Blatina. There were tapes of Croat folk-music and busts of the mustachioed Ban (Governor) Jellačić who in 1849 led the Croat horsemen to the rescue of the Habsburgs. I saw young men in T-shirts with the *Gospa* on one side and the arms of Croatia on the other. (Only when war broke out in 1991 did I realize the implications.) I glimpsed Mostar in the distance, with its twenty-four minarets and that glorious Ottoman bridge across the Neretva.

I left with real regret. I had never seen so many happy people. I asked a girl who came often why she did so. She answered that it was for peace of mind and an end to worry. Many pilgrims testify to a sense of renewed strength. If there have been miraculous cures of physical ailments, cripples walking and the blind regaining their sight, there are even more of spiritual and moral healing.

*

Scepticism and doubts of faith returned within a month, as my friends at the *pansion* had warned. I remembered Pascal's definition of man's condition as inconstancy, weariness, unrest. Like his average man, I am by nature credulous and incredulous. Sceptical about scepticism, Pascal mocks at it. 'Nothing fortifies scepticism more than that there are many who are not sceptics,' he wrote in the *Pensées*. 'If all were so, they would be wrong.' I was also soothed by a Spanish-speaking friend's image of '*rafagas*', of faith coming in light and shade, like sunbeams shining through a Venetian blind.

I read everything I could find on Medjugorje. The most hostile critic had been Mgr Pavao Zanić, Bishop of Mostar. In his view, 'All is the fruit of fraud, disobedience to the Church and disease.' When informed that the *Gospa* had told a visionary he spoke 'hastily', Mgr Zanić retorted that Our Lady would *never* talk about a bishop in such a way. There were some unpleasant stories, such as that of two women (with a history of drug abuse) being pursued down Mount Križevac by 'horrible, disgusting demons'. Critics of the apparitions keep on quoting St John of the Cross, who is adamant that 'signs and wonders' endanger one's faith. 'They can lead to a species of spiritual gluttony . . . if a person does not reject them, they will hamper his soul, so that he will be unable to soar to the invisible.'

But Archbishop Franić of Split thinks the apparitions are genuine. If the Vatican has not so far accepted them as authentic, it has certainly not condemned them. Indeed there are persistent rumours that the Pope himself believes in the Medjugorje visions. The Jesuit Robert Faricy, Professor of Spiritual Theology at the Pontifical Gregorian University, emphasizes the parallels with Fatima:

> The message is the same; an urgent call to repentance, to pray and to do penance so as to co-operate with God's redemptive

> work, to avoid war and to have peace on earth . . . As at Medjugorje, the children of Fatima were shown a vision of hell, to impress on them the evil of sin and of unrepentance.

Pope John Paul II had defined the Fatima message as one which calls people to repentance, gives a warning, invites to prayer and recommends the Rosary. Faricy points out that this is very like the *Gospa*'s message; conversion, warning, prayer, fasting and the Rosary. 'The Fatima prophecies have been fulfilled,' he claims. 'We have now [1984] a new warning and a new call to conversion – in the light of present international tensions and their possible aftermath.' (Though the tensions have of course changed since then, with the collapse of the Soviet Union.)

Faricy is convinced that the Medjugorje apparitions are authentic. He himself has seen the sun dance at Medjugorje, on 24 June 1984 at seven p.m.:

> The phenomenon lasted about five minutes. I could look right into the sun which appeared to be a flat disc, off-white in colour, spinning rapidly. From time to time light pulsed out from behind the disc. I tried to see if my blinking coincided with these pulsations of fire, but it was not so. I found that I could look away without my eyes being dazzled. Afterwards the sun returned to its normal brilliance, and for the next hour, before it set, I could no longer look at it directly.

The Bible is perfectly clear in stating that the sun, the moon and the stars sometimes serve as portents. 'And God said, "Let there be lights made in the firmaments of heaven, to divide the day and the night, and let them be for signs",' Genesis tells us. The star in the East which came to rest over Bethlehem is one example. There were many more during the ages of faith.

Here is what Radbod, Bishop of Utrecht, recorded at the beginning of the tenth century:

> In the year of the Incarnation of Our Lord 900 there appeared a marvellous sign in heaven. For the stars were seen to flow from the very height of heaven to the lowest horizon, well nigh as though they crashed one upon the other. And upon this marvel followed woeful calamities, such as a most notable untowardness of the seasons and frequent tempests, rivers also overflowing their banks as in dread likeness of the Deluge and (what was yet more pestilent than these) ominous upheavals of men boasting themselves against God. In this same year, ere the inter-calary days were ended, Fulk the Archbishop of Rheims and the King Zwentibold were slain . . .

This of course must be dismissed as Dark Age superstition. Or must it?

There are several examples of signs in the sun, of solar omens. The best known is that seen by the Emperor Constantine in AD 312, when he was about to confront his rival, Maxentius, at the battle of the Milvian Bridge outside Rome. He told the historian Eusebius that 'about midday when the sun was beginning to decline, he saw with his own eyes the trophy of a cross of light in the heavens, above the sun, and with the words "Conquer by this sign"'. He ordered jewellers to make a golden banner bearing the sign, which was carried at the head of his army. Maxentius was defeated decisively, drowning in the Tiber. It has been suggested that the sign was what is called the 'halo phenomenon'; the sun's image is refracted through ice crystals suspended in the air, to form a cross with the sun at its centre.

Less well known is the phenomenon seen before the battle of Mortimer's Cross in Herefordshire on Candlemas Day 1461 (the feast of the Virgin's Purification), in which the Earl of March – the future Edward IV – defeated the Lancastrians. Shakespeare describes this in *King Henry VI*, Part 3:

Three glorious suns, each one a perfect sun;
Not separated with the racking clouds,
But sever'd in a pale clear-shining sky.
See, see! they join, embrace and seem to kiss,
As if they vow'd some league inviolable:
Now they are but one lamp, one light, one sun.
In this the heaven figures some event.

A contemporary chronicler says that the Yorkists were terrified, but the noble Earl Edward comforted them and said, 'Beeth of good comfort and dreadeth not: this is a good sign, for these three suns betoken the Father, the Son and the Holy Ghost, and therefore let us have a good heart, and in the name of Almighty God go we against our enemies.'

An old friend of mine – who knows the area well, having fought there with the partisans during the Second World War – wondered if the Medjugorje cult had anything to do with the Bogomil heresy. He remembers sheltering from a German bombing raid beneath the old Turkish citadel at Jajce, once the capital of medieval Bosnia and only a few miles away, in an underground chapel which, so the partisans told him, had been a Bogomil chapel. The Bogomils' religion was the same faith as that of the Cathars or Albigensians in southern France; one fourteenth-century Pope, Urban V, referred bitterly to Bosnia as 'the cess-pool of heresy of all parts of the world', and the people of Herzegovina (in those days called 'The land of Hum' and part of the kingdom of Bosnia) were Bogomils. Most turned Moslem after the Turkish conquest, but their religion lingered on until the nineteenth century, the last Bogomil dying only in 1878. Their *stećaks* (funeral monuments) have strange carvings of men and monsters, of hunting parties, of dancing the *kolo*, together with gnostic symbols which include the sun. The peasants say that anyone who touches these risks being struck by lightning. There are many *stećaks* near Medjugorje while, not far off, the castle of a heretic lord, a Herzegovinan Montsegur, dominates the landscape.

'The sun is the prince of this world and the throne thereof, and the moon is the law of Moses, while the stars are the spirits that, minister unto the prince,' says *The Secret Supper*, a Cathar book from Languedoc – a colloquy between Our Lord and St John the Baptist – whose contents were almost certainly familiar to the Bogomils. 'Christ the son of God is the sevenfold sun and he shall reign.' The Bogomils' favourite Gospel was St John's, because of the words 'And the light shineth in darkness: and the darkness did not comprehend it . . . For every one that doth evil hateth the light.' My friend suggested that a sign of Bogomil influence might be the Virgin's request that seven Pater Nosters be said daily, since Bogomils recited the Lord's Prayer seven times a day.

However, his theory collapses when one looks at Bogomilstvo theology. 'The Son entered the Virgin through her ear, took flesh there and emerged by the same door,' Sir Steven Runciman informs us in *The Medieval Manichee*. 'She did not notice but found Him as an infant in the cave at Bethlehem.' The Bogomil Elect paid her no special honour. 'They declared that each of them deserved the title of the Mother of God, for in each of them the Holy Spirit resided and each therefore gave birth to the Word.' In no sense was she an intercessor. Moreover, they detested the cross instead of revering it.

Someone, who did not accept that the Medjugorje phenomena were supernatural in origin, reminded me of the words of John Henry Newman after he had investigated the liquefaction of the Blood of San Gennaro at Naples. 'The question certainly arises whether there is something in the air,' wrote the Cardinal. 'Mind, I don't believe there is – and speaking humbly, and without having seen it, think it a true miracle.' The disappearing campanile, which I saw from the steps of the parish church at Medjugorje, had given me the impression of a mirage. But, if 'something in the air' was responsible for the sun dancing there, then why had it danced at so many other Marian shrines – and sometimes only on a single occasion?

When I was in my euphoric mood at Medjugorje, I believed in

the visionaries and in their apparitions, and thought that the solar phenomena were supernatural. Later, however, I questioned them, just as I doubted everything else again. Yet if the apparitions were hallucinations, no one could deny that they were benevolent and had done an immense amount of good in changing so many people's lives for the better.

Understandably, everyone concentrates on whether the Mother of God appeared or not. Far less attention is paid to the sun's behaviour. According to the laws of nature, it cannot possibly have danced, yet too many pilgrims besides my painter friend have seen the phenomena. Beyond question, it *appeared* to dance; even in my most sceptical moods I remain convinced of that, at the very least. And while the visionaries at nearly all Marian shrines describe the Virgin in a way which reflects how she looks in religious art, there is no popular image in religious art, let alone secular, of a dancing sun or of a sun emitting rainbow coloured rays. (Even Turner, that great painter of the sun, never portrayed such a thing.)

Mariologists have done comparatively little research on the solar phenomena. On the other hand, a good deal is known about solar *symbolism*. It is a symbolism which has been generally ignored by those who write about the shrines.

In the years immediately after the Second World War archaeologists excavated the grotto of the Tomb of Peter, beneath the Vatican. They found a mosaic dating from not later than AD 250 which showed Christ riding into the sky in the chariot of Helios the Sun God, wearing a radiate crown of sunbeams. The Christians of the catacombs had adopted solar mythology.

In any case, this was already implicit in the Old Testament. 'He hath set his tabernacle in the sun: and he, as a bridegroom coming out of his bride chamber, hath rejoiced as a giant to run the way,' says Psalm 18. 'His going out is from the end of heaven, and his circuit even to the end thereof: and there is no one that can hide himself from his heat.' However, the early Fathers of the Church were more aware of other religions than the Psalmist had been. They took over the imagery of Helios and of Selene the Moon Goddess. (Origen tells us that sun and moon were created 'to perform their stately dance for the salvation of the world'.)

The first Christians were fascinated by the coincidence of the Saviour having risen on Sunday, the day sacred to Helios. In the fourth century the Lord's birthday was moved from the Epiphany to 25 December, the day when the birth of '*Sol Invictus*' (the Unconquered Sun) was celebrated. During the same century St Ambrose would tell the faithful to gaze at the sun and sing praises to Christ.

Similarly, Selene the Moon Goddess was sometimes identified with the Church – the Bride of Christ. The church reflected the light of Christ, just as the moon reflected the sun. And Selene also epitomized perfect motherhood.

In *Greek Myths and Christian Mystery* Hugo Rahner demonstrates how this imagery persisted until well into the Middle Ages. He cites Dante's gaze travelling heavenward in the *Paradiso*, up to the immortal sun, Christ, who gives light to all spiritual stars – '*un sol che tutte quante l'accendea* . . .' In addition, he relates how the Christians of Roman times and of the early Middle Ages saw the mystery of the Church's motherhood as being symbolized by the Virgin, and how 'Mary is the true Selene, in whom all the yearnings of Antiquity after motherly womanhood found fulfilment'.

Meanwhile the number of pilgrims to Medjugorje grew steadily – after 1987 it was over a million annually. Despite Bishop Zanič's attempts to discourage them, ten million pilgrims had come and nearly 25,000 priests had celebrated Mass there by the end of 1990. Groups came from as far away as Peru; there was a very noticeable increase in pilgrims from Eastern Europe – from Hungary, Czechoslovakia and Poland, even from Bulgaria and what was then the Soviet Union. Many travelled on foot, frequently alone, especially those from Croatia, Herzegovina or Western Russia.

Not all saw the sun dance. I heard of a group of half-a-dozen which included an American TV journalist with his camera. While the rest gazed for over half an hour at the sun zig-zagging and pulsating, he kept on asking, 'What are you looking at? What are you watching?' Admittedly, he seems to have been a non-believer. Yet I have met pilgrims who went there to pray, expecting to see nothing but who did, steady practical people without too much poetry in their natures; among them was a chartered accountant from Hertfordshire who saw not only the sun dance but the great cross spin round and round.

Here is a fairly typical account, unpublished, which was sent to me by a former computer correspondent on the *Daily Telegraph*:

> On the first night of my first visit [October 1988], my mother and I both saw the cross on the Hill of the Cross, Križevac, beautifully and brightly illuminated at about 9.30 p.m. We thought nothing of it until the following morning when other pilgrims pointed out that there is no electricity or other means of illumination [save candles] up there. The cross is three storeys high.
>
> On the third day we came out of the church after the 11.00 a.m. English Mass, i.e. at midday. A few people were staring at the sun, which was over the Hill of the Cross – due south. I saw the sun zigzag downwards three times, then zigzag to the left, eastward. It was only much later that I realized the significance of this: the sun was making obeisance to the cross, then to the Hill of Apparitions where Mary first appeared (and still does at Ivan's weekly prayer group on the mountainside).
>
> My mother, standing beside me, saw the sun flash several times. Others described – as we watched together – a dove in the sun and then a host over the sun. I saw neither of these, nor did my mother. The sky was partially obscured by light cloud.
>
> On the third afternoon of my third visit [June 1990], half a

dozen friends and I came out of the church of St James in Medjugorje at about 7.00 p.m. at the end of the Croatian Mass. The sun was at an elevation of roughly 30 degrees above the western horizon in a clear blue sky.

I noticed another knot of pilgrims, including an American priest, looking straight into the sun. I looked up and saw that it had a slightly darker centre, like a disc in front of it, or a filter to cut down the glare. Light streamed from the edges in a variety of colours. It was a majestic sight: I felt as if I was witnessing a demonstration of awe-inspiring power in which the laws of nature were temporarily suspended.

All six of us saw the same phenomenon and continued to watch it for more than twenty minutes, looking straight into the sun without suffering retinal damage. A quarter of an hour later, on the walk back to our lodging, I looked again into the sun. I was unable to do so, nor have I been able to do so since.

Apart from visions and solar phenomena, thousands of men and women who went there broken in spirit, claim that they found the strength to pick themselves up from the ground and start again. Hundreds more insist they were healed physically, from afflictions which range from blindness to infertility, from paralysis to multiple sclerosis. Someone whom I have known since childhood went to the shrine with a blocked artery, awaiting surgery; suddenly the artery unblocked itself. Countless others like myself were given peace of mind. A Benedictine monk told me that what particularly impressed him was the quality of the confessions which he heard there, and the penitents' sincerity.

Beyond question, there is an ecumenical dimension to Medjugorje. Anglicans and Lutherans have seen the solar phenomena. The shrine may be the key to peace in the region. Only the *Gospa* can reconcile Catholics, Orthodox and Moslems, all of whom reverence the Mother of God.

Predictably, misconceptions and false rumours abound. Some Catholics refuse to accept that what is happening at Medjugorje can be true because the Church has not yet recognized the visions as authentic. They ignore the fact that Fatima had to wait for thirteen years until the visions of the little shepherds were officially recognized by the Holy See.

Early in 1991 a new type of phenomenon was seen, small black orbs in the sky which reminded those who saw them of bombs. (With hindsight some think they were omens of impending war.) Then those at the shrine heard gunfire; Serbian troops were advancing, mopping up pockets of Croat or Bosnian resistance. It became almost impossible to get through to Medjugorje, ringed as it was by Serbs, the only way being to fly to Mostar and walk. But early in spring 1992 Mostar fell to the Serbs.

Medjugorje was finally cut off from the outside world in April. The villagers had no illusion about their fate should they be overrun. Women and children were evacuated, but the men stayed, including the friars. They built dug-outs and bomb-shelters, and formed a sort of home-guard, arming themselves with half-a-dozen Second World War rifles, shotguns and even a few crossbows. Much to their dismay, in May the commander of the local Bosnian forces made the village his headquarters, bringing 500 soldiers.

There were 26,000 Serbian and Montenegrin troops or irregulars around Mostar and Medjugorje became a prime target for them. They isolated the area systematically, dynamiting roads and bridges. Telephone lines were cut, only a single generator-powered line remaining in the village, while water supplies were diverted; a little water was available, however, from tanks in the older houses. Cooking had to be done on primus stoves or on charcoal braziers.

The local hospital at Čitluk, the nearest town, was destroyed by Serbian rockets, so an 'operating-theatre' was set up in the basement of an adjoining house; it had two consultants' couches on which two exhausted doctors sometimes amputated limbs without proper anaesthetics – sterilization fluid was re-used, again and again.

Grim reports of what was happening in Mostar filtered through. The city had been reduced to rubble, with corpses lying in every street; old men and old women, little children, who had been shot in the back or had had their throats cut. Hundreds of Croats and Moslems were locked in a church without food or water; in the hospital blood was being forcibly extracted from prisoners until they almost died, for transfusion into 'Federal Army' wounded. The surrounding villages had been razed to the ground, levelled by bulldozers, then covered by soil as though they had never existed. Thousands of people were held in concentration camps. The Serbian commanders were so determined to win that it was rumoured they were hanging troops who disobeyed orders from the great bridge over the Neretva.

Medjugorje was shelled night and day, to surprisingly little effect. Five rockets hit it but the only casualties were a cow and a dog – the former being made into soup. Mortar bombs fell short; rounds failed to explode. The enemy tried hard to destroy the parish church, as a symbol of Croat culture, but failed even though a cluster bomb fell within 500 metres and blew out windows. (The bomb's tail-fin was stamped 'Made in England'.) There were so many unexploded shells and bombs lying around that the locals attributed the church's survival to divine intervention; a captured Serbian pilot said that his bomb-sight had been obscured by a mysterious light. After all, the *Gospa* had promised that Medjugorje would remain an oasis of peace. Every day Mass was celebrated and the Rosary recited in the sand-bagged basement of the priest's house.

*

The situation altered radically in June when the Croats and Bosnians re-took Mostar. In mid-May a convoy from the 'Medjugorje Network' in Britain reached the village: two ambulances, two Land-Rovers and a van, loaded with drugs, driven by a group which included English, Irish, Americans and Croats. Within five minutes of their arrival at Čitluk the drugs were being used in the hospital. The convoy noticed that a rosary served as an instant password – every Croat militiaman wore one round his neck or hanging from a shoulder strap.

On 24 June, led by Archbishop Franić, 10,000 pilgrims from twenty nations marched into Medjugorje where they were rapturously welcomed at tables spread with bread and wine. The parish church of St James was opened for the first time for two and a half months, and the archbishop concelebrated Mass together with forty other priests including Fr Jozo. A Vatican official who also took part, the Czech Bishop Hnilica, promised the pilgrims he would tell the Pope about the march as soon as possible.

Some of the pilgrims commandeered an old bus and visited Mostar. Greeted by a sentry at a check-point with 'Welcome to hell', they soon realized what he meant. An estimated 700,000 rockets, mortar bombs and shells had fallen on the city. Not one building had escaped, Bishop Zanić's palace and the Franciscan friary having been totally destroyed. Only the great Ottoman bridge, built in 1566, survived out of seven which had spanned the Neretva. Unexploded bombs and shells lay everywhere. Houses had been looted, before being blown up or set on fire.

At the time of writing (October 1992) Medjugorje seems reasonably safe, though this may change. The Virgin continues to appear to Ivan and Vicka, as she did in a shelter throughout the siege. Ivanka has been able to return with her child. Planes fly in freely to Split, from where the road to the shrine is quite safe again, and pilgrims are flocking there once more, to the joy of everyone in the village. The friars are encouraging them to pray with their Serbian Orthodox neighbours, whose Patriarch led a demonstration in Belgrade against the war.

Nevertheless fighting goes on. Mostar is still being shelled daily from Serbian positions about fifteen kilometres away and the noise of gunfire can be heard in Medjugorje. Not a single man from the village has been killed so far, although quite a number of them are among the front-line troops and have been in action many times – they all attribute their survival and the preservation of their homes to the *Gospa*'s protection.

In June 1992 Fr Jozo went to Rome, where he was received in audience by the Pope. 'Look after Medjugorje, save Medjugorje,' John Paul told him. 'Don't give up. Keep on!' There could be no clearer indication of the Vatican's attitude towards the shrine. Bishop Zanić's commission was dissolved some years ago, while he himself has recently retired, to make way for a new bishop. The case remains with the Yugoslav Conference of Bishops, who cannot be expected to give a formal pronouncement until the apparitions have come to an end.

Meanwhile, I had to place Medjugorje in the context of those other shrines where the Virgin appeared and the sun danced. I hoped I might recapture that comforting euphoria I had felt in Herzegovina, that I might even find a more lasting escape from my doubts. I had been very struck by Fr Jozo's claim that 'Fatima is coming true at Medjugorje'. Surely there was a link with the Portuguese shrine?

— 2 —
Svatá Hora and Turzovka

'A miracle,' says one, 'would strengthen my faith.' He says so when he does not see one.

PASCAL, *Pensées*

Praised be my Lord God with all his creatures, and specially our brother the sun, who brings us the day and who brings us the light; fair is he and shines with a very great splendour: O Lord, he signifies to us thee!

ST FRANCIS, *The Canticle of the Sun*

In London an exiled Czech Knight of Malta had told me about Turzovka in Slovakia. However he said that although the sun had certainly danced there, the locals would not talk to visitors. Instead he advised me to go to Svatá Hora in Bohemia, a famous Marian shrine. He also spoke of Knights of Malta who had survived in Czechoslovakia under the Communists. I was eager to learn how they had kept their faith.

I set out to Prague from London in a mood of black gloom. I hadn't made a journey abroad without a female companion for twenty years, and don't speak a word of Czech. But when I found myself in that wonderful city my spirits lifted. The flat where I was staying, in a block not far from the River Vltava, had been built in the last decade of Habsburg rule just before the Great War, and paint and plaster were peeling off the building; it looked like a set for *The Third Man*. However my old-fashioned room was immaculate. My hosts, who spoke French, could not have been kinder, especially the sweet old grandmother. They told me, without a trace of self-pity, that the Nazis and the Communists had stolen fifty years from their lives.

Later the grandmother expanded. She described the horrible Nazi régime – the massacre at Lidice and the forcible adoption of Jewish children who looked Aryan; her husband, a telephone engineer, had had to find birth certificates going back several generations to prove that he was not Jewish as soon as Adolf Hitler marched in '*Mais les Russes étaient pires*!' Her parents, who had owned a large shop, died as beggars, while her son-in-law's family farm had been confiscated. 'We were always reactionaries,' she told me proudly, but she was a nervous wreck. None the less, she had managed to teach her daughter, and her very pretty little granddaughter too, some French – of which they were quite enormously proud. (A reversible card on the lavatory door read '*Libre*' and '*Occupée*'.) Learning Russian had been a waste of time.

Such decent and gentle people possessed no defence against Nazism or 'Social Engineering', yet they had managed to keep all the family values, together with beautiful manners. Were they religious? 'No, I know there is no God,' said that otherwise admirable old lady.

I had thought of Prague as a gloomy, even menacing city. My long dead father who lived there briefly during the '20s detested it, though he had been a boon companion of that colourful figure Robert Bruce Lockhart (author of *Memoirs of a British Agent*) and had thoroughly enjoyed the White Russian nightlife. He used to say he had had 'a perfect bitch of a time' there. Perhaps he was biased after seeing a testicle cracker in a museum of medieval torture which, so he told me, had given him nightmares.

Instead the city is full of light. The Old Town has become like a Venice without canals. Still being restored, it is growing daily more beautiful, if daily more crowded. No wonder it was chosen as the location for the film *Amadeus*; the ghost of Mozart can easily be imagined here. One wanders marvelling down cobbled streets with countless Baroque churches, palaces and houses – cream and yellow, dove grey, pale green, tomato red. Over many doors there are cheerful murals of the Virgin and Child, St Nicholas or some other kindly saint, or else the arms (under a closed coronet) of a prince of the Holy Roman Empire. Statues on the Charles Bridge seem to dance above the swans riding on the River Vltava.

Yet at the same time Prague is a complex and indeed secret city. One can well believe it was the world of Franz Kafka. From the window of his little room behind Staroměstské Square, Kafka had to look down, despite himself, into the great Týn church, which is an oddly sinister place. The black Gothic buildings of Prague have a definitely menacing quality in contrast to the gaiety of the Baroque. Over all, on its high rock broods the mighty Hradčany, the royal castle, a surprisingly joyless expanse of cream and green which incorporates the twin spires of St Vitus Cathedral.

The city possesses a quality which appeals to the late twentieth century world at play, perhaps a little too much. Nightclubs are beginning to spring up, while everywhere there are street musicians – English and American, German, French and Italian – who drown the nostalgic accordions and violins of the Czechs. There is a rash of pizza bars. So far nothing has spoilt Prague's beauty though Kafka's world has vanished; to be fair, it must have departed under the Nazis. But the future belongs to the package tour.

*

The atmosphere is uneasy. Behind lie decades of Communist tyranny, when every petty official could bully mercilessly, secure in the knowledge that he had the party's backing; ahead lie years of painful readjustment, of ill-paid toil, of unemployment and near starvation. The old, the middle aged, even the young middle aged, face the future with dread. They know that their country's factories are only fit for the scrap-heap. Yet Czechs are natural capitalists; once their land was the workshop of the Habsburg Monarchy. If older generations are fearful, youth seems undaunted and full of optimism. I have never seen so many smiling young waiters, something unknown under Marxist Socialism.

I had come during the autumn of 1991, a fortnight after the failure of the Russian coup to oust Gorbachev, and was told that had it succeeded there would have been another coup in Prague within a week, which would have been successful. In Czechoslovakia, as in the rest of the former Soviet empire, middle management was still in the hands of ex-party officials, however many top political jobs may have been held by 'dissidents'. In Celetná Street there was none the less a terrifying little exhibition called 'Gulags', to remind people of what they were missing.

In the past it was not easy to be a Christian here, let alone a Catholic. In 1990 a friend of mine heard a small child ask his father outside the Strahov monastery, 'Who's God, Daddy? Who's Jesus?' After the 'Velvet Revolution' of 1989 more than one man informed his parents that he had been a priest for many years but had not dared to tell them.

There was an ancient belief that when a sister of King Vaclav I, the Blessed Agnes who died in 1282, would be made a saint, countless blessings would descend on Bohemia. Within four days of her canonization at Rome on 12 November 1989, a ceremony attended by many Czech Catholics, the Velvet Revolution began. Even agnostics approved of the timing.

*

Despite the new régime, telephoning in Prague is often impossible. Few houses have their own telephones, while those at the underground stations are usually vandalized or broken. After slogging down to the main Post Office, just off Václavské Náměstí, I found long queues stretching behind a mere half dozen boxes for local calls. Two days went by and, for all the pleasures of good food and drink at ridiculously low prices, I grew not merely worried but frantic at failing to get in touch with my one contact in the city, a Knight of Malta. I decided to try calling at his priory, though it was unlikely that he would be there.

In a country where very few people speak English, I knew that I was going to be alone for most of the time. There was small hope of finding kindred spirits in bars and I wasn't interested in other tourists. I intended to spend my evenings writing out notes made during the day or else in reading. I had brought *The Rough Guide*, a pocket Bible, *Conversations with Graham Greene*, Alban Krailsheimer's wonderful study of Pascal, my Everyman *Pensées* and a paperback copy of Blake's poetry. Not everyone finds Pascal pleasant reading. Often he makes me very uncomfortable. 'Men are obliged to believe,' he insists, 'that they belong to this *small* [italics mine] number of the Elect whom Jesus Christ wishes to save.' A Jansenist, he was convinced that most of us would be damned for all eternity. On the other hand he credits Christ with saying, 'Take comfort – you would not seek me if you had not found me.' He was sure that 'Jesus seeks companionship and solace from men . . . Jesus will be in agony till the end of the world.'

However, Pascal is a marvellous friend for a man troubled by the Bat. The doubters' main argument, he says, is that apart from our faith and the Bible we have no evidence for the truth of religion except our own judgement. In Pascal's opinion our judgement can tell us nothing; it can't even tell us if man was created by God, by a demon or by pure chance. No one can be sure he is awake or asleep; he has to believe it, though when we sleep we may think we're awake. Because half our life is spent asleep we have no real idea of truth, whatever we may imagine. Perhaps the half of our life in which we think ourselves awake is only a dream 'during which we know as little about truth and good as we do during our natural sleep' from which we wake when we die. Just as some philosophers argue that we don't have enough intellectual equipment to speculate about eternal truths, Pascal suggests that we don't have enough to query them. 'So there is open war among men, in which each must take part, siding either with dogmatism or scepticism', he claims, dismissing agnosticism. 'He who thinks he can stay neutral is a sceptic.'

William Blake is a poet whom I read again and again, a Christian who despised most other Christians, sometimes even Christianity itself. His verse never ceases to thrill me, with its beautiful imagery and startling insights. One of his drawings is well suited to this book – 'The Red Dragon and the Woman clothed with the Sun'.

Frustration at not finding my friend, or perhaps too much Blake and Pascal, induced a mood of paralysing depression. After a miserable night, my gloom suddenly lifted. The healing was done at breakfast by my landlady, who expressed bizarre theories about our royal family, and was sarcastic about Slovaks. 'Just let them try to support themselves,' she grumbled, 'and stop being paid for by us Czechs.'

As I was crossing the Charles Bridge in the early morning sun, counting swans on the Vltava below – never less than twenty – I saw gilt weather vanes with the eight-pointed crosses of my beloved Order of Malta. The Knights' red and white flag was flying once again over their Grand Priory in Malá Strana, a vast Baroque church and palace, guarded by two stark twelfth-century towers which once formed the barbican of a predecessor of the Charles Bridge. When the Knights recovered the palace, it had been converted into a museum of musical instruments – with the former secret police's bugging devices still in place.

There was nobody in but the caretaker telephoned the Order's ambassador, who asked me to call on him. The embassy, the red and white flag flying reassuringly outside, was at that time off Celetná, opposite the Pariz Hotel. A slight, dapper figure with beautiful shoes, the ambassador had served in the Austrian diplomatic service, spoke perfect English and adored shooting grey partridges in Dorset. His counsellor was tall, bespectacled and slightly stooped, but even more distinguished, with one of the greatest names in Bohemian history. I could easily have imagined either of them in the uniform of the Habsburg Monarchy.

The two Knights told me of the Order's plans for enlisting young people to bring meals to the elderly, shop for them and even wash them. (There are none of the welfare services that exist in Britain or the United States.) In Moravia, under the Knights' direction, teams are being formed to help doctors, driving them if they don't have cars – which is often the case since there are so few private vehicles. Another, longer term project is targeted at diabetes, one of the fastest growing and most deadly of modern plagues; the Knights will first provide and equip a diabetic ward, then finance the training of diabetic specialists, and finally teach sufferers how to live with their disease.

As a very ordinary Catholic, an *homme moyen sensuel* who likes his pleasures and, despite his Hospitaller promise, doesn't do very much to help his fellow men apart from the occasional easy good turn for a friend, I was abashed by this account. The impression made by Catholics who don't agonize about whether they believe or not but get on with the Gospel message is always unsettling. Happily the ambassador ended his account of the Grand Priory's plans and said, 'Why don't we all go out for a damn good lunch?' During a splendid meal, at which I discovered that delicious Czech spirit called becherovka, I told my hosts of my wish to see Svatá Hora. They at once offered to arrange a visit next day.

Over breakfast at my lodgings next morning the grandmother was fascinated to hear that I had met a Lobkowicz. 'And calling himself "Prince" again!' She said she preferred the old nobles to the new sort: ex-party functionaries who buy up real estate and give themselves airs and graces. I was to find that many others in Eastern Europe shared her pleasure at the reappearance of historic names. Like the Church, they give a sense of continuity with a past which might have developed so differently and so much more happily.

My driver was another Czech Knight of Malta, a young geologist. Despite party policy, he had managed to go to the Charles University and then find a job there; because of his name he had not been allowed to do field research in case workers should meet him. A devout Catholic, he told me that it had been easy enough to practise his religion in Prague, where one could could go to confession and communion without being noticed, unlike small towns and villages where during the '50s people were arrested for attending Mass. A keen demonstrator under the old régime, he admitted that when the Velvet Revolution began he had never suspected that it would succeed in toppling the Communists.

The Czech countryside, with beautiful woods and mountains, is undeniably inspiring. I have been told that the Catholicism of Dvořák is expressed not just in his *Stabat Mater* but in every piece of music in which he evokes the landscape. This may be so yet, had I been a Czech, I don't think I would have dared to call myself a Christian under the former régime.

Svatá Hora lies forty or fifty kilometres south-west of Prague at the foot of the little mountains known as the Brdy. The road from Prague goes through woods full of deer – and former rocket sites – and past huge fields created by the collective farms. This area is comparatively unspoilt, unlike northern Bohemia or northern Moravia where exquisite Gothic towns such as Most have been destroyed by open cast mining for coal – exported to Russia.

My friend explained how one of his family's castles, Jezeři (a place of great importance in the history of Czech Renaissance music), was now in danger of disappearing into the ground because of this sort of mining. The landscape of northern Bohemia is everywhere pitted by poisoned holes. The Czechs are very bitter but can do nothing.

The country around Příbram has also suffered, though not to the same extent. Silver has been mined here since the Middle Ages and where there is silver there is uranium. Slave gangs of political prisoners, serving sentences of up to twenty years, had dug the metal out with their bare hands; many prisoners did not live to see their release. The little town is full of dirty concrete flats but the Svatá Hora, the Holy Mountain, is another story.

It is not a very big mountain, being no more than a low hill, but on it stands an elegant Baroque monastery. Dark red, white and cream stucco, with exuberant statuary, it was built by the Jesuits between 1655 and 1707, after the Thirty Years War when Bohemia was very poor; each of the eight chapels around the original medieval chapel bears the name of the city which paid for it. The altar of the miraculous statue of the Virgin and Child is a mass of precious metal – Bohemian gold and silver from Příbram. Above it, there is a golden sunburst.

According to pious legend, a chapel was built here in the thirteenth century by the Knight Malovec, in gratitude for his rescue from highwaymen, but there is no documentary evidence before the sixteenth century when it acquired the miraculous statue.

This is believed to have belonged to the first Archbishop of Prague, Arnost of Pardubice, who died in 1364. Some say he carved it himself, inspired by the Madonna at Klodz. As a dissolute young man, when praying to the Virgin he had been horrified at seeing her turn away; on his promising to reform, she turned to face him. For the rest of his life he never went on a journey without taking a statue or a painting of her with him, but the statue which he carved always stayed in the chapel of his castle at Příbram. During the Hussite wars of the fifteenth century it was moved to the oratory of a local hospital. It remained there until about 1550, when it was in danger from immigrant Lutheran miners and was placed in the chapel on the Holy Mountain.

Pilgrims came to pray, and there were miraculous cures, hermits settling in huts around the shrine. The first recorded miracle was in June 1632 when a Prague tailor, Jan Próchazka, who had been reduced to beggary by blindness, came here to pray for the return of his sight; it was restored after three days of prayer and he became a hermit, spending the rest of his life at Svatá Hora. The news of his cure spread throughout Bohemia and pilgrims arrived in thousands; among them was the Emperor Ferdinand III, who came in 1646 to pray for victory over the Swedes. However, only two years later the statue had to be hidden in the woods when the Swedes sacked Příbram.

The shrine was entrusted to the Jesuits and in 1652 the statue was taken on a week's visit to Prague, to encourage devotion to '*Panni Marie Svatohorske*'. She was brought back in triumph in a red velvet carriage drawn by four magnificent grey horses, the gift of my driver's ancestor. In 1658 an Italian architect called Carlo Lurago designed the present building. It became the most venerated shrine in Bohemia, over 30,000 pilgrims flocking to it annually on the third Sunday after Pentecost; The Holy Roman Emperor Leopold I came in person in 1673 to pray for protection against the Turks, who were threatening central Europe once again. In 1732, the centenary of Jan Próchazka's cure, Pope Clement XII gave formal permission for her solemn crowning, both Virgin and Child being given the diadem of the Holy Roman Emperor which they still wear.

Most of the frescoes in the cloisters, charming and naïve, were painted before 1750 and commemorate a hundred or so miracles performed by the Madonna of Svatá Hora. A good example is the cure of a soldier, Jan Láska in 1689. ('What a name'! whispered my friend. 'It means "laughter".') Fighting before Belgrade – shown, literally enough, as a white castle – Jan was knocked off his horse by a Turkish sabre cut to the head; his companions thought he was dead but he retained just enough consciousness to pray to Our Lady of Svatá Hora, promising to go to the shrine if he was healed. Other frescoes are of rescues from plague, shipwreck or highway robbery.

The Jesuits were evicted in 1773, when they were dispersed, their role as guardians of the shrine being taken over by secular priests and then, in 1861, by the Redemptorist Order. The shrine continued to flourish and in 1905 Rome declared Svatá Hora one of the world's great Marian basilicas.

A very well attested miracle took place in June 1940. A factory girl from Upice, Marie Milota, had had a bad leg injury at work in October 1937 and spent three years in bed, including one in hospital; her knee had been broken to re-set it but refused to heal. She tried to go to Lourdes but was prevented by the war. Wheeled in to hear Mass in the basilica at the 'Silver Altar' she suddenly felt her strength returning, rose from her chair and walked.

Persecution began in 1950. The Redemptorists were turned out and the statue had to be hidden once again. Nevertheless, the pilgrims kept on coming and the Archbishop of Prague saw to it that there were always priests to say Mass for them, though no less than six were arrested during the years which followed.

Then there was the Velvet Revolution, and the Redemptorists returned. 'We're back,' said the superior, Jan Zemanek, 'invigorated by our forty-year holiday.' Graham Greene considered the Redemptorists the least attractive order of any, 'with an obligation to dwell in all their sermons and retreats on the reality of hell', but I took an instant liking to Fr Jan. Barrel-chested and barrel-stomached, in his late sixties with strong, peasant features, a cropped white head and an iron hand clasp, he greeted me with a cheerful bellow, demanding, 'Why can't you speak a nice, easy language like Czech?' This man had been tried in the fire. Even the most besotted atheist could see that here was someone incapable of compromise.

Men like him had not only been shot out of hand or sent to the uranium mines, but had suffered more subtle persecution. During Mass one day a brave and popular – too brave and popular – parish priest, Fr Cihost, saw the crucifix on the altar move from right to left, then from left to right. His congregation gasped but he refused to accept it as miraculous. The secret police, who had been using magnets to move the crucifix, then attached cords and wires to it, after which they arrested him for faking a miracle. In prison he refused to sign a confession, his finger-nails were torn out and he died from torture. The official cause of death was 'tuberculosis'.

The superior told us that there had been several miracles in the recent past, including one only a week before our visit; a girl with a tumour on the brain, declared to be a hopeless case by the doctors, had had it successfully removed after praying to the Lady of Svatá Hora before the operation. 'What about curing doubts of faith?' 'Oh, we have many miracles of that sort but we don't talk about them,' replied Fr Jan, with a grin. His unquenchable optimism was symbolized by the shrine's sympathetic restoration after years of neglect.

He showed us the miraculous statue, small and black, with fat cheeks; I have to admit that I found it ugly and unattractive. Yet somehow this makes it even more impressive; the massive silver ornaments which frame the altar on which it stands seem only fitting – they express trust in the Lady of Svatá Hora's healing powers and gratitude for her miracles.

But although I liked Svatá Hora very much indeed, and could feel that it was genuinely holy, I could sense none of the reassurance given to me at Medjugorje.

Throughout my visit to Bohemia I was surprised by evidence of a vigorous, popular Church. Although largely Catholic, before 1938 the Czechs were not noted for fervour and since then there have been campaigns to destroy Christianity, in particular by the Communists. During a single night in 1950 all monasteries were occupied by the police, every member of a religious order, male or female, being sent to a concentration camp. All Catholic schoolmasters were sacked. Most of the secular priests were made to work in the mines, to dig the Prague Metro or to become street cleaners. In country parishes the few who survived were isolated and spied on, deprived of bishops to back them up – although urban laity came out from the towns to encourage them. Yet the calibre of the men who emerged from the rare seminaries which survived as window dressing was first-class despite deliberately poor teaching. The late Primate, Cardinal Tomašek, never compromised and won wide respect. Persecution proved counterproductive, as it has throughout history.

The Cardinal was a keen supporter of Medjugorje. In 1987, still under Communist rule, he declared, 'I am deeply grateful to God for Medjugorje. It all fits in very well with what has happened in the seventy years since the Fatima apparitions.'

Since the Velvet Revolution the monasteries have re-opened, though their lands have not yet been returned. Crucifixes are displayed ostentatiously in television programmes. There is definitely a Catholic revival, even if some of it is due to nostalgia for a pre-Marxist world.

As he drove me back from Svatá Hora, my friend told me about his hopes of helping fellow countrymen further east, such as the Czechs in the Ukraine. There are several thousand in villages near Chernobyl, who speak their ancestral tongue with difficulty; being without priests, they have become more or less godless. What really interested him were the Czechs in the mountains of the Banat in Romania, cheerful, unspoilt Catholic hillmen who speak the Czech of two centuries ago.

That night I could not sleep. Faith was returning. 'When I remember thee upon my bed and meditate on thee in the night watches.' I rose before dawn and went to the Central Station; I could get breakfast there, even at six a.m. A solid meal was available in the pre-1914 buffet, ham and wafer-thin slices of cheese. I noticed that others were drinking huge glasses of beer but I didn't join them. Since alcohol was on sale, there were plenty of drunks, including a pathetic bespectacled Englishman mumbling what appeared to be T. S. Eliot. Three junkies marched in, one with a bandaged stump in place of a hand.

Then I walked to my appointment with Count X, who had promised to tell me about a nobleman's life under the Communists.

Elites are usually religious, if only because they benefit from the old order of things. The patrician families of dying Rome were among the last to cling to paganism, while a few years ago *The Times* was astonished to discover in a survey how many members of the British Establishment were Christians. This is no less true of the historic nobility of Central Europe, natural targets for Communist persecution. Much has been written about the Czech intelligentsia's sufferings, very little about those of the aristocracy, whom secret policemen regarded in the same way as the Cheka had seen Russian nobles – *byvshie ludi*, 'former persons' without rights. Being born with a great name was to be born into an under-class, whose members were barred from higher education or decent jobs and who were under constant surveillance. Ironically, as in past centuries they continued to marry each other because they lived in a species of social ghetto. They trained themselves to be anonymous and impersonal, never asking personal questions, never carrying the addresses of relatives or friends, let alone letters from them. Above all, they stayed Christian.

In 1950 Count X, who was studying to be a biochemist and who had just married, was sent to a labour camp for 'military service'. The service was normally for two years but many people spent at least four years in such camps. Other inmates included seminarians, young priests, landowners' sons and of course youthful noblemen. Not allowed to handle weapons, by a ridiculous anomaly they were paid wages far better than a soldier's pay. The rest of the army called them the '*Černi Baroni*' or Black Barons. (Svanderlik wrote a novel of this name about them, which was dramatized for Czech television.) The Count told me that here he learnt the meaning of Catholicism. Sundays were free so Mass was said in a barrack room, the priest using a slice of bread as Host and a small bottle as chalice, saying the prayers silently; the rest of the room sat on their bunks or lounged around, pretending to read newspapers or singing. He himself did not have too bad a time, spending his second year as the camp doctor's assistant, after which he was released and allowed to continue his studies. He qualified as a microbiologist, joining a laboratory though never allowed out on field research. His wife was a doctor, a general practioner. When the 'Dubček Spring' of 1968 ended in a Russian invasion, they were on holiday in Italy but decided that they must go back. On his return the Marxist head of his department told him emotionally, 'It's the duty of a man with a name like yours to stay in Prague.'

He said that he had been lucky, but it was easier for doctors to survive than for lawyers or historians. Noblemen had been made to work as lavatory-attendants or as window-cleaners; the head of his family was made to sweep the streets of his village. Some were sent to the uranium mines, like Count Joseph Kinsky or Count Friedrich Strachwitz; others were in the labour gangs which dug the Prague Metro. Yet not one joined the party and not one committed suicide.

The Catholic nobles of his country have returned to public life. Prince Schwarzenberg conducted protocol at the Hradčany for President Havel, while a Lobkowicz was recently appointed auxiliary Bishop of Prague; it is not inconceivable that one day he may become Primate. Such families have rendered a very real service to the Church by their fidelity, which emphasizes the historic continuity of Catholicism among Czechs.

*

However, the reappearance of a few great names should not lull one into underestimating the survival of an enormous Marxist network, which remains rooted like ground ivy. Only senior officials with a high profile are at risk. The network reaches far beyond those in office in 1989. Many so called dissidents were Communists in the pre-Dubček days of the 1960s, and have always retained their links with those who stayed slavishly obedient.

Although I can quite understand Graham Greene deriving a good deal of fun from being bloody-minded, I have never been able to fathom his tolerant attitude towards Communism. 'A writer who is a Catholic cannot help having a certain sympathy for any faith which is sincerely held,' he once explained. Finally even he despaired of finding Communism with a human face. What shocks me, genuinely shocks me, is the number of ex-Communists I have met who admit that they never believed in their 'faith'. Those who believed it were bad enough.

The Reds have ruined Czechoslovakia, just as they ruined Russia. On the old black and white TV in my bedroom I watched a programme about Czech industry, which showed factories reminiscent of Britain in the early 1950s. It will take decades to rebuild the economy.

Yet there were good delicatessen shops bursting with rich food in Na Příkopě, the street leading to the Václavské Náměstí, and in Wenceslas Square itself. They were full of Czechs – I wondered they could afford to buy anything at all. Just where Celetná enters the great square of Staroměstské Náměstí I strayed into what turned out to be an exceptionally expensive restaurant, a *vinarna* full of fat Germans, and by mistake ordered 'Icelandic smoked salmon'. I watched a young Czech couple at the next table, who could only afford a bottle of beer between them, and was cheered at seeing how amiably the waiter served them.

A new entrepreneurial class is emerging, recruited from former black-marketeers and ex-party officials, who will develop a peculiarly unlovely form of capitalism. If I blame Graham Greene for 'looking for Christ within Communism', I can't imagine anyone trying to look for Him in the new materialism about to hold sway in Prague.

Great Baroque churches, such as Sv Mikuláš in Malá Strana, are full of tourists, but just off Náměstí Republiky there is a little Franciscan church which really is a house of prayer. Outside, in a small courtyard filled with flowers, there is a statue of Jude Thaddeus – the Apostle chosen to replace Judas. He is the patron of hopeless causes in Prague as everywhere else, which is why there are so many flowers and so many supplicants here.

One of the grandest Baroque churches in Prague houses the Prazké Jesulatko, the Infant of Prague. This tiny statue of the child Jesus was brought to Prague in the sixteenth century, during the Emperor Rudolf II's reign, by a Spanish lady, Countess Manrique de Lara, who married a Bohemian noble, Count Bernstein. Their daughter Polyxana married Prince Zdenko Adalbert Lobkowicz; both were staunch supporters of the Counter-Reformation. After the defeat of the Protestants at the White Mountain in 1620, they gave the statue to its present home, the church of Panna Maria Vitezna, which had been confiscated from the Lutherans and given to the Carmelites. (During the eighteenth century it was used by Knights of Malta, hence an eight-pointed cross on the façade.) The statue, wearing an Imperial crown and carrying an orb with a Maltese cross, has seventeen sets of baby clothes, of velvet, silk and fur, which are changed regularly. It attracts many pilgrims, especially from South America – though why I have never discovered – and is credited with numerous miracles. Nothing repels me more than cults like that of the Infant. They make me wonder how I can go on being a Catholic.

Many people leave the Church because of too great a demand on their credulity. Recently, while writing a book on Sussex, I came across the sad story of a seventeenth-century English friar, Thomas Gage, a missionary in Central America. During his years in the Guatemalan jungle he became fascinated by the Holy House of Loreto; according to pious legend this was the house of the Virgin at Nazareth where Christ was conceived, and in 1294 was carried through the air by angels to Loreto near Ancona to save it from demolition by the Turks. When Friar Gage eventually visited Loreto, he was so disgusted that he renounced Catholicism, preaching a recantation sermon at St Paul's in 1642 – *The tyranny of Satan, discovered by the teares of a conuerted sinner* (in which he declared 'I was like a foule and ugly monkey'). I have a good deal of sympathy for Thomas Gage.

Yet I encountered one of the most moving representations of the Madonna which I have ever seen at the Prague Loreto, a superb Baroque complex on the Hradčany. Its cream and buff façade, with a cupola whose bells play a hymn in honour of the Virgin every hour, was built in the early eighteenth century; the church and six chapels joined by a double decker cloister are from the end of the seventeenth. The exquisite '*Santa Casa*', modelled on that at Loreto, was built by a Prince Lobkowicz in 1631. Its Black Madonna, glimpsed through a massive silver grille, was carved from limewood in 1671; she is far more moving than the Virgin of Svatá Hora or the *Gospa* in the parish church at Medjugorje. If I cannot accept the legend of the Holy House, I have to admire the beauty of the Prague Loreto and revere its Madonna.

Turzovka is a village in north-eastern Slovakia, on the slopes of the Beskinden mountains beside the River Kyusca. It was part of Hungary until 1918, with the rest of Slovakia. During all my reading about Medjugorje I could find nothing on Turzovka, though there were plenty of references to Garabandal and even to Hriushiw. I was unable to trace anything about it in German let alone in English. At the Jesuit headquarters at Farm Street an expert on Marian shrines could only tell me that he thought he had heard of it.

At last I came across a reference. It said that between 1 June and 14 August 1958 the Virgin and Child had appeared near Turzovka to a forty-two-year-old forester, Matthias Laschut (usually spelt Lašuta), a married man with three children. However, a mariologist, writing in 1987, stated that he had been unable to secure enough information about the shrine – 'communications are poor in the Eastern Block countries. Both bishops and witnesses live in fear.' He mentioned a booklet, *Turzovka, Slevensky Lurd* (Turzovka, the Slovak Lourdes), by S. Sensick but, try as I might, I failed to obtain a copy.

Nor could the Czech Knight of Malta in London tell me very much, despite having been there himself. He described Turzovka as an ugly little place, with factories and concrete flats, though there was a forest full of roe deer across the river. Its church was unremarkable save for being full for the six o'clock Mass on a weekday after work. The parish priest was uncommunicative. The locals would say nothing except one old woman. 'Have you seen anything?' my friend asked her. 'Living here, I'd be a real fool not to go into the woods and watch what's going on,' she replied, but she refused to elaborate.

In order to reach Turzovka, I would have had to go by rail to Vienna and then hire a car to drive up over the border, both expensive and time consuming. I was so discouraged by what I had heard from the Czech Knight that I abandoned the idea.

However, when I returned to London, the Knight sent me an unpublished account of the phenomena at Turzovka which is so important that I have decided to give substantial extracts from it. I have never met the author, who does not want to be named, but apparently he is a former Bohemian magnate, once the owner of great estates, who went through the usual hellish experience of his class under Communism. All I could learn about him was that he is a devout Catholic, highly educated and 'a man of rugged probity'. While convinced by what he saw at Turzovka, he none the less remains detached, refusing to be influenced by it. 'Sincere faith in God must be able to do without miracles,' he warns, 'otherwise it simply becomes mere speculation.' Pascal couldn't have put it better. What follows is based on his account, which has never been published before.

The account says that on a June Saturday in 1958 Lašuta was on his normal rounds, walking through the forest. He had reached high ground, being about a thousand metres up, where the spruce trees began, when suddenly he saw a beautiful woman in white who appeared to floating in the air. According to statements he made later, the forester – who at that time was only a vague believer – stopped dead in his tracks, incredulous and very frightened. The beautiful young woman moved towards him and said that she was the Mother of God and, for the time being, he must not speak of her appearing to him. He must pray for reconciliation, for atonement by the whole world. She added that she would come to him again in seven days' time, at the same place and at the same hour. Then she dissolved into nothing before his eyes.

Lašuta could not bring himself to believe that what he had seen was real. He tried to drive the vision out of his mind, almost convincing himself he was the victim of a hallucination. Nevertheless he went back to the same spot in the woods on the following Saturday, in a state of feverish anticipation. In all, 'this fascinatingly beautiful lady' (*fazinierend schönen Frau*) appeared to him seven times, always on a Saturday in the same place at the same hour, the last occasion being on the vigil of the feast of the Blessed Virgin Mary's Assumption.

The 'lady' always held a white rosary in her hands and spoke to him in very clear, intelligible words – requests, admonitions and warnings which closely resembled those of the apparitions at Lourdes and Fatima, though this extremely simple, more or less illiterate man had never heard of Lourdes or Fatima. Afterwards he repeated sayings by the beautiful lady whose substance and content were very much above his intellectual capacity. Although particularly impressed by the final apparition, and knowing that he was now free to speak of what he had experienced, at first he told only his wife and children. But when they repeated it to their neighbours, the story spread very fast. Since Lašuta was respected by everyone who knew him, and as he also had a reputation for telling the truth, nobody at Turzovka thought he was crazy. A mixture of curiosity and hope drew many people to the place where the apparitions had occurred, high in the forest. They brought with them statues of the Virgin, crucifixes, holy pictures and candles, which they fastened to the trees or stood on the ground.

Up till now, everything had depended on what one simple man, Lašuta, claimed to have seen, so that the miraculous 'happenings' at Turzovka could arguably be dismissed as autosuggestion, hysteria, coincidence or even fraud. However, there then began a series of strange phenomena, experienced by large numbers at the same time, which seemed to make the idea of subjective hallucination or illusion at least questionable. Where the forester – who had meanwhile changed totally and become a deeply believing Catholic – claimed to have seen and heard the Mother of God on seven occasions, a spring suddenly burst forth from the forest soil, hitherto generally supposed to be arid; the water flowed out of the ground from the highest point of the mountain, something considered most unusual by experts on hydrography. Still more spectacular were strange lights and solar manifestations which astonished the pilgrims.

News of these 'miraculous occurences' spread like wildfire and the number of pilgrims increased by leaps and bounds. On Sundays and on holidays motor coaches came to the mountain from far and wide, while there was a continuous flow of people on foot up and down the steep mountainside.

Cures started to happen, the healing of serious and seemingly incurable illnesses, some of them apparently verified by doctors. Stories about Turzovka reached Prague, even crossing the Czechoslovak frontiers into neighbouring countries; pilgrims arrived from Hungary and Austria. By now even the hard-boiled sceptics and realists who so far had had only pitying smiles for the 'gossip from Turzovka' were finding considerable difficulty in thinking of a rational explanation.

Then the Communist authorities began to pay attention. They realized – or thought they realized – the danger of so much spontaneous enthusiasm for religion among the 'deluded masses' who, irritatingly, did nothing worse than spend their free time climbing up a wooded mountain where they prayed, drank water and sang songs in praise of the Virgin Mary. There were too many of them doing it and there was no sign that 'this blind mob-madness' would end of its own accord. Nothing could be done through the law, even through the 'People's law', so the authorities tried violence. One moonlit night a bus arrived, filled with Communist Youth, full of zeal, who scrambled up the slopes into the forest and laid waste the site of the apparition – the spot where the Virgin was reported to have appeared to Lašuta. All the makeshift altars, crucifixes, pictures and statues, together with the wax left from innumerable candles, were thrown on to a great bonfire, soaked in petrol and burnt. The night was illuminated by a bright red light. Next day pilgrims found a scene of charred devastation. The villagers were outraged. No one admitted the crime but it wasn't too difficult to guess the identity of the culprits.

There were several raids of this sort, but none of them had any lasting effect. Each time, within a few days devoted hands had erected bigger and better altars, cleared away the ashes and the wreckage, covered the scorched earth with pine branches. The blocked-up stream gushed forth once again into the light of day, while enthusiasts brought up bricks from the valley below with which to build a permanent chapel for the Mother of God.

The authorities decided that more serious measures were needed. Lašuta was arrested and brought before a court, charged with whipping up 'inflammatory popular hysteria'. Before the trial he was interrogated and tortured many times by the police.

Against all expectation, the court found him not guilty; he was released and allowed to go home. However the state forestry department sacked him shortly afterwards and, on instructions from senior party officials, he was confined in a lunatic asylum. Following intensive examination, the asylum doctors decided there was nothing wrong with him, no mental abnormality, and he was again released and permitted to return to Turzovka.

The infuriated authorities could not let this muddled business go on. A man who was in contact with the Mother of God at Turzovka had to disappear; while people were conscious of his existence the 'disturbance' would continue. Lašuta was seized by the secret police and taken to an undisclosed prison far away from Turzovka where he was kept in solitary confinement. Even his unfortunate family were not allowed to know where he was imprisoned.

None of these measures had any effect whatever. The steady flow of pilgrims showed no sign of diminishing in the slightest. Despite the activities of the security organizations who policed all access roads, demanding to see identification papers, more and more people came to the mountain. On Sundays and on holidays when the crowd was especially large the police blocked access roads over a wide area, but the pilgrims made long detours across fields and meadows and through the woods.

On the high ground above, Masses were celebrated, brass bands played Marian hymns, the crowds of faithful singing with them or else saying the Rosary. There were many strange tales of 'miracles of the sun' which had been experienced by pilgrims.

Then the Church spoke, for the first time. The local bishop (of Nitra) ordered his priests to read a pastoral letter from their pulpits in which he sternly forebade the faithful of the diocese to take part in pilgrimages to Turzovka. The letter had little effect since everyone knew that it was not inspired by Rome, suspecting that the régime had bullied the bishop into writing it.

*

The author of the account on which this narrative is based visited Turzovka for the first time on Trinity Sunday 1963, almost five years after the lady appeared to Lašuta. He went by train, noticing that nearly all the passengers left it at Turzovka station. No one needed to ask for directions about the way up the mountain, since everyone was going the same way. He joined the crowd. The villagers shouted cheerful, friendly greetings to the pilgrims as they passed their houses. There was a monotonous murmur as the pilgrims said the Rosary. Walking fast, he overtook group after group of pilgrims praying aloud. He reached the summit of the mountain at about noon. It was a fine, sunny day.

The whole of the high ground, a forest clearing amid the tall trees, was covered by a vast, colourful multitude, candles flickering everywhere. Near the place where the forester Lašuta was said to have seen the Mother of God, people stood packed in a wide, deep circle. The air itself seemed almost as if saturated by devotion, a spontaneous expression of religious faith, of a sort he had never experienced before or since. The sound of singing came through the forest. A priest stood on a tree-stump, preaching fervently to a group of pilgrims, after which they all knelt to say the Rosary.

He pushed his way through to the site of the apparition with some difficulty. A great deal was going on at the spring. A very fat bus-driver in uniform was organizing the bottling of the water, people waiting patiently for their turn to fill their bottles. The writer queued for a long time as the sick and disabled were coming every minute and willingly given precedence. When he drank it, he found the water refreshingly cold with an earthy taste. He drank so much – it was a hot day – that the bus-driver joked, 'Leave some for the others.'

Walking away, the writer passed through dense ranks of pilgrims. There were some altars and many wayside shrines. He found himself speaking to strangers. Everybody was speaking freely and without any restraint to everyone else; all felt bound deeply to each other by the emotion which they shared. The themes, which recurred over and over again, were the Mother of God together with people's worries, hopes and expectations. 'She has come to us, into our vale of tears,' said a cripple who had been dragged up the mountain by his family. 'I can't ask her to heal me – I just want to be happy that she's here.'

A dozen young men were struggling with a home-made crucifix, fashioned from tree-trunks. They dug a deep hole in the stony ground and erected the crucifix which was at least six metres high. When the work had been finished, the pilgrims stood round admiring it and shaking the young men's hands gratefully. One of them called out to the crowd, 'They'll find it hard to burn a big crucifix like this!' Everyone understood only too well whom he meant by 'They'.

Growing tired, the author went a little way off to lie down on a mossy patch. He had almost fallen asleep when suddenly the sound of distant singing and the murmur of the Rosaries was interrupted by shrill cries. He rose quickly and went up to the high ground near the site of the apparition. This was what he saw:

> Everybody was standing as if lost in ecstasy, gazing at the sun. The fiery orb in the sky had lost its sharp circular outline and seemed to be ablaze, burning, with flames bursting out of it. The contrast to the sun we all knew and had seen countless times was so striking that among over 500 people who were watching in consternation there was only shocked astonishment. After a few moments an enormous cone-shaped light spread above and around us, like some over-sized tent made of long, vividly hued strips. It consisted of every colour in the spectrum from red to violet, but those magnificent strips of colour glowed so brightly and intensely that one could not compare it to a rainbow. All around, coloured strips covered the sky, the trees and their branches, the ground and the people. The strips fanned out from a single focal point in

> which was the sun. I saw deep blue and bright yellow people next to me, whose colour changed when they moved . . .

From his account it is obvious that the spectators thought that this was a divinely inspired miracle and that the Mother of God was present. Some of them stood motionless, as if turned to stone, gazing thunderstruck at the sky. Many there believed that their worries and needs would certainly be attended to, since, after all, the sign from heaven was so unmistakable. They were desperately anxious not to lose this precious moment of mercy, shouting, even screaming, their pleas to heaven.

Four state foresters in uniform, ordered to carry out fire-protection duties on their day off because of all the burning candles and therefore not too well disposed to what went on at Turzovka, stood rigid at attention, saluting. Three local brass bands, which had come with the pilgrims, formed up, raised their gleaming instruments to heaven and began to play fortissimo the well known Marian hymn '*Tisickrát pozdravujeme tebe . . .*' (We salute you a thousand times, Mary.') Everyone joined in the singing and the joyful Marian chorus rang through the brilliantly coloured forest. The writer describes the scene as 'strange and deeply moving, overwhelming . . . God related.'

It was a good twenty-five minutes before the display began to fade gradually. After another fifteen minutes it was all over. The writer took a careful look at the sun; it was already setting in the west and it seemed quite normal again. 'As if waking from some beautiful, happy dream, I felt myself coming back to the reality of everyday life. But that blessed feeling of contentment from what I had just experienced stayed with me. From every face around me there radiated happiness . . .'

I find the writer's attempts to produce a natural explanation for the phenomena so interesting that I give them in full. He asks:

Illusion or reality? Hysterical psychosis or supernatural manifestation? Phenomena consistent with the laws of nature or a sign from the Other World? I don't know. I have merely described what I experienced and I saw.

One might argue plausibly that certain conditions of light with suitable degrees of temperature and humidity, together with the right conjunction of certain physical parameters, might produce a fairly simple dispersal of light which could result in a special colour effect. Yet why did this always happen in the same place?

One might argue too that the human dioptical apparatus, the eye, when exposed to strong sunlight is a conduit for visual sensations which do not accord with the real object seen, but are illusionary pictures. Later I tried this a number of times, gazing long into the sun. The eyes hurt intolerably but I never saw the colours of the spectrum. Moreover this theory is contradicted by the fact that the light phenomena at Turzovka have been photographed several times in colour and the developed prints have invariably produced the colours in their full intensity.

One might also point to hysterical mass-psychosis, but then again one cannot answer the question as to why this state of emotional mass delusion should always recur in the same place.

He says something about the way in which he relates his experience at Turzovka to his religious faith which, I must confess, hits me very hard indeed. As I have explained, my search for the dancing sun has really been a search for reassurance about my own beliefs. He admits that he went to Turzovka to see a sign from the next world for use as a crutch to support a lame faith – 'precisely the problem of the Apostle Thomas for which he received an unmistakable rebuke from Our Lord'. He points out that *to know for certain* would deprive our faith of a great deal which is very valuable. Looking up to heaven should not become 'a greedy gaze searching for a divine confidential secret, so that we can snatch something concrete which will enable us to calculate the profit and loss account of our lives'. The question 'illusion or reality?' is simply a waste of time.

It is a pity he does not go into more detail about the Virgin's message to the forester Matthias Lašuta. Significantly, it reflected that of Fatima – there must surely be a link between the solar phenomena at the two shrines. But the testimony of so cautious and level-headed a witness is of particular value.

I have tried in vain to find out more about Turzovka. Does the sun still dance there? Have there been more cures at the 'Slovak Lourdes'? But, sadly, my friends tell me that its inhabitants are obdurate in their refusal to talk.

Nevertheless, Turzovka was of great importance in my pilgrimage. It rebuts some of the arguments put forward by John Cornwell in *Powers of Darkness, Powers of Light*. 'The Medjugorje and Garabandal apparitions are . . . unfolding stories in the context of the folk religion of Mediterranean communities,' he concludes, adding that generally such apparitions are first seen by young girls at about the age of puberty. Turzovka (of which Cornwell does not appear to have heard) is rather a long way from the Mediterranean, while Lašuta was a man in middle age. Yet the Lady, the sun and the message have everything in common with Medjugorje and Garabandal. Above all, there seems to be a link with Fatima – the resemblances are unmistakable, including the behaviour of the sun.

— 3 —

Kraków and Częstochowa

Reason says Miracle, Newton says Doubt –
Aye that's the way to make all Nature out –
Doubt, Doubt & don't believe without experiment:
That is the very thing that Jesus meant
When he said, Only Believe Believe & try
Try Try & never mind the Reason why

William Blake, *Resentments*

the face that most resembles Christ

Dante, *Paradiso*, 32: 85–86

I had always wanted to visit Częstochowa since I had heard it praised so often, and so fervently, by my many Polish friends. If there were no reports (as far as I could tell) of apparitions by the Virgin or of a dancing sun, I was certain that there must be something else at this Marian shrine which attracted millions of pilgrims. But what? When I asked my friends they simply laughed or shrugged, replying, 'The Black Virgin.' Could she heal, like the *Gospa* at Medjugorje, I wondered. Did she banish doubts of faith?

Częstochowa, the town beneath the shrine of the Black Virgin, is an industrial slum, so I decided to visit the 'Bright Mountain' from Kraków. I had been told that the old capital was a beautiful city; that its castle on the Wawel Hill was the heart of Poland; and that it had a famous church, the Mariacki, which possessed another wonder-working icon.

One cannot begin to understand the Poles without knowing a little history. In the fourteenth century Poland joined with Lithuania to form a mighty realm which included the entire Ukraine. In 1610 the Poles even occupied Moscow. But then there were wars with the Swedes, with Turks, Tartars and Cossacks, and with Russia; half the Ukraine was lost in 1667, though the Poles remained strong enough to save Vienna from the Turks in 1683. Ruin followed, the country being divided between Russia, Austria and Prussia at the end of the eighteenth century; politically the Poles ceased to exist. A Polish state reappeared in 1918 and again in 1945, but was pushed steadily westward; after the Second War Russia seized what was left of the Polish Ukraine, compensating Poland with German territory.

Kraków was an independent republic from 1815–46, a city state. A mingling of Gothic, Renaissance, Baroque and Biedermeyer, it is marvellously preserved; only a single bomb fell on it during the 1939–45 war. It has a gentle, irresistible charm, despite the sulphurous proximity of Nowa Huta, an industrial suburb with crumbling tower-blocks and archaic steelworks. Stalin had Nowa Huta built to create an 'urban proletariat' which would tame the Catholic dons of Kraków University; instead, workers allied with intellectuals against Marxism, the local branch of Solidarity marching beneath the banner of the Virgin. The Order of Malta has built a magnificent church at Nowa Huta, with the eight-pointed cross much in evidence.

My hotel, the Pollera in Szpitalna Street, was within walking distance of both station and city centre. Dating from Habsburg days, it had 'hot and cold running water in every room', with friendly staff who enjoyed a joke, and reminded me of the Dublin hotels of forty years ago. It also had a really excellent restaurant, with ash blonde waitresses.

I had an introduction to another Knight of Malta. The Count was not a native of Kraków – his father came from what was formerly 'Russian Poland' and had been in the Uhlans of the Russian Imperial Guard of the Tsar – but clearly he loved the city. First he took me to an art nouveau café, Jama Michalika in Floriańska Street, all green, mauve and amber glass; it was sad to reflect that its clientele must have known so much misery. We went to the Mariacki church in the great, windy, Italianate market-place at the end of Floriańska; every hour, from one of the Mariacki's two tall towers a trumpeter sounds the long, wailing '*hajnal*' – there is a break in the middle, commemorating a thirteenth-century trumpeter who was shot in the throat by a Tartar arrow. Inside is a copy of the Black Madonna of Częstochowa, a copy so perfect that many locals are convinced it is the original; it inspires deep devotion and is credited with miracles. At midday huge wooden rods open the Mariacki's other treasure, a gigantic tryptich of gilded wood over the high altar which Veit Stoss carved during the late 1400s, with scenes from the lives of Christ and his mother; the most touching shows her falling asleep before her assumption into heaven – the dormition.

In the square nearby there is a very ancient church, dedicated to St Wojciech, who was martyred by Prussians a thousand years ago. It too has an icon of the Virgin, though not a copy of the Lady of Częstochowa. If scarcely a great painting, her long narrow, wistful face is one of exquisite tenderness and very moving when seen from a certain angle.

Finally we climbed the Wawel Hill. Looking down over the River Vistula, the rock which is Poland's very heart has both a castle and a cathedral; the former with a courtyard of the sort one might expect to see at Urbino rather than in Northern Europe, the latter holding the tombs of over forty kings of Poland – here too is the shrine of St Stanisław who, like Beckett, was murdered by his sovereign. It was the cathedral church of Karol Wojtyła before he became Pope; he called it the 'sanctuary of the nation'. At the side of the kings lies Tadeusz Kościusko who fought for George Washington in the American Revolution and who led the heroic Polish rising of 1794 against the Russians.

Describing his own life under Communism, the Count said that he had been very lucky. Naturally he lost his estate but he was never persecuted and found a good job in a housing department. (His father, a true Pole, joked that it was the first time that he had had no money worries, he told me.) He could not shoot any more – that became the *nomenklatura*'s privilege – but he did not mind. No stauncher believer could be imagined; there was no need of adversity to strengthen his faith.

However, a Polish Knight whom I know in London had a very different experience of Communism. Arrested for having too many foreign friends, after months of interrogation he was given ten years' hard labour; a fastidious man, he cleaned the camp latrines to spare elderly prisoners who had been given the job. One day, spread-eagled against the camp hospital's wall awaiting an injection, he found himself beside a priest to whom he made his confession. After this they met regularly. There was no wine for the Christmas Mass so the Knight prayed for raisins; they came in a few days, in a food parcel from Sweden – though they had never been in previous food parcels. On Christmas Day, lying on his bunk, the priest celebrated Mass with a host made of flour stolen from the hospital and with raisin wine – using a tin spoon for a chalice. (Long afterwards Archbishop Wojtyła confirmed that the Mass had been valid.) Even supposed atheists in the camp asked for communion.

I envied those two men. I wished that I had their serene religion instead of my own flickering, tormented faith. Like Francis Quarles, in the seventeenth century, I doubt even my doubting:

> It is the ship that moves and not the coast.
> I fear, I fear, my soul, 'tis thou art lost.

Yet friends often ask me, infuriatingly, 'How can you be so certain in your beliefs?' Of course I'm not, as any one who reads this book must realize. Sometimes I have what Cardinal Newman called *certitude*. He wrote that *certainty* is impossible; however rational and well thought out, no belief can be proved logically. (He quoted St Ambrose: 'It pleased not God to save his disciples by logic.') In Newman's judgement there was no such thing as a totally convincing argument; there is always a margin of objection, just as there is with any proof in higher mathematics. But the Cardinal's certitude is a state of mind which everybody has come across in other people – reached through intuitive perception, and from the cumulative effect of considering probabilities. What 'to one intellect is proof, is not proof to another', Newman reminds us; the 'certainty of a proposition does properly consist of the certitude of mind that contemplates it'.

Only rarely during the last few years had I known Cardinal Newman's certitude.

I must admit that it is fear which makes me go running back to religion, though it has not yet changed my way of life. I am fascinated by the story of Armand de Rancé, a Frenchman of Louis XIV's time, who inherited a titular abbey but took no interest in religion. Returning from a visit abroad, he found the corpse of his adored mistress displayed in segments on a table, like meat and offal in a butcher's shop; she had died during his absence – there had been an autopsy. He fled to his abbey of La Trappe. It was roofless, inhabited by four monks who supported themselves by poaching, but he made it into the strictest community in Europe – the Trappists. I doubt if my conversion would have quite such an impact.

Some argue that religion functions by creating fear and then dispelling it by ritual. 'A man of timorous disposition and in great doubt of his acceptance with God, and pretty credulous, might be glad of a Church where there are so many helps to heaven,' Dr

Johnson observed in the year before he died. 'I would be a Papist if I could. I have fear enough, but an obstinate rationality prevents me.' Well, I too have fear enough. Am I irrational? Perhaps. But, as Pascal asked, what has that got to do with it?

In the modern world one has to pay for religious belief with a certain degree of isolation. Although sympathetic, Arnold Toynbee confessed that he dared not become a Catholic, because no historian would take him seriously if he did. (Yet the academics whose opinion Toynbee so valued regarded Marxism as 'intellectually respectable'.)

In the past there was blind faith, which still survives in the 'backward' areas of Eastern Europe and the Mediterranean, but in the West religious belief is increasingly seen as eccentric; atheism or agnosticism is the proper condition of educated minds. Nowhere is this truer than in Britain, the least Christian country in Europe.

I am well aware that my beliefs seem to many of my friends ludicrous, morbid, even monstrous. I admit that there is something very strange indeed about Christianity, about a God who, having created men and women, allows some to go to hell for eternity, and saves others by undergoing a frightful, agonizing death.

Catholicism attracts fewer and fewer thinkers and artists. Its abandonment of beauty and mystery, its de-mythologizing, its refusal to let men be awed, is at least partly responsible; the new emphasis on the ordinary can lead all too easily to a suspicion that the Church's perception of God is second rate. Even before the present malaise many Catholics found the going hard. Graham Greene wrote (in *A Sort of Life*) how 'many of us abandon Confession and Communion to join the Foreign Legion of the Church and fight for a city of which we are no longer full citizens'. Nowadays many of us do not bother to join the Foreign Legion.

Nowhere have I felt less of an oddity (and, momentarily, ex-doubter) than in the churches of Poland.

Częstochowa had stirred my imagination as a very young man,

when I first read Henryk Sienkiewicz's *Deluge*. I had known and liked the Poles since Ampleforth where there were many Polish boys. I call myself a 'Franco-Irishman' because of my background; and the Polish temperament has a lot in common with that of the French and the Irish. I was intrigued when I heard that Częstochowa was the favourite shrine of this most God-haunted and romantic of nations. I had heard of the Black Virgin's miracles and knew that her pilgrims – no less than those at Medjugorje – were convinced that she had personally overthrown Marxist Socialism.

I had underestimated the distance between Częstochowa and Kraków. There was no morning train so I decided to go by bus. The twelfth person whom I accosted at the terminal spoke English and showed me where to board, while I gave the driver a scrap of paper on which I had written in Polish, 'One ticket one way to Częstochowa.' The journey was supposed to take three hours. At first we went through beautiful country, with forests and manor houses, but then we came to a gloomy little town called Mislowice, and then to Katowice – a hellish place of monstrous factories and filthy high-rise blocks. Even Katowice's buildings from pre-war or Imperial German days are hideous, for it has long been an industrial town. A dark cloud overhung it and there must be fearsome pollution. Everything here is black with soot or worse, including the white bark of birch trees – pregnant women are terrified of breathing, lest the air harm the children in their wombs.

We drove on through a ruined landscape, farmed after a fashion, great woods alternating with factories or pylons. Eventually the country opened up, there were men and women working in the fields – some were using scythes.

When we approached Częstochowa, half an hour late, it was in drenching black rain. The town looked like Katowice all over again, having been industrialized by the Communists. A taxi driven by a robber took me up the main thoroughfare three kilometres long, re-named 'Hitler Street' and then 'Stalin Street', but once more 'Najświętszej Marji Panny' – 'Lady Mary Boulevard'. It leads to the Jasna Gora ('Bright Mountain'), a significant name because the monastery regards itself as separate from the town. First one sees a tall, rectangular campanile then one realizes that the Jasna Gora was a fortress as well as a monastery; it is ringed by a deep, brick-lined moat and has frowning gun emplacements.

Before going in, I visited an exhibition in a hall just outside. It showed the collapse of Communism and revival of Christianity in Eastern Europe, starting with the 1980 strike at Gdansk. What was striking in these photographs were the changing expressions on the faces of the high party officials; first arrogant contempt, then bewildered apprehension and finally fear as the Mother of God overthrew Marxism.

Entering the monastery, I found myself in an imposing Baroque church. At the communion rails of the chapel where the Blessed Sacrament is reserved, there knelt a familiar figure in blue; it was a life-like statue of the Virgin. Everywhere there were rapt faces, almost terrifying in the intensity of their devotion. Yet the faces were even more rapt in the chapel of the Black Madonna, a church in itself. The altar is of black ebony with gleaming silver ornaments, the icon hidden by a silver gilt screen. The walls too are all but concealed by silver, covered with *ex-votos* in gratitude for cures, together with discarded crutches and artificial limbs. Mass was being celebrated, the congregation singing a haunting Polish hymn with wild emotion.

Many miracles have been worked here, the earliest in 1396 when a blind painter from Lithuania recovered his sight. The community opened a *Liber Miraculorum* in 1402, to record favours granted by the Virgin; it was continued till 1885, after which a separate file was kept on each case. Among them were several victories; in 1514 Bishop Jan Konarski offered Mass before the icon for King Zygmunt, campaigning against Grand Duke Vassily of Moscow – the Russians were defeated during the Mass. One of the most dramatic cases of healing was in 1540 when a Lublin shopkeeper, Marcin Lanio, wheeled the corpses of his wife and two small sons into the chapel where Benediction was taking place; as the congregation sang the *Magnificat*, suddenly the icon glowed and the three sat up in their coffins.

There has been healing at Częstochowa in more recent times, often of supplicants who have overcome great obstacles to reach the shrine, or in response to unusually fervent prayers. In 1929 an elderly man paralysed from the waist down, Michal Bartosiak, crawled from the railway station to the Jasna Gora – then rose to his feet before the icon. In 1955 a woman, haemorrhaging and near death, was totally restored to health; in her view 'It was because I believed so firmly that the Lady of Częstochowa would be kind to me.' There have been many, many, other cures including cases of thrombosis and encephalitis. Careful records are kept; depositions by those cured, priests' testimony and doctors' reports. In 1977, not an exceptional year, forty-eight miracles were documented. However the *ex-votos* of those healed are a better indication of what is believed to occur – these range from 1500 to 2000 annually.

In the downcast mood in which I had arrived after my gloomy journey, I reflected – not for the first time – that despite all the raptures of the cured, he or she must still have to fear other illnesses, old age with its pains and indignities, and endure the unravelling of death. But I was heartened by being told that here the Virgin specializes in cures of mind and spirit.

The chapel is the centre of a huge complex, a highly organized pilgrim centre which is run by Pauline fathers. It is also a national shrine. In 1655 4000 Swedish troops were routed before it by the Black Virgin. Sienkiewicz describes what happened:

> A white fog hid the summit of the Jasna Gora, and according to the normal order of things should have hidden the church too, but by some strange phenomenon the church with its tower was raised not only above the cliff but above the fog, high, high – just as if it had left its foundations and was hanging in the blue under the dome of the sky. The cries of the soldiers announced that they too saw the phenomenon.

Then the garrison, 250 peasants led by a handful of local gentry, charged downhill and routed the Lutheran besiegers. From the faces which I saw in prayer before the icon of the Black Virgin, I can well understand why the Swedes fled. Moreover, she herself was seen in the sky. From that moment onwards the war went in favour of the Poles.

Later I was shown a painting of the siege; the Virgin stands on a cloud above the Bright Mountain, while to the right there appear to be three suns – as at Mortimer's Cross (see p. 19).

Although moved, my first impression was that though the place was undeniably holy, it was for Poles alone. So much did I feel this that I had a strong urge to leave at once and return to the pleasures of Kraków. Luckily I stayed. I had a letter of introduction from the Polish Knights of Malta which persuaded the Prior's secretary to take me on a tour.

Ever since Ampleforth I have respected and liked monks for their concentration on what really matters, and for their humanity. They are one of the reasons why the Bat finds it hard to flit. Fr Simon was a prime specimen, scholarly, absent-minded, talkative and very funny. There could have been no better guide.

'The first thing you must see is the Virgin's unveiling,' he told me. This is done four times a day. We went to the chapel where thirty monks were about to say Mass. Trumpets sounded a majestic if melancholy fanfare as the silver curtain rose slowly. She wore a robe studded with diamonds, the 'diamond robe'. (She has other robes, including one of rubies.) I could easily believe that the exquisite face revealed was that of a sinless creature, the ultimate human being after Christ. Two scars on her cheek emphasize that this is someone who has been hurt, agonizingly. Graham Greene called it 'the most convincing portrait ever painted of Our Lady', quoting Belloc's words 'Help of the half-defeated'.

I had read Belloc's 'Ballad of Częstochowa' long, long ago.

Help of the half-defeated, House of Gold,
  Shrine of the Sword and Tower of Ivory;
Splendour apart, supreme and aureoled.
  The Battler's vision and the world's reply.
  You shall restore me, O my last Ally.
To vengeance and the glories of the bold.
This is the faith that I have held and hold,
  And this is that in which I mean to die.

Only when I had seen the icon did I realize how well the ballad suits the Bright Mountain.

No wonder pilgrims come. At Częstochowa they have 'a picture of Mary, Most Glorious Virgin, Queen of the World and of the Poles, which has been painted with strange and extraordinary skill, with a serene expression on her face from whatever direction you may gaze,' wrote Canon Jan Długosz of Kraków in about 1475. 'Contemplating this picture, one is filled with an intense feeling of piety, as if looking at a person who is alive.'

To say that I felt that the Black Virgin had a message for me is much too simple. It would be truer to say that she made me think; there was a sense of dialogue. 'What do you want?' she seemed to say. 'What *do* I want?' I asked myself, and then 'Do I really want it?' Her answers were very strange, in that they were so enigmatic and even contradictory, like those from some pagan oracle in Antiquity. On the one hand 'I can't help you' or 'I won't intervene'; on the other, 'Yes, but not in the way which you expect.' This inconsistency might appear to have been a reflection of my own confused mind, yet I know that it wasn't. At the same time, I was aware of being reassured by the Virgin as she had reassured me at Medjugorje, though differently – the dimension (if that is the right word) was altogether new. I left her chapel with real peace of mind. As at Medjugorje, my doubts had been swept away. I felt something more, a sense of protection. My feeling of reassurance was to grow with the days, the weeks and the months – if it would fade with the year.

The icon's origins are shrouded in mystery. According to Canon Długosz, it was 'painted by St Luke the Evangelist himself'. The most favoured theory, however, is that it began as a copy of an icon of the *Hodegitria* (the 'Virgin who shows the way') which is known to have been venerated at Constantinople by harbour pilots from the fifth century until the fifteenth, when it was destroyed by the Turks. As a copy, it could therefore have been painted at any time between the fifth century and its arrival here in 1384, when it was brought by Ladislas of Opole, the Palatine of Ruthenia. But since then it has changed. In 1430 Hussite heretics, raiders who were sacking the shrine, tore away the icon's jewels and slashed its face. (The scars are not from 'a Swedish lance-thrust' as Graham Greene wrongly believed.) It was re-painted about 1433, on the old boards. The restoration made it far more Western, since the portrait is no longer two-dimensional, and is much softer in both tone and outline than any Byzantine icon. Something has been added, akin to the art of Giotto – and also something which is indefinable.

Hitherto, I had prized equally four other images of the Mother of God, all of them Byzantine. One was the immensely tall and slender mosaic Virgin who soars over the Apostles at Torcello in the Venetian lagoons. (A child described her to Jan Morris as 'a thin young lady, holding God.') There was Our Lady of Vladimir from about the same date, the twelfth century, an icon whose haunting face wears an expression of the sort which the Russians call *umileniye* – 'loving kindness'. In 1986 I saw the Virgin of the Annunciation at Mileševa in Serbia, a fresco which some think is the most beautiful fresco in all Byzantine art. Two years later, in a cave church at Ugento in Puglia – hollowed out by Greek monks – I glimpsed by candle-light the fading outline of a once lovely Madonna painted on the rock face about 1000 AD.

However, all these were eclipsed by the Lady of Częstochowa. Hers is the sort of countenance which inspired Dante to write

la faccia che a Cristo
piu si somiglia

in the *Paradiso*, 'the face that most resembles Christ'. The Ampleforth prayer book used to contain St Bernard's prayer to the Virgin, as imagined by Dante. 'Thou art she who didst so ennoble human nature that its maker did not disdain to be of its making':

tu se' colei che l'umana natura
nobilitasti si, che 'l suo fattore
non disdegno di farsi sua fattura

Yet at the same time the unknown restorers of 1433 did not entirely dispel her Eastern quality. She is still Orthodoxy's 'Most holy Lady, Mother of God, light of my darkened soul, my hope, my shelter, my refuge, my consolation, my fount of joy.' The Black Madonna belongs to both East and West.

Even so, in 1717 she was formally crowned as Polish Sovereign in a ceremony decreed by the Seym, the nation's parliament. That coronation has never been forgotten by the Poles. When some years ago a person whom I loved had died, I received a letter from a Polish friend who told me that he was praying for her to 'Our Lady Queen of Poland and Grand Duchess of Lithuania'.

*

'Our community numbers eighty priests and thirty brothers,' Fr Simon told me, as he took me round the monastery. 'We attract almost too many novices.' He explained that the community's main work was hearing confession; there were countless penitents, shattered by their encounter with the icon, who all needed counselling, spiritual or psychological or both. In August 1991 1,300,000 pilgrims had come to the great open-air Mass celebrated here by the Pope. Nearly as many came every August, often whole parishes together, on foot; those from Warsaw would spend nine days on the road. When at last they reached the Jasna Gora many of the groups prostrated themselves, lying face down on the ground.

One of the most famous penitents in the history of the Bright Mountain was Prince Mikołaj Radziwiłł, head of the renowned Lithuanian family. After his conversion from Calvinism to Catholicism, his confessor ordered the prince to walk to Jerusalem as a penance; it took him two years, from 1582 to 1584; when he died, he left the monks his rock crystal rosary and his carved walking stick. The latter is among the few modest items in the monastery's treasury, one of the most amazing hoards of gold, silver and precious stones in all Europe. Not only does it contain sacred vessels and reliquaries but there are swords and maces – even captured Tartar bows and horsetail standards. Perhaps the most moving items are a crown of thorns woven out of barbed wire in Dachau and a rosary made of bread pellets in Ravensbrück.

Fr Simon then showed me the magnificent Baroque library, a sublime room completed in 1739. The books are cased in mock volumes of wood and tooled leather; among them are many illuminated manuscripts and incunables. There is also the manuscript of the 'Ballad of Częstochowa' which Belloc wrote during his visit here in 1928.

We then went into the refectory, a noble room of about the same date. It was five p.m. 'Tea time,' said the monk. He insisted on my consuming a vast bowl of cabbage soup and then a cold pork chop in batter, washed down with glasses of tea. Luckily I had missed lunch and expected to miss dinner too, but I balked when he pressed an even bigger chop on me.

Then he drove me to the station, warning me against pickpockets. Only last week an American priest had lost $80. 'I thought ninety-five per cent of Poles were Catholic,' the priest had shouted. 'Don't worry,' Fr Simon told him. 'It was the other five per cent who stole your dollars.' During a photo-finish he insisted on buying my ticket, after which he put me on the wrong train, retrieving me at the last moment. Finally he pushed me on to one which was leaving, thrusting a piece of paper through the window and explaining 'You must change there, Professor.' On the paper was written, 'ZĄBKOWICE' and 'TRZEBINIA'.

I decided that my chances of sleeping at Kraków that night were nil. I tried pronouncing the names to two passengers, old women who shook their heads, looking at me with deep suspicion. The train lumbered on into the dusk, through the by now familiar pattern of idyllic landscape and ecological disaster.

However the Black Virgin was looking after me. Somehow I managed to get out at Ząbkowice, if only because the train went no further. On the dreary, ill-lit platform I asked a small bespectacled young woman whether she spoke English. 'Of course,' she replied. Her name was Zofia and she was assistant curator of a museum at Kraków, besides being an Arabist who was writing a thesis on the Barmakid vizirs of eighth-century Baghdad. She shepherded me home. Her conversation during the journey was fascinating. She told me that there were 6000 Tartars in northern Poland but her researchers had convinced her that their language had died out, even if they still prayed in Arabic.

Next morning I felt as I had at Medjugorje – euphorically happy and, rare for someone of my temperament, optimistic. Was this the 'Częstochowa effect'? Several Poles have told me that it was. Less heady and evanescent than the Herzegovinan sort, it deepened as time passed instead of diminishing, though eventually coming to an end. I have met Poles who visit the Bright Mountain every year to recharge their batteries, just like the Medjugorje pilgrims.

I called on Zofia at the Wyspiański Museum in Kanonicza Street. (Still only partially restored, with its medieval and Renaissance houses, this is one of the prettiest streets in Kraków.) At the museum, her dark hair dragged back in a bun, rimless spectacles over enormous green eyes and in a long black dress, the assistant curator looked like a turn-of-the-century blue-stocking, a character from Joseph Conrad's *Under Western Eyes*. Curiously enough, I discovered afterwards that she was a relative of Conrad, who spent his childhood in a nearby street.

Stanisław Wyspiański, who died in 1907 aged only thirty-eight, had been a leader of the *fin-de-siècle* cultural revival in Poland, a playwright and a painter of genius, a symbolist who turned to Polish folklore for his inspiration. 'Very beautiful man,' Zofia told me earnestly, 'but he catched syphilis from one of Gauguin's models.' At the end he could only draw in bed, sketching what he saw from a window. He worked mainly in pastel. Most of his paintings were away at an exhibition but those which remained were undeniably impressive. Zofia also showed me some fine stained glass designed by him, at a Franciscan church not far away.

She was very proud of being an *alumna* of Kraków University, with its Gothic Collegium Maius and Baroque church. It is a university which has always been staunchly Catholic. I soon learnt that my new friend's religion was unquestioning, something I had noticed in other Polish intellectuals. Occasionally I wonder how they believe so passionately that their country is under the Virgin's protection when it has suffered so terribly. Perhaps they will be recompensed in the next world.

In the chapter 'Soldiers of the Virgin' in *The Polish Way* Adam Zamoyski (Hospitaller of the Polish Knights of Malta) writes:

> A powerful myth grew up of Poland as the predestined bulwark first of Christendom, the *Antemurale Christianitatis*, a phrase first applied to it by Machiavelli. 'Lord, You were once called the God of Israel,' Jakub Sobieski prayed in the 1650s: 'on bended knee we now call You the God of Poland, our motherland, the God of our armies and the Lord of Our Hosts.'

In his book on the 1919 war Count Zamoyski describes a mounted duel between a Polish cavalry officer and a Bolshevik trooper in front of their respective units. The officer changed his sabre from his right hand to his left, so that he could make the sign of the Cross, and then back again, before cleaving the Russian from neck to shoulder with a single stroke. The other Red troopers shouted 'The Devil!' and bolted. The crusader instinct is far from dead among modern Poles, since their Catholicism is the faith of men and women incapable of compromise.

I spent a last afternoon in Kraków, Zofia taking me on a whirlwind tour of any churches I might have missed. I can still do my twelve miles in three hours but I found it hard to keep up with that human whippet. The one I liked best was SS Peter and Paul, built in the 1580s. A noble piece of early Baroque, its façade is guarded by statues of the Twelve Apostles in a row; they are copies, the originals having been removed because of pollution – fumes from Nowa Huta.

In a vault below the high altar of SS Peter and Paul lie the bones of a sixteenth-century Jesuit, Piotr Skarga. A priest who converted Mikołaj Radziwiłł and who was the king's confessor, who published many books which are still read, and who made historic speeches in the Seym, he was also admired for his saintly life. Credited with working miracles, his tomb is covered by scraps of paper – petitions for intercession.

So I was surprised to learn that Skarga had not been canonized because of a suspicion that he had committed suicide; when they opened his coffin to beatify him, they found that he had been still alive when buried – in a coma. Had he given way to despair? The tale seems very unlikely. A Polish friend in England was outraged when I mentioned it. Yet I remember hearing the same story about Thomas à Kempis when I was at school, that when they opened the coffin of the author of *The Imitation of Christ* they found bony fingers fastened round a bony neck; the inference being that having been buried alive at ninety-one after a life of spiritual perfection, Thomas despaired when he awoke and supposedly strangled himself, which is why he had never been canonized. I hope that neither story is true.

I know a similar tale with a happy ending. My godfather Bertie Seward told me that when he was a boy at Bordeaux, a hundred years ago, the cardinal archbishop often came to lunch at his father's house. A rich nobleman, strikingly handsome, the cardinal was adored by ladies. Bertie asked him why, when the world offered so much, had he chosen to become a priest? 'As a young man I was a rake, almost a debauchee,' replied the archbishop.' 'One day I woke up in darkness, not knowing where I was; I couldn't sit up, nor move my arms or legs. Then I heard the sound of horses' hooves and of men's marching feet. It was the *pompe funèbre* – I was in my coffin, about to be buried alive. I screamed, I bellowed. No response, only the noise of hooves and feet. Finally they stopped. I was being lowered into my grave. Then I prayed. I would become a priest were I saved. At that moment sunlight streamed in; the coffin-lid had been opened. But my hair had turned from black to white. So, I am a priest.'

I cannot help wondering what might have happened if the cardinal had not kept his promise.

I made a final visit with Zofia to Jama Michalika, the prettiest of coffee houses. Sadly, it, was time to leave Poland. I had had no presentiment that I would like the country and its people quite so much. No doubt my visit had been a failure. I had found no evidence of a sun dancing over the Bright Mountain. Nor was there any obvious link with Fatima.

On the other hand I had experienced Częstochowa's power to heal. Above all, I could take with me the memory of that marvellous icon. Surely Dante must have been dreaming of such a countenance when he wrote of 'the face that most resembles Christ'? I shall never forget the Black Virgin.

4

Lvov and Hriushiw

Atheism shows strength of mind, but only to a certain degree.

PASCAL, *Pensées*

And there appeared a great wonder in heaven: a woman clothed with the sun, and the moon under her feet, and upon her head a crown of twelve stars.

REVELATION, 12:1

I had come east to Poland, from Prague, but there was a Marian shrine still further east, in the Ukraine, which I wanted to see. It was not too far across the frontier. I did not appreciate how difficult that wretched little journey would prove.

Just before leaving England I said goodbye to an old friend who was dying. A former member of the *Wehrmacht* (and a survivor of the Officers' Plot against Hitler) he had been on the Russian Front and had vivid memories of the Ukraine. He spoke of interminable journeys eastward over the steppes through mile upon mile of sunflowers, of wild parties. (Finding captured Ilyitch vodka too fiery, the Germans refined it by leaving the stuff on corrugated iron roofs in the blazing sun, lacing what was left with sugar and egg yolk.) Less agreeably, he recalled commanding a hospital train from Mariupol to Berlin after a Soviet offensive; he could never forget the cries of the wounded, of a full general screaming for his mother. He described two Knights of Malta – he belonged to the Order – putting on surcoats with the eight-pointed cross beneath their tunics before a Russian attack, so that they might 'face death with happy hearts'.

A convert from Lutheranism to Catholicism, he was a religious man, though very much in his own way. He had spent a good deal of time in North Africa (he had hoped to raise the Touareg, the nomad warriors of the Sahara, for Rommel) and there was an eastern, almost Sufi tinge to his faith; for him religion was 'the soul's intuition', 'music of the spirit'. He owned an icon which had a curious provenance. One day in 1943, not far from Field-Marshal von Manstein's Ukrainian headquarters, he heard 'beautiful, glorious singing'. It came from a thatched barn; entering, he found Mass in progress – the peasants had brought their icons out of hiding and hung them on the walls of this makeshift church. They would disappear again when the Russians re-occupied the territory, but not before he had succeeded in buying one. He was always convinced that the Ukrainian people remained deeply spiritual at heart.

'Goodbye,' said old Karl, raising himself on his pillow and saluting. 'Take my compliments to the Russian Front,' I never saw him again but I would remember him at a Ukrainian shrine.

During 1987 the Virgin was seen at Hriushiw in the Ukraine, in a pillar of light 200 metres tall, by half a million people. Among them was Josyp Terelya who suffered for over twenty years in Soviet prisons as a 'Greek Catholic' and who had apocalyptic visions of the future – 'a sea of blood and fire'. He stresses the Virgin's role in overthrowing Marxism and Hriushiw's links with Fatima, warning that the Second Coming is almost upon us.

No country has had a more terrible history than the Ukraine, not even Poland. Nowhere have there been bloodier wars, massacres, witch-hunts or pogroms; no people are more violent and none more Christian. Never until now have the Ukrainians had their own state, save for the Cossack Hetmanate during the seventeenth century or for a few months in 1917–18. Their language is as close to Russian as Slovak is to Czech but there are differences in vocabulary and pronunciation; the Ukrainian for 'charming' means 'ugly' in Russian, and Lvov is 'L'viu'. During the 1930s twelve million Ukrainians died from artificially induced famine and they formed fifty per cent of the Gulag population. From 1944 to 1947, led by Stefan Bandera, they fought from forest bases a little known war against Germans, Russians and Poles. It was hopeless. 'They took our land,' Terelya says of the Russians. 'They stole our culture. They stole our spirit.'

The nuclear disaster at Chernobyl in the Eastern Ukraine sent many to their Bibles, where they read in Revelation: 'And the third angel sounded, and there fell a great star from heaven, burning as it were a lamp, and it fell upon the third part of the rivers, and upon the fountains of waters: And the name of the star is called Wormwood; and the third part of the waters became wormwood; and many men died of the waters because they were made bitter.' The Ukrainian for wormwood is '*chernobyl*'. Terelya was not just voicing his own opinion when he linked Chernobyl to the Apocalypse. Nor was it the first apocalyptic event. 'We must always think back to Fatima,' he warns. 'The miracle of the sun – when it seemed to come crashing towards the earth – may have been a warning of nuclear warfare.' He reminds us that the atom bombs dropped on Japan looked like a falling sun.

On 26 April 1987, twelve months after Chernobyl, a thirteen-year-old peasant girl from Hriushiw, Marina Kizyn, saw a strange light hovering over the derelict 'chapel of the three holy ones'. (A name commemorating three supernatural candles seen burning here during the last century.) Inside the light was a woman in black who carried a baby in her arms. The woman spoke, telling her that because of their sufferings God had chosen the Ukrainians to lead the Soviet Union back to him. Marina called her mother, Myroslawa, and her sister, Halia. The Lady bowed to them. 'It's the Blessed Virgin,' said Marina's mother. 'Kneel down and pray.' Within minutes people were flocking to the chapel, an ever increasing flood as the days went by. What made the apparitions so different from those at Fatima or Medjugorje was that the crowds saw both the light and the '*Bohoroditsa*' – the Virgin.

There was general agreement about the Mother of God's message: 'Teach the children how to pray. Teach them to live in truth, and live in truth yourselves. Forgive the nations who have harmed you. Don't forget those who died in the disaster at Chernobyl, which was a sign for the whole world. Say the Rosary constantly. It is the weapon to use against Satan. He fears the Rosary. Say the Rosary every day, anywhere where people gather.

'I have come purposely to thank the Ukrainian people because during the last seventy years it has suffered most for the Church of Christ. I come to comfort you, and to tell you that your suffering will soon end. The Ukraine will be an independent state.

'Repent and love one another. Those times are coming which have been foretold, the last times.

'Look upon the desolation which envelopes the world – the sin, the sloth, the genocide. I come to you with my eyes full of tears, beseeching you to pray, to strive for goodness and for the glory of God. The Ukraine was the first country to acknowledge me for her Queen and I have taken her under my protection. Strive to do God's will, for without this there can be no happiness and no one may enter the kingdom of God.

'You shall win my heart and you shall live in unity. Obey firmly those who lead the Church, and you shall gain your own country, and be respected among the nations of the world. I love the Ukraine and the Ukrainian people for their suffering and their faithfulness to Christ the King, and I shall defend the Ukraine for the glory of the kingdom of God upon earth and its future.

'The Ukrainians must become apostles of Christ among the peoples of Russia. If there is not a return to Christianity in Russia, then there will be a Third World War.'

(One should remember that this was in 1987 and by 'Russia' the Virgin was understood to mean the then Soviet Union.)

'A mass of people come to Hriushiw on foot, in cars – whether their own or the Party's – by bus or train' reported *Lvovskaya Pravda*. 'Not just from the surrounding districts but from far-off regions. They come . . . to see the Virgin Mary's face.'

'Each day a stream of people, old men and women, boys and girls, young parents with or without children, flow into the Kizyn farmstead, on a little hill about a hundred metres from the chapel,' said another Lvov paper, the now defunct *Leninska Molod*. 'Only from here, if rumours are true, can one see the Blessed Virgin Mary's silhouette.' On 13 May (the anniversary of her appearance at Fatima in 1917) her outline appeared on the screen during a television broadcast.

As at Medjugorje, the authorities grew alarmed. When a psychiatrist examined Marina and found her quite normal, they ordered her parents to keep her at home. The crowds became so big that there were articles in *Pravda* describing the apparitions as the work of extremists determined to wreck perestroika.

For three months troops surrounded the chapel. They tried to block the road by cutting down a tree but it fell on their trucks. A KGB colonel swore he was going to bulldoze the building, laughing when told that his son's cancer would be cured if he spared it; he left the chapel alone on hearing his son had been healed. It was rumoured that a sniper had been detailed to watch the windows and shoot the Virgin if she appeared, how he tried to shoot her but dropped dead.

Far more impressive than these lurid tales were accounts of

KGB personnel kneeling down and crossing themselves, and reports that Orthodox Christians as well as Greek Catholics were convinced that they had seen the Virgin hovering over the chapel.

Lvov, capital of the Western Ukraine, is less than 200 kilometres from Kraków. I wanted to see its fine buildings. In any case, I had to go through it to reach Hriushiw.

I asked the red bearded curator of the Wawel for advice. (Like some castellan in a Sienkiewicz novel, he was a nobleman and a Knight of Malta.) 'Make no mistake, you're embarking on an adventure,' he began. 'Nasty things happen to people in Lvov – they disappear without trace. I don't think it will happen to you but be careful. Remember, you're going to be a very rich man there, as the average wage is a dollar a day.'

I hate adventures and was especially alarmed since I knew I would arrive an hour after midnight, when there might not be any taxis. I had a booking at one of the two Intourist hotels, though which one was not clear from my voucher.

'You may not be able to get a train back,' added the castellan soothingly. 'If so, take a taxi to Shegini and walk across the border at Przemysl, ten kilometres away.'

He explained that the Western Ukraine had been Polish from the fourteenth century till 1945. Then the frontiers were redrawn, the Polish population being deported to the former German city of Breslau (now Wrocław) and replaced by Ukrainians from the East in a typical piece of Stalinist 'social engineering'. If the Poles reclaimed it, Germany would demand a large chunk of Western Poland.

I emerged from the Wawel in such a state of nerves that I did what a Pole would have done – I went straight to the Mariacki and prayed to the Black Madonna for a safe return to Kraków.

I am a bad traveller, nervous and pessimistic. Arrival, not the journey, is what makes travel worthwhile. When uneasy about it, I instinctively pray for protection, generally to the Virgin. Yet is this belief? My faith wavers again as soon as I feel safe. I have a friend, an agnostic who doesn't believe in God (though sometimes I suspect he would like to) who prays whenever he goes to the dentist.

My train left from Kraków Plaszow, not from the cheerful central station. A gloomy, run-down place, more of a goods junction than a passenger stop, it had served a Nazi concentration camp on a nearby hilltop. In a donkey jacket and jeans, unshaven, with a shabby old airline-bag for luggage, I was doing my best to look inconspicuous; later I would be rewarded by being mistaken for a steel-worker. Unlike the Polish trains on which I had so far travelled, the carriage was filthy; the blankets in the three-bunk sleeper in which I was incarcerated at one p.m. were verminous. Then I realized I was on a Russian train. I shared the sleeper with a young working couple, obviously just married, a blonde and her adoring husband. It was a shock when the blonde, peering down from the bunk above me, showed a thin face of ethereal beauty.

That train took twelve hours to cover 180 miles. Throughout I worried whether there would be taxis. How should I find my hotel without one? I spoke only one or two words of Russian – the conductor nearly put me off at the wrong stop. At last Lvov was heralded by plumes of green smoke in a dark blue night. In Polish I whispered 'Goodnight', so as not to waken my companions if they were asleep. A whisper came back from the girl, '*Dobranoc*', such a gentle, supportive whisper. It quickly became clear that I was going to need support.

Stepping down on to a normal enough continental platform, I went down further steps – emerging into a nightmare. In the yellow sodium light, like some scene from Gustave Doré's sketches of the slums of nineteenth-century London, hundreds of ragged men, women and children were sleeping packed together, almost in heaps; there was a low hum of faint, melancholy voices, together with an all-pervading smell of human excrement – an old man was defecating into a rubbish bin. The station, I learnt afterwards, did duty as the city's only refuge for the homeless; what it must be like in winter, I dare not think. I pushed through, cursing.

Outside, to my joy, I saw taxis and jumped into the first one. Its driver, unpleasant and very drunk, yelling all the way how he loved Margaret Thatcher but hated Gorbachev (still just in power), drove me to the wrong hotel and, having wolfishly snatched a dollar, sped off into the dark. Then I found myself ringed by a group of young thugs, also drunk, who plucked at my jacket and kicked my bag, but decided I wasn't worth mugging. After lengthy bargaining in broken German, another young man led me to a small Lada with flat tyres, only one front seat, no windscreen wipers and no brakes. He too was drunk, laughing wildly as we lurched and jolted through the night over the cobblestones down incongruously dignified streets.

Even at that hour the hotel, the *right* hotel, was full of sad babushkas, sweeping the majestic stairs with birch besoms. A relic of Habsburg opulence, it had been built in 1904. Not only did my vast bedroom have a big bathroom but there was even a bath-plug under its once chromium-plated taps. I knelt down, thanking the Lady of Hriushiw for my safe arrival.

Next morning I had a hot bath. I was privileged since there was water for only four hours a day. The word for restaurant in most Slavonic languages appears to be '*cavernia*' and the hotel breakfast room lived up to it. The meal was slices of dry sausage on rye bread, followed by buckwheat cakes with sour cream, and a glass of tea.

In the hotel corridors a few chipped pieces of reproduction

Biedermeyer furniture survived from before the 1939 war. The one indisputable antique was an aged porter, poor old Vladimir Gennadeyitch. A diminutive figure, with his long white moustaches and gold-braided cap, he looked like a character actor from some Hollywood version of a Chekhov play.

When I went outside, however, my first impression was of a *Klein Wien*, a little Vienna. In my imagination I thought that I could just see ghostly *Kaiserjäger*, fast stepping riflemen, swinging through Mitskevitch Square to a lilting Strauss march. This was not too fanciful since, as 'Lemberg', Lvov had been the capital of Habsburg Poland (Galicia) from 1773 to 1918. Closer inspection revealed leafy tree-lined streets and squares, pleasant parks and a score of Baroque churches, with the remains of turreted medieval walls. There is an imposing campus – until 1939 Lemberg was among the great European universities. On further exploration, the city appeared more like a larger Kraków than a little Vienna, despite the Habsburg imprint. It is surprisingly big, with more than three-quarters of a million inhabitants compared with 300,000 fifty years ago. As at Kraków there is plenty of hideous industrial development, aged factories belching forth evil fumes. Yet, worn and faded through it may be, Lvov retains much of its ancient beauty.

The Western Ukraine, of which Lvov is the capital, is the more fiercely nationalist half of 'Ukraina'. In 1989 Lvov was the first city in what was then the Soviet Union to pull down a statue of Lenin, another, in a suburb, took longer to topple than expected so a poster was hung round its neck, apologizing for 'inconvenient delay'. Hammers, sickles and red stars disappeared the same year. Statues of the guerrilla leaders of 1944–7 were erected; for a while the KGB blew them up at night, the last time being in 1991. The blue and yellow flag now flies from every public building. I saw men wearing the cream coloured Ukrainian uniform of 1918 – it was odd to see them walking the streets with Soviet soldiers in khaki.

What this brave and generous people have endured for three-quarters of a century is frightful. Their spirit remains unbroken; far from being surly or apathetic, they are warm-hearted, welcoming strangers and giving lavishly of their meagre best. One should not patronize them. The Ukraine's vast potential wealth, agricultural and mineral, is matched by the calibre of its inhabitants. This could become one of the richest countries in Europe.

For all their potential, the citizens of Lvov seemed apprehensive. In the hotel foyer I met a short, dark, plump woman in her forties, who spoke English and who was clearly one of the *nomenklatura*, the former Soviet ruling class. Even by Western standards she was elegantly dressed, in a pink tweed suit and Gucci scarf, with a smart coiffure and good jewellery. 'Lvov has so much to offer,' she told me with obvious pride. 'Everything is here – Gothic, Renaissance, Baroque, Biedermeyer – and pretty country is in easy reach. But,' she added sadly, 'there is nowhere to stay, nowhere to eat, no proper hotels or restaurants, no cafés.' Life had been infinitely better five years ago, let alone twenty. It would be a decade at the very least before the Ukraine developed a capitalist economy.

Dinner at the hotel was in a once noble room, where *K. und K.* officers and Polish gentlemen had entertained their ladies. Guests were now waited on – if that is the right phrase – by shambling, half-shaven, jacketless tramps in baggy trousers and shirtsleeves, with crumpled, unbuttoned waistcoats as a pathetic symbol of status; they could have doubled as old-fashioned railway porters. There were half a dozen dishes on the menu, three of them 'off'. The first course was either sliced tomato and onion, without a dressing, or borsch; what appeared to be green vegetables in the borsch was aged horsemeat. The main course was a rissole in thick batter, with lightly boiled potatoes. For drink there was beer, vodka (excellent) or sickly sweet Russian 'champagne'. The amiable Tadzhik with whom I shared a table was studiously ignored by the waiters, two of whom were slumped at another table over a bottle of champagne.

*

The next day was a Sunday so I went to Mass at St George's Cathedral, of the Ukrainian Catholic Church of the Byzantine Rite – the Uniates or 'Greek Catholics'. Two superb Baroque statues stood over the main door, one of a Pope in his tiara, the other of a Patriarch in his Byzantine crown, symbolizing the happy relationship between Rome and the oriental Churches. From outside, the building is an eighteenth-century confection of cream and dove grey, of buff and chocolate, with dark green cupolas. Inside, jade green and gold, the decoration emphasized links between Uniates and Roman Catholics. There were pictures of Christ exposing his sacred heart, of the Last Supper (over the royal doors of the iconastasis) and the Stations of the Cross.

The cathedral was packed. Some girls were in Ukrainian folk costume: striped black or brown skirts, long and tight, with embroidered white shirts, and sometimes a red sash round their waists. A few men, and many small boys, had shirts embroidered round the neck in brown and red.

Being familiar with the Orthodox Liturgy, I was able to follow a good deal of the service, outwardly so different from the Western Mass, which lasted for over two hours. I have seldom heard such fervent singing. Its emotion made me choke, and many Ukrainians near me were weeping. They had only recovered their cathedral a year before. The Church is all that they have, now that the Marxist dream has vanished into very thin air indeed. Few of today's Ukrainians appear to be non-Christians. Sitting in his cage in hell, Stalin is at last aware of the extent of the Pope's divisions.

There are about five million Ukrainian Uniates, most of them in the Western Ukraine, where they regard themselves as preservers of the nation's language and identity. In the old days before 1939 the big landowners were Poles and Latin Catholics, so that their priests were spokesmen for the peasants who were Ukrainians and Uniates; the best educated and on the whole richest of the smallholders in this predominantly peasant society, they were very much its leaders. Outwardly, Uniate Catholicism is almost indistinguishable from Orthodoxy; admittedly the priests are clean-shaven, the iconastasis doors are open throughout Mass, there is the occasional three-dimensional statue of a saint and the Latin Rosary is used, but that is all. There are, however, more subtle differences. The words 'and the Son' have been added to the Creed, there is no warm water in the chalice at Communion and blessed bread is not distributed after Mass. Even so, apart from that and their acceptance of the Pope's jurisdiction, it might seem there was very little difference between Uniates and Orthodox.

In 1946 Stalin tried to force Uniates to repudiate the Pope and to merge with the Orthodox. They went underground and were persecuted savagely; bishops, clergy and laity were hunted down, imprisoned, tortured and murdered. The Mass had to be celebrated in forest clearings, priests being hidden in barns by the faithful. Meanwhile the Orthodox took over their churches, 250 in the Lvov region alone. St George's Cathedral was only handed back to the Uniates in 1990, an event celebrated by a crowd which is said to have numbered 250,000.

Later someone at Lvov told me that the survival of their religion was due to a factor which no amount of 'social engineering' could hope to overcome – the indomitable babushka or grandmother, who instilled the eternal truths during a child's early years. In *Auguries of Innocence* William Blake anticipated just the sort of silent conflict which must have taken place between a babushka and a school teacher trying to replace Christianity with Marxist dialectic:

He who mocks the Infant's Faith
Shall be mock'd in Age & Death.
He who shall teach the Child to Doubt
The rotting Grave shall ne'er get out.
He who respects the Infant's faith
Triumphs over Hell & Death.
The Child's Toys & the Old Man's Reasons

Are the Fruits of the Two Seasons.
The Questioner who sits so sly,
Shall never know how to Reply . . .

Here at Lvov I saw a triumphant victory over militant atheism.

But the ecumenical spirit was absent. Nothing saddened me more during my visit to Eastern Europe than the bad blood between Uniates and Orthodox. Admittedly the Russian Church had not behaved very well in the Ukraine in recent years. Subservience to Stalin and his heirs was the price of its survival; undeniably, it co-operated in suppressing the Uniates after 1946, occupying their churches, cathedrals, monasteries and seminaries, attempting to force them to disown the Pope. When the Uniates emerged from the catacombs, the Russian Orthodox restored their property with the utmost reluctance.

Even so, the Uniates forget that Orthodoxy too has very real historical grievances. During the thirteenth century Crusaders sacked the cathedral of Hagia Sofia at Constantinople, the Orthodox equivalent of St Peter's, after which the Pope installed a Latin Patriarch. (How would Catholics feel if Greek troops had sacked St Peter's and installed an Orthodox Patriarch in place of the Pope?) For centuries Ukrainian Orthodox were forced to accept Uniate jurisdiction, those who refused being persecuted. Few Catholics, whether Uniate or Roman, did anything to help the martyred Orthodox Christians of the Soviet lands during the dreadful years which followed 1917. Nevertheless, when all is said and done, the Church of Rome has infinitely more in common with the Orthodox Church than with the 'reformed' Churches of the West.

I revere the Orthodox Church. An occasional visit to its Liturgy does wonders for one's belief in bread turning into Christ's Body and wine into his Blood, the Real Presence. Many people single out the Creed in Russian (in fact Church Slavonic) as the most moving moment of the Liturgy, but for me it is the Cherubic Hymn – the Orthodox *Sanctus* – which is sung at the Great Entrance, when gifts of bread and wine are brought to the altar. I recall a Greek Liturgy at a church in the Mani in the Peloponnese recommended to me by Patrick Leigh-Fermor; the iconostasis was low enough for one to see the priest fanning the gifts with the chalice veil, to symbolize the fluttering wings of the descending Holy Ghost; like the '*Cherubimska*', that fluttering helped immeasurably to confirm my faith in the Real Presence. I value too such Orthodox prayers as that to the guardian angel: 'O Holy Angel, that keepest guard over my despondent soul and passionate life, leave me not a sinner, nor depart from me to my undoing.'

That evening the mineral water ran out. When I asked in the restaurant for a bottle to take to bed, I was told '*woda, nyet*'. There was no beer either. Since no water came out of the taps in my room, I had to clean my teeth in Russian champagne – a dollar a bottle.

I spent a wretched, fearful night. Perhaps it was the champagne. Once upon a time Catholics used to pray for deliverance from the *Timore Nocturno*, 'The Night-time Fear'. Many people, and not just Catholics, experience it. The hours when vitality is at its lowest can play very strange tricks with the mind – especially if one has low blood pressure, and mine is fish-like. Napoleon considered 'five o'clock in the morning courage' as the yardstick of bravery. It is a time when my mind is only too free from doubt and I try desperately to pray. I lay awake in that huge, gloomy bedroom, wondering why I had bothered to come to Lvov.

It was Hriushiw (pronounced 'Hrooshoo') thirty-five miles south-west which had brought me to Lvov, a place where the Virgin appeared to half a million people. I knew that it was near Lvov but I could not find it on the map; understandably, because in Russian it is written 'Grouchevo'. I had written to a prelate at the cathedral but received no reply – scarcely surprising, since he was ninety and retired. However, at the cathedral chancellery a young Canadian Ukrainian, Fr Kowalski, had at once informed me that 'Hriushiw is very famous', promising to find me an interpreter and a car. He also told me proudly that over 400 seminarians enrolled between 1990 and 1991, that the monasteries were attracting many novices. In the green archbishop's palace opposite the cathedral, the chancellery was a hive of activity.

Next morning, what passed for breakfast was unavailable at the hotel till eight thirty a.m. but the interpreter brought sandwiches and a flask of coffee. Anatoly Vassilievich Shevel, thirty-one years old, holder of a doctorate from Lvov University, was small, fair-haired and likable. He worked for the Ukrainian–Canadian Joint Venture, financed by emigré money; in a pioneering bid to attract tourists, they were building a motel at Shegini just across the border from Poland, together with a four-star hotel at Derevatch in the Carpathians, eight miles from Lvov. As we drove towards Hriushiw he told me that the Soviet Army was still being taught Marxist ideology (this was in 1991) while there were many caches of Nationalist weapons from the 1944–7 war, but he did not expect trouble. Despite sixteen years in prison as a dissident, the chairman of Lvov regional council, Vyacheslav Chornovil, was implementing a bloodless revolution without any recriminations or attempts to settle old scores.

Minor roads in the Ukraine are atrocious. There are few signposts. Often Anatoly stopped to ask the way, receiving on one occasion the helpful advice, 'Follow that old man on the bicycle.' Eventually we came to the long, straggling villages of Hriushiw Krasna and Hriushiw Stara (the Red and the Old) which have about 2000 houses between them. My driver pointed out a dismal village shop, with detergent, soap, carpet-beaters, paint and cereal cans in its window, and the collective farm's machinery park where aged tractors were rusting into the ground. Very long and very muddy, the single street was bordered by wooden or concrete cabins, some with only one window; dogs, horses and pigs roamed everywhere. In the fields there were sunflowers and huge haystacks like tumuli – the ponds were crowded with geese. It was a lucky place, Anatoly told me, since it had natural gas as well as electricity, though so remote that the red stars had not yet been torn down. There were two Uniate churches and a chapel, an Orthodox church and a Baptist tabernacle.

We gave a lift to a white-headed, ruddy-faced little man, on his way to church. He informed us that he had been born in 1916 and had fought in the Red Army, that he worked as a wagoner, how he hated Germans but loved Mrs Thatcher. 'If I'm illiterate, I know enough to realize the value of religion for a community,' he added. Laughing, he described how the Communist teachers had tried to stop their pupils from going to watch the apparitions. 'The children took no notice – sometimes they climbed out of the school windows.'

The wooden church of St Semeon at Hriushiw Krasna, in design a Greek cross with a central cupola and free-standing bell-tower, was packed with worshippers. Outside it was painted in various shades of ochre, inside in rainbow hues and newly gilded. There was a nineteenth-century daub of the '*Bohoroditsa*' on the ceiling, with the Child peering out of her womb; what made it disquieting were the eyes. In vestments of rose silk, a gold stole reaching to below his knees, the priest chanted the Liturgy's opening prayers before the iconostasis, a clean-shaven man in his late thirties with piercing brown eyes. Behind him stood ten men carrying candles in three-branched candlesticks and a dozen women bearing white banners embroidered with the faces of saints, the poles crowned with flowers, which they lowered at the more sacred moments.

We stood in the gallery among a choir of about twenty, whose gnarled brown features seemed as if carved out of wood. The men were in their awkward Sunday best, the women in shapeless skirts and woollens, with headscarves. There was a strong smell of sweat, garlic and sausage. They sang from books which had clearly been printed long ago, swaying backwards and forwards, some with their eyes shut. A woman cantor with two gold teeth led them, giving the pitch in a piping, bird-like soprano.

While the priest read the Gospel, the very old knelt at his feet, rising to kiss the book when he had finished. The choir sang the '*Cherubimska*' at the Great Entrance of the Gifts, 'exulting, singing, proclaiming, chanting the triumphal hymn, "Holy, Holy, Lord God of Hosts . . ."' The candle-bearers marched through the iconostasis into the sanctuary, to emerge escorting the gifts of bread and wine. The choir sang too of the Mother of God, 'more honourable than the Seraphim'. Perhaps it was my imagination but, since this was Hriushiw, I fancied that they did so with particular fervour.

As it was a weekday, there was no Communion. Holding a cross, the priest ended the Mass by preaching an emotional sermon, which Anatoly translated for me. He congratulated his flock for staying steadfast to the Faith during the dark, cruel days of persecution, begging them to pray for those who had not lived to see the reopening of the churches. He then began long and musical prayers of intercession for the souls of the dead.

Most of the congregation trooped out. We chatted with them while waiting for the priest. A man told us how the church of St Semeon, built in 1922, was closed after the war. There had been four churches in the village but only the smallest was allowed to stay open, the priest being forced to turn Orthodox and celebrate the Orthodox Liturgy; an old man who liked a quiet life, he did so because he was frightened he might starve. St Semeon's had remained derelict till 1959 when an Orthodox priest took it over, throwing out the Uniate icons; no one would go to his services so it was closed again. It had only been given back to the Uniates in 1990.

Outside that wooden church, standing in the mud surrounded by peasants, I felt as if I were on a set from one of those sad Soviet films I had watched ever since I was a boy. I was brought back to the present abruptly. 'How long before civilization reaches us?' the self-appointed spokesman asked anxiously. He meant the consumer society. I dared not tell him what I really thought.

The priest came out. Fr Zinovi Stepanovich Mykut, introduced himself with diffident authority. Making light of persecution, he said he had been here for ten years, that life had been difficult at first. Now there was a large congregation every Sunday, with many devout young people. Fifty Catholics were arriving from Austria in the spring; called by the Virgin, they would live in the village.

We drove to the chapel of the Holy Trinity over which she had appeared. Wooden, painted ochre, it was very like the parish church – a Greek cross with a metal cupola and free standing bell-tower. Abandoned for many years, it had only recently been restored.

It is important to put Hriushiw in the context of the Ukraine, which has known countless visions of the Mother of God since medieval times. Some were associated with springs of healing water. In 1240 a monk fleeing from the Mongols' sack of Kiev took refuge at a lonely hamlet called Zarvanystya. He committed himself to the care of the Virgin, then fell asleep. She appeared to him during the night, with a host of angels. When he awoke he found that he was in a beautiful meadow over which there was '*a strange glimmering light*' (italics mine). In it he found a spring, above which there was an icon of the Mother of God holding the Child. Many miracles took place down the centuries at the shrine which he built, while another icon (of Christ Crucified) was found nearby in 1740. The icons were hidden at the Bolshevik invasion in 1939, and taken to Lvov in 1944. Their present whereabouts are unknown, but their place has been taken by copies. Pilgrims still come and there are continuing reports of miracles.

The early history of Hriushiw has similarities to that of Zarvanystya. During the eighteenth century an icon of the Virgin was seen here, hovering over some willow trees which bordered a well fed by a spring. There is a very pretty, very primitive, painting of the incident in the chapel, a picture which is clearly contemporary. Another account says the Virgin appeared in person and that the locals planted a willow tree to commemorate the vision, an icon being hung from it in 1806. Pilgrims came. One day a spring of pure water with healing powers began to flow from the trunk. It was desecrated in about 1840 by a ne'er-do-well who dumped offal and rotting fruit into it, preparing the way for a cholera epidemic during which he and his entire family died, together with many others in Hriushiw. Then the Lady came in a vision to a sick woman, telling her to have the well cleaned and a Mass said to dedicate it to Christ. This was done and the cholera stopped. In 1856 a chapel was built round the spring, to be replaced by another edifice in 1878. There was a constant stream of pilgrims, who drank from the well; on one occasion three supernatural candles were seen floating above it. In 1914 the Virgin came again, appearing to twenty-two peasants mowing in the fields a fortnight before the outbreak of the Great War, warning them that the Ukraine would undergo terrible suffering for eighty years and that Russia would become a country without God.

Three days after Marina Kizyn's vision, the martyr-seer Josyp Jaromyr Terelya arrived at Hriushiw. Born at Kelechyn in the Carpathian mountains of the Western Ukraine in 1943, he was the son of dedicated Communists; his father was a zealous servant and friend of Stalin, while his mother had worked for the Ukrainian Communists' anti-religious bureau so keenly that she denounced her husband for owning an icon. Nevertheless Josyp was brought up a Christian by his Greek Catholic grandmother. At eighteen he joined the Ukrainian Nationalists and the Uniate Apostolate of Prayer, distributing Bibles bound as the *Communist Manifesto* and organizing religious services in the woods.

Called up for military service, he was arrested on declaring that he was a Christian. He then spent nine years in concentration camps and fourteen in prison.

His autobiography describes a world in which prisoners were herded into cells with standing room only – at Vladimir sometimes twenty men were put into a cell ten foot by ten – on floors running with mud and water, routinely starved, beaten and tortured. They included hard-core criminals, murderers and sexual deviants. (During an uprising at a camp renowned for homosexual rape, 240 homosexuals were pushed into a wooden barrack room and burnt alive.) On one occasion five cell mates tried to kill him while he slept, by cutting the veins of his arms and legs. Very tough – a former middle-weight boxing champion of the Ukraine – he survived, even escaping once or twice. He says he met the Swedish diplomat Raoul Wallenberg (the saviour of so many Hungarian Jews) in 1970, at Vladimir, though the Soviet authorities claimed that Wallenberg died in 1947. A guard told him of a massacre at Mordovia in 1945, when 2300 nuns and novices from the Baltic and the Ukraine were bayoneted after being systematically raped by drunken executioners.

Every means was used to break Terelya. During the autumn of 1967, in solitary confinement, and having gone without food for days, he had a vision of Russia as a drunken, dirty woman in a red dress, foaming at the mouth, her eyes burning with hatred for Christ; she stripped off her dress, to reveal a blackened body covered in revolting scabs. 'A voice said to me, "Pray to Our Lady of Fatima and this woman shall be saved."' Eighteen months later, in a concrete punishment cell three foot by seven, he had a vision of Christ the King on a white throne – fair haired and about thirty years old.

His praying and preaching, attempts to convert the guards – not always without success – and distribution of religious literature exasperated the authorities. He was too well known to be murdered so they tried to kill him by an especially severe régime. At Vladimir in February 1970 he was placed, thinly clad, in Cell

21 into which cold air was blown deliberately; the damp on the walls froze to ice.

He awoke in the middle of the night of 12 February, feeling strangely warm. There was a light in the room, not so much silvery as 'like the aureole around the moon on an exceptionally moonlit night'. The Virgin was standing in the cell. In an azure veil, with dark blue eyes, she was 'a very pleasant young woman' yet also, Terelya tells us, 'like a huge jewel in the shimmering light – majestic beyond words, as real as the walls and the hermetic door'. She came as a messenger of Christ, warning that if the Ukrainians did not forgive the Russians they would be punished, but there could be no peace until Russia turned to Christ. She showed Josyp a vision of flames and tanks, a prophecy of war between Russia and some other country. She also told him to pray to 'the Angel of the Ukraine'. Then, promising 'I shall always be with you', she disappeared. The light remained in the cell for a few more minutes.

Precisely two years later, on 12 February, even weaker physically, Josyp Terelya was put back in Cell 21, wearing only a thin shirt. The walls were thickly coated with ice – the camp authorities meant to kill him. Suddenly the cell began to feel warmer and there was a powerful light. The Virgin looked just the same as before, except that she wore a dark blue dress like a Carpathian country women and a heavy veil. Josyp knew that when people are freezing to death they can have hallucinations so he put out his hand to touch her – a body was there. Besides consoling him, she showed him visions of the future. Russia was on fire. The faces of the people in Moscow were twisted with fear, while horrible creatures ran through the streets, as big as dogs, with faces like rats and spitting venom. He realized that the flames were part of a war which would break out before the year 2000. Again he saw Christ the King. Then the Virgin disappeared in a great flash of light. By now he was so hot that he had to take his shirt off. The guards burst in – they thought the cell was on fire.

*

One night in 1983 Terelya was leaning against the wall of his cell, when he woke up in a meadow at the old miracle shrine of Zarvanystya. There was bright light everywhere and a smell of apple blossom. A white eagle flew down, telling him not to be afraid. Then the eagle turned into an old man in white, who also told him not to fear, since he was under the Mother of God's protection. He warned Josyp that far worse times were coming for Christians, far worse than in Luther's day; even bishops would become neo-pagans. In the end God would punish the apostates, because only through punishment would He be able to bring humanity back to reason. Faith and love would be reborn, but then Satan would inspire a new persecution of Christians. The world would be divided into messengers of God and messengers of Antichrist. Asked his name, this 'ancient, celestial man' answered, 'I am the Archangel Michael.' When Josyp came to, he did not know whether he had seen an archangel or dreamt it. But his cell smelt so strongly of apple blossom that the guards turned it upside down looking for apples.

Elsewhere in his writings Terelya refers to the fabled dream of Pope Leo XIII that Satan had been given a hundred years in which to destroy the Church. He laments the abandonment of Leo's prayer after Mass: 'Holy Michael, archangel, defend us in the day of battle, be our safeguard against the wickedness and snares of the enemy.' 'And look what has happened since then [1884]: toxic chemicals, radio-activity, huge wars and the threat of larger wars, the occult, drugs, abortion, humanism, wanton sex, and theories of Godless evolution.' Churches are empty; cinemas showing violent and pornographic films are full. But the Devil's reign is almost over. 'Our Lady's apparitions are the precursor of the Second Coming of Christ.'

When Terelya arrived at Hriushiw on 9 May 1987 he was staggered by the sheer size of the multitude. He estimated that 80,000 pilgrims were arriving daily, some of them from the Baltic and even a few from Central Asia – Uzbeks and Tadzhiks. So many candles had been lit near the chapel that there was a carpet of wax two feet deep, while the ground was covered in offerings; scarves, flowers, loaves of bread and banknotes.

People were pointing at the Virgin but for some hours Josyp was unable to see her. He says the light over the chapel's cupola was 200 metres tall, enveloping the building, the grass and the crowd in a silver glow like moonlight, yet, it was not a reflection of the moon. 'The glow of the moon is silver, but this was a different colour, a very soft silver. The unusual light grew more intense. Each blade and leaf of grass were electrified,' he recalls. 'In the heavenly radiance even the most homely people looked like beautiful angels. It was as if we were transfigured.'

There was another, brighter light within the aureole over the chapel, an orb of 'silver-lilac' which after oscillating and shimmering to and fro, came to rest on the cupola. Then he saw the Virgin within the orb, in flaming robes. 'It was if the robes were on fire and out of this only a face could be seen.' He describes this fiery light as 'like putting alcohol on a shirt and setting it aflame'. She was a woman of between eighteen and twenty-one, beautiful, not like a film star but in her simplicity. She exuded goodness and peace, although in tears. Some saw her in black, bearing the Infant Christ, others in white. She carried a rosary, often saying the words, 'Praised be Jesus Christ.' She did not have a set timetable, as at Medjugorje, but came unexpectedly. About half the crowd could see her though to many, including some monks and nuns, she remained invisible.

The Mother of God frequently spoke to the pilgrims, to 'My daughter, the Ukraine'. 'I see fire,' she warned. 'The villages are burning. Water is burning. The very air is on fire. If people do not convert to Christ, there will be war. There shall be a great conflagration.' The world was still travelling down the road of self-indulgence, Antichrist was still very powerful. They must pray to Christ the King and the Archangel Michael for 'ravaged Russia . . . if Russia does not accept Christ the King, the whole world faces ruin'. She begged them to say the Rosary, to avoid drunkenness. She warned that some pilgrims would see a third world war; evil times were coming, far worse than any they had known. But she promised the Ukrainians that 'The time is here when this nation of yours which loves God shall become a state and be a haven for those who remain faithful to Jesus Christ.'

The Virgin promised too that the third secret of Fatima would be revealed to them, if they stayed loyal to the Pope. Terelya claims that the Hriushiw apparitions are closely linked to those at Fatima, though he thinks that the Mother of God disclosed more at Hriushiw than at Fatima. He stresses that the 'Great Persecution' began in 1917, the year of Fatima.

At the end of July 1987 a shining figure of Christ Crucified was seen by peasant children taking cows to the meadows and then, when the vision faded, his Mother appeared in a wonderful white dress. The *Bohoroditsa* continued to appear at Hriushiw until 15 August, the feast of the Assumption. She was also seen at thirteen other shrines in the Ukraine, including Zarvanystya where Josyp had spoken with the Archangel Michael. At Hoshiv, preceded by 'celestial spheres' which could be seen a dozen miles off (and were at first mistaken for some form of nuclear weapon), she was visible from a distance of twelve miles, standing on a hill where there was a ruined monastery. Often she told priests to amend their lives.

Other figures appeared. At Hoshiv Josyp and four friends saw someone 'giving out light' whom a priest with them said was the Angel of the Ukraine. Marina Kizyn, the first to see the Virgin at Hriushiw, met a much older woman, dressed as a nun, who told her to pray in the chapel, and whom she is convinced was also the Mother of God. A beautiful young nun appeared at the chapel, miraculously healing a sick child. There were many cures, ranging from cancer and eczema to psychological disorders. At Lvov in June Josyp and his friends saw five luminous crosses, 'silver with a blue edge', moving through the midnight sky.

In his *Powers of Darkness: Powers of Light* John Cornwell is particularly sceptical about Hriushiw. He sees similarities with the Zeitoun apparitions of 1968, when a figure in white, surrounded by a bright light, was seen by 250,000 people over a Coptic church in a Cairo suburb. There were reports of luminous globes and 'explosions of light'. He stresses that the Cairo police had insisted that such phenomena were freak illusions caused by faulty street lighting. (Though this had been hotly denied by many witnesses.) 'Was the Hriushiw phenomenon a copy-cat instance of the Zeitoun visions?' he asks. 'Was there some sort of stage managed hoax, in which clever crowd psychology had been employed?' He concludes, 'The parallels between Zeitoun and Hriushiw seemed to me to be too numerous to be coincidental.'

However, he had not been to Hriushiw. Had he been there, he would have seen that – unlike Zeitoun – there is no street lighting, and that it would have been impossible to project, without being detected, beams of light 200 metres high over a tiny building which was surrounded by the KGB. 'If Hriushiw was a case of mass hallucination . . . how could so many onlookers describe the same thing without talking to each other during the apparitions?' asks Terelya. 'Yet, at times she appeared somewhat differently, and many saw the phenomena on a much smaller scale, but the essential experience – and many of the messages – were identical.'

Cornwell went to Canada where he had an interview with Terelya. He did not take to him, commenting 'In Josyp Terelya I had encountered, I felt, the dark face of popular mysticism.' But he was writing before the publication of Josyp's autobiography in 1991, and is mistaken on several points. Terelya was never the 'leader of the Ukrainian nationalists'. He says that Terelya had spoken of seeing the Lady in a glow of orange and blue lights – 'I remembered that orange and blue, the colours of his virgin, were the Ukrainian national colours.' In his own book Terelya makes no mention of an orange and blue glow, while in any case the Ukrainian colours are yellow and blue. Cornwell tells how Terelya spoke to him of a colonel in the Soviet militia who fainted when he tried to shoot at the Virgin and awoke converted, who now 'spend his time travelling round the villages relating what he saw'. Josyp writes that, though there were such rumours, the officer was merely moved from the Ukraine by his superiors.

I agree with Terelya when he claims that sightings by so many people argue for authenticity rather than otherwise. Far from being a copy-cat instance of the Zeitoun visions, those at Hriushiw had a remarkable feature. The Lady shone like the *moon*, not the sun – 'it was like something between the silver glow of the moon and a fluorescent light', are Josyp's actual words. ('It was like moonlight, but it wasn't like moonlight' is how he describes the illumination of Cell 21 at Vladimir. 'The closest thing I can relate it to is the aureole around the moon on an exceptionally moonlit night.') Reading this, I recall Hugo Rahner's words on the Virgin: 'irradiated by the Easter sun, she illuminates, like the full moon, the darkness of this world with her spiritual splendour.'

If there are resemblances to the phenomena at other shrines, they are with the solar display at Turzovka. 'The leaves, the twigs, the people, the blades of grass, everyone and everything was phosphorescent, everything that was within that gargantuan field of light,' Josyp recounts. 'On many leaves there was a silver glow. This could also be seen around the hair, around the heads of many faithful. The air appeared 'alive, imbued with energy. Streams of light seemed to issue not only from the trees and grass but from our very finger tips, which were surrounded by aureoles.'

Some things in Terelya's strange and very moving book can be challenged only too easily. He cannot have met poor Raoul Wallenberg since we now know that Wallenberg had been shot in 1947. He claims, incorrectly, that the Orthodox teach that God is not one in three persons but two. (This is a misunderstanding of that ancient bone of contention between Catholics and Orthodox, the *Filioque* clause in the Creed.)

A man methodically starved, tortured and exposed to cold for many years might well see things. 'As Catholics, we do not need or demand miracles,' he says himself. 'I don't need to see the Blessed Mother to keep my faith alive . . . It is not up to God to prove Himself to us; it is for us to prove ourselves to Him. Our faith in Christ the King carries us through life. Our beliefs do not hinge on supernatural phenomena.' Yet he believes in his visions: 'neither do we reject such signs from God once we are convinced the signs are authentic, edifying, and not a device or deception of Satan.' Some of his prophecies are demonstrably wrong, others unlikely, but so were many made by the prophets in the Bible. Nevertheless, the Ukraine *has* become an independent country, just as the Virgin promised, something seemingly unthinkable in 1987. One should remember his charity towards his enemies. His book's dedication is scarcely that of a fanatical Nationalist: 'To the Mother of all humanity, and to the victims of persecution – that which has already occurred and that which is to come.'

What on earth do I, the sophisticated, 'sceptical' Catholic, make of Terelya? Is he in truth John Cornwell's 'dark face of popular mysticism'? Certainly I cannot accept a good deal of what he says, especially some of those visions of the future which seem to be inspired by the Book of Revelation. Often his imagery is both horrible and terrifying. Undoubtedly his mysticism is popular. Yet does it truly have a dark face?

One should hear him in his own defence. Why doesn't the Virgin appear at the Kremlin or on television if what she has to say is so important, he himself asks. His answer is that she is only concerned with the devout, the very simple – she herself was a peasant girl. The 'secular humanists' who worship sensuality, materialism and science would never listen – Hriushiw is the antithesis of sophistication.'

Are *all* his visions to be dismissed? He was right about Ukrainian independence. As for troubles ahead, one should recall what a great nineteenth-century statesman, Prince Metternich, said about revolutions; once they start, they go on to the end, generally accompanied by civil wars or wars abroad or both. Yugoslavia may well be the blueprint for the future of what was once the Soviet Empire, with its ruined economy, dissolving society and Nationalist divisions. Stripped of their imagery, the warnings by the *Bohoroditsa* at Hriushiw are not unlike those by the *Gospa* at Medjugorje.

It is important to remember that Terelya was only one among tens of thousands who claimed to have seen the Mother of God at Hriushiw. As for other sightings, the curator of the Wawel, a sober, hard-headed man if ever there was one, told me that there had been reports of visions from all over the Ukraine.

The Virgin still appears at Hriushiw, though only occasionally. Some pilgrims – and there are often a hundred a day, from Moscow or Siberia, from America or Italy – see her outline on the chapel balcony or in the windows. It has changed those who live there. When they recovered the chapel in 1990, everyone in the village gave 200 roubles towards refurbishing it, and every able-bodied man gave his labour free.

I went into the pretty chapel, repainted and gilded until it dazzled. I admired the painting of the icon of the miraculous well surrounded by the local nobleman and the village elders. I drank the healing water from a tin mug. Beside me a pale woman with wispy grey hair under a black hat, said with awe to be a Muscovite, was in a trance.

At first I had no sense whatever of the other world. During Mass in the church, the painting of the *Bohoroditsa* on the ceiling and the beauty of the singing, had moved me. Here I was quite unmoved. Nevertheless I made my petition. Then, at last, I felt something. The answer seemed to be that I was unlikely to get what I wanted though, as if to tease me, it was not impossible. I would have to pray, or rather open myself to the divine will, which is not at all the same thing as praying that God's will be done; it simply gives resignation a new dimension. I was given none of the reassurance which I had at Medjugorje or Częstochowa. Sadly, I asked Anatoly to drive me back to Lvov.

On the way Anatoly told me of his grandfather, a Ukrainian peasant born in 1909. The old man said that life was better under the Poles. Before 1939 he owned two hectares, two cows and two horses. There were few drunks in the villages in those days, whereas drinking and slacking were the norm on collective farms. He had been made head of his *kolkhoz* and in consequence was nearly shot by guerrillas, spared only because of his reputation for kindliness.

As a boy Anatoly enjoyed staying with his grandparents, though they lived on potatoes and sour cream. They were Orthodox but he himself was not a believer. 'I can only accept religion when people live it,' he told me. 'And the last person I knew who did that was my grandmother.' He was sarcastic about arguments as to whether village churches should be Orthodox or Uniate in the new climate of religious freedom – one priest had tried to be both, on alternate days.

At Lvov he took me for a late lunch to one of the two private restaurants, the Vidpochynok Caffe opposite the Polytechnic, run by some of the prettiest young women I saw in the Ukraine – or anywhere else. We had really good borsch, delicious boeuf stroganoff and vareniki (like ravioli but with hot bacon fat), fruit and excellent coffee. The place was unlicensed, so a charming manageress brought me a teacup of vodka on the house. She and her partners were clearly successful, despite having to pay eighty per cent tax to the state.

No impractical man can survive here. Moving into a new flat, Anatoly had had to learn welding to install the sanitation and make all the furniture. (I can't even change a washer on a tap.) The flat had three rooms, one of them a workshop for the moment, in which lived Anatoly, his wife, their newborn child and a stepdaughter, but he considered himself well housed. He spoke of queuing for nine hours for petrol, of trains a day late. He had always refused to join the party, though offered a job in the Foreign Service or the KGB if he did so – with the prospect of a better flat, a car and foreign currency. (What would I have done?) He was fascinated by the death of Communism and wondered if Lenin had ever been sincere; he told me that even before perestroika out of thirty members of his faculty at Lvov University only one was a convinced Marxist. Yet he was without bitterness, full of cheerful optimism.

On my last evening at Lvov I was asked to dinner at the Dniestr Hotel (the *other* hotel in Lvov) by Sonya, a dynamic young blonde with Slav good looks, who worked at the Patriarchate. The Dniestr waiters wore bow ties, and the food wasn't too bad, with reasonable *zakushki* (hors d'oeuvres) and vodka. The other guests were a young sophomore, an American Ukrainian like my hostess, and a dark haired Russian girl.

The sophomore told me excitedly that medievalists had just discovered that as early as Charlemagne's reign Frankish clergy had been trying to widen artificially the differences between Catholicism and Orthodoxy, which was why they encouraged the addition of the *Filioque* clause to the Creed. The Russian said she loved Budapest restaurants but was never going back to Hungary because the Magyars were 'so horrid' to Russians.

Very well informed, Sonya admitted there were serious tensions in the Ukraine. It was the first time the eastern and the western regions had been united, and decades of repression had induced an inability to compromise. Political power had evaded the former dissidents whose experience was of protest, not of governing; even middle management was monopolized by ex-party members. All the churches had a high profile, she continued, as they had defended human rights. But the Uniates disliked the Orthodox, comparatively new arrivals at Lvov, for having occupied their buildings and co-operated with the Soviet régime.

I found the 'Latin' cathedral by chance, very early on my last morning. Apparently there are still 10,000 Poles in the city and recently they have regained not only their cathedral but also an archbishop. (The Armenian Catholics too will soon have their church again.) A Gothic building, the cathedral was 'baroqued' in the eighteenth century; the effect is delightful. Suddenly I realized how Latin I am in religion, how much a man of the West. There is another Gothic church in Lvov, on a hill, the fourteenth-century St Elizabeth, once noble but now a wreck; the figure of Our Lord on the great pietà high on the wall outside has lost its legs – probably by design, as the Christ on a crucifix inside has also been desecrated in this way. Its brick walls are pitted by shell holes and the windows are without glass. For forty years it was derelict, fenced off, but recently attempts have been made to rehabilitate the nave – there is a tiny makeshift altar, with a postcard of the Black Madonna.

On a hill opposite is the Baroque church of the Carmelites, full of lovely, faded frescoes; crude icons have been hung over some of them because it has been given to the Uniates. The Dominican church (near the medieval arsenal of the kings of Poland) is the finest Baroque edifice in Lvov, even better than St George's cathedral, with a vast cupola; until 1990 it was a museum of atheism but now it is a museum of religion – the same curator as before dolefully selling tickets.

So obviously do these churches hold the ghosts of departed Poles that the inscriptions have been removed from tombs, as if for fear that the descendants of the dead might return to claim their lost inheritance. Many still alive in western Poland must recall the dreadful day when they were forced to leave here for ever.

At the hotel the Intourist office booked me a seat on a train to Przemysl. I realized that I would have to use that terrible station again – I made the clerk write Przemysl on my ticket in the Russian spelling, in clear Cyrillic capitals. Even then I was uneasy. Just before my departure I went to the Latin cathedral and prayed to the Black Madonna. When I got back to my room the phone rang. Anatoly had decided to come and see me off.

At ten o'clock on a rainy morning the station was marginally better than on the night of my arrival but it still stank of human excrement. A policeman was dragging a screaming tomato-faced drunk along by his ear. Anatoly asked me if the police would treat us like that in England: 'Only if we were very poor,' I reassured him. By myself I would never have found the train, '*Przemysl*' being written in Ukrainian instead of Russian. There were no prison guards, yet getting on to it was like entraining for the Gulag; most of my fellow passengers, a wild horde, were smugglers and they boarded that train like pirates. (Each day 15,000 of them try to cross the Polish border.) A twenty-stone woman conductor in a shiny blue uniform, her half-dyed red hair piled high like a red beehive, shrieked at them unavailingly. Anatoly coaxed her into letting me ride in her service compartment instead of in the 'first class' carriages with their torn, filthy rexine benches. He himself was shaken, afterwards writing to ask, 'Did you get out safely to Poland in that terrible train?'

Once the passengers settled down, it was not so bad. I even saw two violinists with their violin cases, a mother and daughter apparently, knapsacks on their backs – though perhaps they too were smugglers. We trundled through flat, occasionally rolling country, sometimes enlivened by deep woods or an onion-domed church. The train stopped, started, over and over again.

Eventually it crawled across the border, into the lovely little city of Przemysl.

I may not agree with Josyp Terelya that the apparitions of the Virgin at Hriushiw were to warn us of the Second Coming. Yet I cannot help being moved by some words at the end of his book. 'They will persecute us but it will not be for long. All the atheists' fancy tools cannot stand up to the tools of Christ – two pieces of wood.' This was written by a man whose fingers were deliberately smashed by his gaolers to prevent him writing letters to the outside world, who was made to drink from lavatory bowls in order to break his spirit.

Although the sun did not dance at Hriushiw, there was more than a hint of activity by the moon, with lunar rays instead of solar transfiguring the landscape. I had found something of that for which I had been searching, if only a little. My doubts had been weakened, my faith strengthened. And Hriushiw had convinced me that there was a definite connection between the Virgin's appearances and the miraculous collapse of the Soviet Union. Most important of all, she had spoken of Fatima.

5
Walsingham

But Mr Unbeliever was a nimble Jack; him they could never lay hold of, though they attempted to do it often.

JOHN BUNYAN, *The Holy War*

They are all gone into the world of light!
And I alone sit ling'ring here

HENRY VAUGHAN, *Silex Scintillans*

It is odd how often what one is looking for turns up on the doorstep. I never suspected that the sun might have danced in England. Yet a monk told me it had done so at Hazlewood Castle in Yorkshire and at Walsingham in Norfolk.

I was surprised, because to me the English landscape seems so heathen. Writing a book on the county where I live, I have been struck by the survival of paganism in place names and in local legends. The Anglo-Saxon worship of Woden (or Odin), similar to that of their Norse cousins, was very nasty indeed; its rites included human sacrifice and rape. No mythology has a more horrible concept of the sun; according to the *Edda* she (Northerners saw the sun as female) is continually chased across the sky by the wolf Skoll who will eventually run her down in the Iron Wood, when he will seize her in his jaws and devour her, spilling her blood all over Asgard. The Odin worshipping Vikings conquered northern England, and I would have thought Yorkshire the last place in which to see the sun dance.

However, I hurried north, to be met by a friend at York station. I had already been to Hazlewood for a weekend during the 1980s, on a retreat with the Knights of Malta. A classic recusant house, it was the seat of the Vavasour family, who were given it by Edward I. The medieval chapel has two splendid tombs, those of Sir Thomas, who died in 1632, and Sir Walter, who died in 1713. Despite harassment as suspected agents of Spain or the Stuarts, they saved the chapel for Catholic use; 314 children were confirmed here by Bishop Leyburne in 1687. The Vavasours died out in 1826 but the branch of the Stourtons who inherited the estate took their name. Today the rambling castellated mansion is run by Carmelite friars as a retreat house.

I need not have hurried. The sun had certainly been seen to dance here, by many people, but ten years earlier. On 11 September 1982 a large group of Catholics, who had come for a public recitation of the Rosary, watched phenomena similar to those at Medjugorje, though there were no apparitions by the Virgin. Disappointingly, I was at once informed that the local bishop had asked everyone who saw the phenomena to say nothing about it and I have been unable to secure detailed information. My excited journey had been in vain.

Those who watched the sun dance at Hazlewood had been devout Catholics. Pilgrims to Medjugorje would say that this shows that the phenomenon was genuine. Sceptics might argue that it indicates auto-suggestion – but although Catholics have continued to pray here, the sun has not danced at Hazlewood since that day in 1982, making auto-suggestion an unlikely explanation.

I had mixed recollections of my first visit to Walsingham, on a pilgrimage in 1978. The scene was a cross between a pageant and a race-meeting, bishops, priests and faithful milling round and round in a pious scrum. What saved it from being ridiculous was the determination to honour the Virgin and the care taken of crippled pilgrims.

Walsingham has been called the 'English Loreto'. In 1061, five years before the Norman Conquest, a devout young widow, Richeldis, had a dream; the Virgin took her to Nazareth, showing her the Holy House where the Annunciation occurred – now supposedly at Loreto. The vision was given to Richeldis three times, so that she could measure the house and build a replica at Walsingham. The Virgin told her it would be a place of healing. When Richeldis set about building it, she found two sites marked in the dew; the builders chose the wrong one but after she spent a night in prayer, angels moved the house to the right site. English hagiographers suggest that Walsingham inspired Loreto, since it was in existence long before 1291.

By 1169 a priory of Augustinian canons was guarding the shrine. From Henry III every king of England until the Reformation endowed Walsingham Priory, embellishing the Holy House. The priory church was magnificent, especially the Lady Chapel which was a separate building. The chapel enclosed the Holy House, which stood on a stone platform but may have been a timber structure. No details of the shrine survive, save that it held a small wooden statue of the Virgin about three feet high (standing on a 'toadstone' to symbolize the conquest of evil); and was encrusted with gold, silver and jewels. It had two famous relics; a finger of St Peter and a vial of 'Our Lady's Milk' – earth from a grotto at Bethlehem where she had rested, which turned white when exposed to the sun. Among its jewels was a superb collar of rubies presented by Henry VIII; the 'King's Candle' burnt perpetually before her altar lest she forget him. Walsingham was the national shrine of a country which in those days called itself 'The Dowry of Mary'.

A ballad printed by Richard Pynson (printer to Henry VII), dating from about 1495, explains why Walsingham attracted so many pilgrims: 'All that me seke there shall find socoure.' Our Lady had worked countless miracles at the shrine, so that ballad tells us, 'ever lyke newe to them that call hir in dystresse'; for the sick, the dead ('agayne revyved, of this is no dought'), the lame, the deaf, the blind, the wounded, the leprous and the tempest tossed. In addition,

> Folke that of fendys have had acombraunce
> And of wycked spyrytes also moche vexacyon
> Have here be delivered from every such chaunce
> And soules greatly vexed with gostely temptation . . .

I envy the chance of being healed from fiends, wicked spirits, vexation and temptation. The ballad gives good advice, of a sort which is followed by the pilgrims to all the modern shrines of the Virgin:

> Lo here be the chyef solace agaynst all tribulacyon
> To all that be seke bodely or goostly
> Calling to oure lady devoutly.

That was how they dealt with depression in those days – Erasmus records the cure of a mental defective at Walsingham.

However, the shrine of Our Lady of Walsingham went down with the abbeys in 1538. The Virgin's statue (called 'Our great sybyll' by the Anglican martyr Bishop Latimer) was burnt at Smithfield and the shrine's jewels went to swell King Henry's coffers. There was a pitiful attempt at protest, described as a rebellion by the authorities, eleven men being hanged, drawn and quartered in consequence, including the sub-prior. The 'rebellion' had never been more than muttering.

The Holy House and the Augustinian priory were demolished. Today only a few haunting ruins remain. A ballad written by an unknown Elizabethan recusant laments:

Bitter, bitter oh to behold the grass to grow,
Where the walls of Walsingham did show . . .
Sin is where Our Lady sat, heaven is turned to hell,
Satan sits where Our Lord did sway, Walsingham oh farewell.

It had been a thriving pilgrim town. Besides the priory and a Franciscan friary, just like at a modern shrine, there were souvenir shops and guest houses with such cheerful names as *The Moone and Sterr, The Sarassyn's Hede, The Madynhede* or *The Crownyd Lion*. There were guest houses along the roads to it. The road from London was known as 'The Milky Way', after the famous relic of the Virgin. When pilgrims came within a mile of the Holy House they left their shoes at the Slipper Chapel and walked the rest of the way, as did Henry VIII in 1511, the year when he presented his necklace. The shrine had a wonderful reputation; there was a rumour that despite having destroyed it the king entrusted his soul to the Lady of Walsingham when he lay dying, as had his much injured Queen, poor Catherine of Aragon.

The great humanist Erasmus gives tantalizing glimpses of the old Walsingham, which he visited a year after King Henry. He left a votive prayer in Greek, to hang before the shrine:

But the poor poet, for his well-meant song,
Bringing thee verses only, all he has,
Asks in reward for his most humble gift
That greatest blessing, piety of heart . . .

In 1524 he published the *Colloquy on Pilgrimage*, a dialogue with a pilgrim who had been to Walsingham: 'At the uttermost part of all England, betwixt the North and the East, not far from the sea, scarcely three miles. The town is almost sustained by the resort of pilgrims.' Erasmus recalls 'the house where Our Lady dwelleth . . . The light was but little, and she stood at the right end of the altar in the dark corner.' Despite the devotion he had shown during his own visit, he mocks 'such as run upon pilgrimages under pretext of religion', even if he rebukes those who remove statues from churches.

The shrine was remembered well into Queen Elizabeth's reign, when there were references to it in a number of songs:

As ye came from the Holy Land of Walsingham
met you not with my true love
by the way as you came?

Or:

As I went to Walsingham
To the shrine with speed
Met I with a jolly palmer
In a pilgrim's weed.

But by the seventeenth century all save a few antiquarians had forgotten it, though the wells near where the Holy House had stood were used as wishing wells; a wish was made after drinking water from them in one's hand – a memory of the days when pilgrims had knelt between the wells to pray for relief from pains in the head or belly.

In 1897 the little Slipper Chapel, a fourteenth-century gem which had been turned into a cow-house, was bought by a Catholic. Pilgrims began to come to Walsingham again. The chapel was restored and given a statue of the Virgin modelled on the Lady on the priory's seal. The pilgrimage – called the Dowry of Mary Pilgrimage – is now a national event in the Catholic calendar, attended by thousands; after Mass at the Slipper Chapel, there is a procession to the priory ruins where prayers are said over the site of the 'Holy House of Nazareth'.

Early in August 1988, during the hottest summer in living memory, there were reports of solar phenomena. A monk – a mariologist – obtained several accounts which he afterwards passed to me. They have never been published before.

One of the fullest is by a Catholic scientist who was attending a conference in a marquee next to the Slipper Chapel. He says that he did not like what he had heard about Medjugorje – the Marian piety, the solar phenomena and 'all the business of "Secrets" and impending disasters' – stressing that he had read none of the literature about it and had no idea of what he was supposed to see. 'I know that what was reported at Fatima was a rotating motion [of the sun] and the appearance of a zig-zag plunging to earth, but I saw nothing like this, nor any flashing lights in the sky.' He continues:

> I have seen eclipses both of the sun and of the moon. This appeared to me to be something more like an eclipse *by* the sun of something even brighter. The sun itself was still very bright but could be looked into without the eyes being hurt. Whatever the sun appeared to be 'eclipsing' gave it a brilliant white line around its rim. This had a shimmering effect which might have given the impression that the sun was 'rotating'. The impression I got was that of a large host being suspended in the sky with a brilliant light from behind being 'filtered' through it. There also appeared to be an 'activity' within the sun, which at times was very pronounced, like a heart beating. The surface seemed to have a 'mottled' effect, possibly due to small cloud formations. This speckled effect also extended into the immediate area around the sun, rather like a mass of tiny smaller suns. The general overall colours were gold and rose pink. I also on occasions got a similar impression to that gained when looking at the sun from under water . . .

This took place between seven thirty and eight p.m. on Thursday, 4 August.

Others watching mention a prismatic effect. One woman speaks of

> a wonderful view of constantly changing colours, blue, green, golden, red circles, coming out of the sun towards us. At one

> point the sun appeared to be dead white, like a host, and at another to 'spin' – to come towards us and then return to its position in the sky. At one moment I saw five or six small red suns revolving around the sun, which was red, with lights flashing behind it.

A third person says, 'The sun seemed at first sight to be pulsating (growing brighter – less bright – brighter – less bright, and so on). After a few seconds I thought it appeared to be rotating in the way that one can spin a globe. This seemed to be taking place against the background of a brilliant white disc . . .'

A fourth describes the sun 'blazing in the sky, surrounded by reds, purples, blues, greens, yellows, changing colours all the time . . . It was a shining white luminous circle spinning rapidly. At one moment it seemed to move forward towards us, then it was back in place again.'

Nearly all who saw the phenomena were put in mind of a gigantic Host – though a child compared it to 'a Disprin'. Most thought they were witnessing a miracle. Some sang the Fatima *Ave Maria*, others the *Salve Regina*, while others recited the Rosary. A priest who was there estimated the crowd at about 500; no one had difficulty gazing at the sun without dark glasses.

Several saw solar phenomena on the following evening. They were not so colourful, save for that described by an education lecturer from Yorkshire, which occurred between five thirty and six thirty p.m. She writes:

> In the sky which was white in colour there appeared an enormous bright yellow sun, and within its boundaries a magenta-pink coloured bird whose head had the curve of a dove's and whose wings were spanning the sun's diameter. Each wing had within its span darker coloured, magenta-red pulsating arteries. This had the appearance of life-giving blood coursing through . . .

Most of the little group with her could see the yellow sun but not the dove. Then, when she tried to draw it, a child came and said, 'I saw that big bird in the sun as well.'

On the same evening the sun was seen rotating near Hazlewood. However there have been no further reports of solar phenomena at either Walsingham or Hazlewood. At no time did anyone claim to see the Virgin, though one woman thought she discerned the word 'PEACE' in the clouds above Walsingham. It has to be said that, so far as I know, all those who watched the sun dance were devout Catholics.

Just after I obtained these reports, I showed them to a young painter, a strong-faced girl with deep black eyes and a rare smile. 'Oh,' she said, 'that's what I watched at Medjugorje.' She described how the sun had become a white disc, revolving like a Catherine wheel, emitting prismatic rays. Hitherto everyone I had met who saw the phenomena was convinced they were supernatural, but she was an exception.

The painter had gone to Medjugorje in 1987, when she was fifteen. She had heard, in a vague way, of the sun dancing but did not expect to see it herself. A very strong minded and fiercely independent person, she had been dissatisfied with her convent school, angry at being confirmed at an age when she was not properly equipped to understand Catholicism. As for a dancing sun, like the witness at Turzovka, she considered that if she was to have faith, it was better to have faith without a sign. At the same time she admitted that the vision had been beautiful and impressive; she prized it enough to try to keep it in her head. She felt that it was cheapened when, as she was leaving Medjugorje, from the bus she saw the sun dance again – and cheapened still further when she watched it do so 'somewhere in England' two years later. When she returned to the convent, she did not mention the sun, not wishing to make certain nuns jealous, or to be laughed at by other girls.

By the time I spoke to her, she had become an agnostic. On the whole she was inclined to think that there must be a natural explanation for what she had seen at Medjugorje, even if it was one which had not yet occurred to the scientists. She had made herself stare into the sun, and thought that this might produce similar effects if done in the right light. But as a true agnostic she kept an open mind, ready to accept it as a miracle should the evidence suggest it, mirroring her attitude to God.

As I left this very honest and clear-headed young woman, I realized that meeting her had forced me to re-examine my own position. Had my attitude changed since visiting Medjugorje? Physically, the sun could not have danced. After long reflection I could not see the likelihood of a natural explanation, however much I respected the painter. But, as yet, neither could I altogether accept a supernatural cause. I saw no answer.

Walsingham is in Norfolk, for me *terra incognita*. I was met at Thetford by a Knight of Malta, of sound recusant ancestry. A career soldier, he had left his beloved regiment some years earlier, in order to write a life of Christ; at present he was working on a biography of Mary Tudor. His house was adorned by portraits of austere, grim-faced Catholic forebears. I was reminded of Lady Marchmain's brothers in *Brideshead Revisited*; they had had 'the harsh features of a race at war with its environment'. He himself recalled Charles Dickens's description of the recusant Mr Haredale in *Barnaby Rudge* – 'a burly, square-built man, negligently dressed, rough and abrupt in manner, and, in his present mood, stern and forbidding'.

However, there was nothing austere or forbidding about his hospitality. There was good roast beef at dinner, in the candlelight beneath the gaze of the grim-faced ancestors, and a very good bottle of wine. He inquired if I had ever read Clement of Alexandria on 'The Rich Man's Salvation'?

*

Now the story of the rich man has always disturbed me. As we know, he asked Christ what he must do to receive life everlasting. When told to keep the Commandments, he replied that he had done this from his youth. Our Lord answered that one thing was wanting – that he should sell his goods and give them to the poor, then come and follow him. The man went away, Christ commenting that it was easier for a camel to pass through the eye of a needle than for a rich man to enter into the kingdom of heaven.

I was alarmed by this even as a boy. When I was fifteen I met Monsignor Ronald Knox and asked him about it. He answered soothingly that the 'Eye of a Needle' had been the name of the narrow entrance of a street in Jerusalem in Christ's time. But years later I read Georges Bernanos on the street-name theory. 'So the rich only scrape their shins or wear holes in the elbows of their smart coats! I find that rubbish,' wrote that royalist yet fiercely anti-bourgeois writer of the 1930s and '40s. 'Our Lord should have put "Danger of Death" on every money-bag, just like the warnings on electric pylons.' (It would be hard to think of anyone with less money than Bernanos.)

I am a poor man by the standards of most of my friends and relations, but I own a nice little flat, belong to a pleasant club in London, travel a good deal, buy any book which catches my fancy, and entertain my friends. Yet by the standards of many in the Western world I am rich; by the standards of the East I am rich beyond the dreams of avarice. Am I going to hell? When (after my visit to Norfolk) I read Clement of Alexandria, a second-century Father of the Church, I found he argued that the wealth whose possession Christ condemned was a 'a brood of sins in the soul', not money itself but love of money; what he wants rich men to do is to spend their money on helping poorer neighbours. I take more comfort from Christ's words when the disciples inquired who then could be saved? 'The things that are impossible with men are possible with God.'

*

We discussed a subject which never fails to fascinate me, recusancy – the history of those who, after the Reformation, refused to conform to the Church of England but stayed loyal to Rome. My host related how during the seventeenth century his forebears had owned two manor houses, in parishes served by the same parson; they always spent Sunday in the parish from which he was absent, to avoid having to attend the Anglican service. What he did not mention was the harried life they lived – the priest-holes and Masses in hidden chapels, the ostracism, ruinous fines and chance of a hideous death. He showed me a pistol carried at Marston Moor; some of the Cavaliers' best soldiers were Papists. I noticed a portrait of an officer of about 1770. 'I thought all your family had been Catholic?' I asked. (At that date no Catholic could hold a commission in the British army.) 'So they were,' he said. 'That chap served in the Hanoverian army, which took Papists.'

I have to admit that there is something a little comic about fantasies of a long-dead Catholic world. Evelyn Waugh made fun of them in *Officers and Gentlemen*, in which a rabid old Papist tells Guy Crouchback about a crusade against the Nazis: 'A great rising was imminent throughout Christian Europe; led by the priests and squires, with blessed banners and the relics of saints borne ahead. Poles, Hungarians, Austrians, Bavarians, Italians and even plucky little contingents from the Catholic cantons of Switzerland would soon be on the march to redeem the times. Even a few Frenchmen . . .' But no one can deny the heroism of England's Catholic squires down the centuries. In such a house it was surprising that I did not dream of plots against Bloody Bess, or of the Kings over the Water and risings against the Georges, when I went to bed.

Walsingham is in 'High Norfolk', a long strip of rolling ground along the coast. ('Norfolk Highlanders' are said to look down on the inhabitants of the flat Breckland.) Most of the roads used by the pilgrims during the Middle Ages have ceased to exist or have declined into grassy tracks. Some pilgrims crossed the Wash, pausing outside Kings Lynn to offer thanks for a safe crossing at the lovely little chapel of the Red Mount, which still stands near Kings Lynn station. For it was fourteen treacherous miles across the Wash, a route threatened by unpredictable tides, sea-mist and quicksands; guides were available at Walpole Cross Keys, carrying wands with which to test the sand – they were compared to Moses leading the Israelites over the Red Sea. Many northern and Midland pilgrims came this way, though some northerners arrived by ship.

In the unspoilt green valley of the River Glaven, this is surely one of the prettiest villages in England, full of ancient houses of great charm – black-and-white medieval or Tudor or red brick Georgian. At the first glimpse it is obvious that it has become a place of pilgrimage, from the many shops selling *bondieuserie* (oleaginous holy pictures, garish statuettes and pious books) and from all the hospices and hostels. The beautiful priory gatehouse is still intact, while though only a single Gothic arch survives from the church it is deeply impressive, with an undeniably poignant quality. There are Catholic, Anglican and Orthodox churches, each one attracting pilgrims. Beyond question, this quintessentially English village has a quality which is reminiscent of Medjugorje or Fatima, though, despite the shops, it has escaped any trace of vulgarity.

Yet for me Walsingham is a little too perfect. It shows just what the English can do with a shrine. Curiously self-conscious, it is not unlike the set of an old Ealing Studios' film; at any moment I expected to come across 'Our Lady's Tudor Tea Room'. However I admit that I feel somewhat ungracious in saying so. In no way do I want to question the pilgrims' devotion, let alone the central reality – that the Mother of God is here and intercedes for sinners, not infrequently healing them.

One of Walsingham's merits lies in reminding visitors how well Catholicism suits the English temperament. It is too often taken for granted that Anglicanism is the natural religion of this country. Listen to the music of Thomas Tallis and you are listening to music composed by a recusant – even 'Greensleeves', regarded as the most English of tunes, comes from a Catholic England. A Papist reading Shakespeare is soon aware that this is the work of a man born into a Catholic country. John Donne was a former recusant, Ben Jonson a Catholic convert for twelve years, Dryden a convert who remained staunch and Alexander Pope a steady recusant. The deep, ineradicably Catholic roots of English culture are part of the reason why so many writers and historians have become Papists. The Church of England itself has grown much more Catholic over the last hundred and fifty years, all but extinguishing that candle lit by Cranmer and Ridley, if it has not yet learnt how to pray to the Virgin – the Anglican shrine here being a rare exception among a communion whose members are on the whole contemptuous of 'mariolatry'.

We went first to the Anglican shrine, in Holt Road. In 1921 the local vicar, an 'Anglo-Catholic', installed a statue of Our Lady in Walsingham parish church and introduced pilgrimages. The statue was moved here after the shrine was built in 1931. Today the village is a stronghold of what used to be called the High Church, thousands flocking to it on the annual Anglican pilgrimage. A guide book tells us proudly that 'the daily devotions, though nominally Anglican, are indistinguishable from the most elaborate Roman Catholic ritual'.

The church containing the shrine is an Italianate building in chocolate brown and cream, with a pretty bronze Virgin on the roof over the main door. The shrine itself is an imaginative reconstruction of the Holy House, with an effective statue copied from the image on the old priory's seal, but the decoration is excessive – I counted at least twenty silver sanctuary lamps. There are votive lights and ex-votos everywhere, some of the latter naming the cures for which they give thanks – rheumatism and weak eyes seem to predominate among the ailments healed. Under an elaborately carved *pietà* a gilt letterbox is labelled 'intercessions'. Much about the shrine is attractive, especially the side chapel of the Ascension.

A Catholic man who prayed here on New Year's Day 1983 claimed to have seen a veiled woman in grey, like a nun, who filled the shrine with her presence – he was convinced that it had been the Virgin. I myself did not respond to the atmosphere, could sense nothing which was holy, though this may have been due to my cautious attitude towards Anglican Christianity.

Once I had a certain affection for Anglicanism. I descend from a host of Church of Ireland clerics, including Jeremy Taylor, Bishop of Down and the author of *Holy Living, Holy Dying*. (His great-grandfather Dr Rowland Taylor, Cranmer's chaplain, was burnt at Smithfield during the reign of Queen Mary of Blessed Memory.) But I had thought of it as the Anglicanism of Donne, George Herbert and Traherne, of Launcelot Andrewes and Bishop Ken. A keen supporter of ecumenism and 'reunion' during the 1960s, I later grew nervous that any step towards Anglicanism might take us further away from Orthodoxy. However, since the decision to ordain women, I have been delighted by the prospect of Anglo-Catholics joining the Church of Rome and reinforcing its beleaguered conservatives.

This is recusant country. As late as the eighteenth century a family called Parker kept a secret chapel at their house in the neighbouring village of Great Walsingham. The poem 'The Wracks of Walsingham' may have been written by St Philip Howard, the martyr earl of Arundel, a Norfolk man who is known to have visited the shrine. Another Elizabethan martyr saint, Henry Walpole, was born at Docking not far away. Converted by witnessing Edmund Campion's execution at Tyburn in 1581, when he was splashed with blood from the scaffold, Walpole went to Rome where he became a Jesuit. He was arrested as soon as he returned to England in 1593 and spent two years in the Tower, during which he was tortured fourteen times – hung up by his hands from iron clasps. Finally he was hanged, drawn and quartered at York, which meant being hanged till half-dead, then cut down to be castrated and disembowelled; what remained was beheaded and hacked into four. Hundreds died in this way, priests and laymen. No doubt the Protestants have their Smithfield martyrs, like my unhappy ancestor, but Catholics went on being executed for their religion until 1681 and were fully emancipated only in 1829.

Some are convinced that the medieval anchoress and mystic, Julian of Norwich, came on pilgrimage to Walsingham. It is quite likely that she did, though there is not a scrap of evidence. The bookshops here are full of her *Revelations of Divine Love*, since she has become increasingly popular among Anglicans as well as Catholics during the present century. In particular, her boundless optimism appeals to the former. Her best known saying is 'All shall be well and all manner of things shall be well.' I wish I could believe it.

I felt more aware of God in the Orthodox church of St Seraphim. What was once Walsingham station had been converted into a small monastery, the booking hall serving as a chapel. It is odd to see a gilt onion-shaped cupola on top, adding a flavour of Eastern Europe to the Norfolk landscape. Inside, I could have thought that I was in some tiny Balkan church, so much is contained in so small a space without over-crowding; the iconostasis and its icons are impressive, tapers of unbleached wax burning before them in iron bowls filled with sand.

There are more Orthodox Christians in Britain than there are Baptists and Methodists, their numbers concealed by division into national churches; Greek, Russian, Serb or Romanian. One day the differences will blur and there will be an English Orthodox Church. Over thirty years ago the Russians began to celebrate the Liturgy in English.

Orthodoxy is an indestructible faith. It has survived centuries of Turkish occupation and then decades of atheist persecution. The Catholic Church has not been a kind sister, often trying to convert its members by force. She did nothing to help after the Russian Revolution. (My mother remembers a Russian girl being harried by nuns at one of the Sacré Coeur convents in Brussels during the 1920s; at the end of every Mass they would twitter '*Maintenant, prions pour la conversion d'Irène*'.) Yet Orthodoxy remains vibrantly alive. The real priority of ecumenism must be rapprochement between Rome and Constantinople, and not just because they are the largest Christian communions. We share so much, including devotion to the Mother of God.

We met a man who knew all the Walsingham gossip. I explained why I had come, asking him if there were any recent reports of a dancing sun. He replied that he knew a woman with a little oratory in her garden who had seen tentacles reach out of the sun, almost down to earth, after which the dance had begun, accompanied by prismatic rays. I wanted to meet her, but he would not give me her address – she was too shy.

Over-restored, the Slipper Chapel had lost the forlorn appearance which made it so appealing in old photographs, though its statue of Our Lady of Walsingham was convincing enough. A sacristy added between the wars had been converted into a chapel of the Holy Ghost. The Slipper Chapel was now the centre of a 'pilgrim complex' which possessed a bookshop and a cafeteria. The most recent addition was a new church, designed to blend with the landscape. Outside it looked like a big, red-tiled flint barn; inside like some farm building turned into a smart modern restaurant, all dull red brick and shiny yellow wood.

We went to Mass, celebrated by priests in vestments of bright purple, clashing with the red brick and the yellow wood. There was a lack-lustre sermon, barely audible despite a microphone. At the end of the service, much to my surprise, they sang an ancient Latin hymn:

Ave Regina Coelorum
Ave Domina Angelorum . . .

(Hail, Queen of the Heavens
Hail, Lady of the Angels . . .)

It was the only moment of beauty in the entire performance.

Afterwards my host told me that, despite his conservatism, he was not altogether displeased by the new Mass. He also made the point that if you go on pilgrimage to a Marian shrine, when you arrive you will find that it is not so much the Mother of God who is present there as her Son. You end up in front of His altar. This time I had seldom been aware of either, save at the church of St Seraphim, though I was able to believe that the sun had danced over the Slipper Chapel.

I bought a guide to Walsingham, written by someone who was obviously convinced that the Lady is much in evidence. He knew at least three people who had seen her. 'I have never left the village of my choice,' she had told one of them. 'Many who loved me had left me, despite the Scriptures, and turned their backs on me.' The author listed the miracles which had taken place in 1983 alone:

> This year's claims include a woman who came to give thanks for a cure from cancer, a man for a cure from a growth on his hand, another who claims that since she came to live in Walsingham her failing eyesight had been restored, and a little boy cured of very bad deafness after being sprinkled at the Anglican holy well.

A Catholic priest, who dipped his leg in the holy wells at the ruined priory, had a two-inch gap in a leg-bone healed; his doctors were certain that no human agency could have cured him. A crippled girl, bed-ridden for fifteen months, rose from her stretcher and walked after being wheeled to Mass at the Slipper Chapel. 'I shall never get well unless I go to Walsingham,' she had said repeatedly when she was in hospital, although she had no idea where Walsingham was. The miracle converted her non-believing mother to Catholicism.

The book contains a grim little anecdote. 'Every pilgrim who seeks the help promised by Mary must be ready to accept God's will,' the author warns. He relates how a pilgrim who came in an ambulance and was too ill to leave it, attended an open-air Mass in the priory's grounds, fervently praying for a miraculous solution to his problems. Two days later the miracle duly occurred – he died.

Sadly, this otherwise informative work had nothing to say about solar phenomena, no doubt because it was published five years before the display of 1988.

For all my carping, I left Walsingham with real regret. Something of the Old Religion still clings to it: 'Walsingham, oh farewell.'

On the train back to London I fell into conversation with a middle-aged spinster. I couldn't stop her. She turned out to be a fanatic High Anglican, like some character in a Barbara Pym story, who babbled happily about 'reunion'. 'I do so admire the Romans' discipline,' she gushed.

Discipline? All that went out after the Second Vatican Council. There are no rules now of the sort one encounters in the novels of Graham Greene or Evelyn Waugh. No longer are there obligations to abstain from meat on Fridays or to fast from midnight before receiving Communion. Confession is becoming a matter of personal choice. The problem of divorce and remarriage, which tormented so many of Greene and Waugh's heroes and heroines, usually finds a solution nowadays; not only is annulment much easier, and much more likely, but those who marry outside the Church are discreetly given the Sacraments – as one English bishop put it recently, there is a 'divergence' between theology and pastoral practice.

I had enjoyed my visit to Walsingham though my sense of the Virgin's presence there was more akin to what I had felt at Svatá Hora than at Medjugorje or Częstochowa or even Hriushiw. It gave me no feeling of tranquillity and did nothing to reassure my faith. Yet at the same time I remembered the young painter telling me that the reports of the sun dancing at Walsingham reminded her of what she herself had seen at Medjugorje. In particular I recalled how some of the visionaries outside the Slipper Chapel in August 1988 had responded to the solar phenomena by singing the Fatima *Ave Maria* as though by instinct.

— 6 —
Garabandal

Certainly there be that delight in giddiness,
and count it a bondage to fix a belief . . .

BACON, *Of Truth*

Last night did Christ the Sun rise from the dark,
The mystic harvest of the fields of God . . .

SEDULIUS SCOTTUS, *Carmen Paschale*

I recommenced my pilgrimage a few weeks later, at the end of April 1992. By then I knew that the sun was dancing at more Marian shrines than I had time or money to visit. The most interesting seemed to be Garabandal in northern Spain and Oliveto Citra in southern Italy – both with apocalyptic warnings, miracle cures and solar phenomena. Which should I choose?

Oliveto is twenty-five miles inland from Salerno, a small town above the River Sele, dominated by a medieval castle. Late on the evening of 24 May 1985, preceded by 'a falling star', the Virgin appeared to children playing near the castle gate. Since then many people had seen her at the gate – in blue and white, with a crown of stars and carrying a baby. One girl reported how a small orb of light exploded, to produce an immense, dazzling glow within which was the Madonna. It was rumoured she would give a sign and at eleven p.m. on 20 July 1985 'a luminous red cloud' materialized, visible ten kilometres away.

She gave messages to twenty persons, visiting several. They were calls to penance, with urgent warnings. Since humanity's faith had been shipwrecked, 'I can no longer hold back the righteous arm of my Son ... The world stands at the brink of the abyss.' In January 1986 she declared that time was very short. 'There will be earthquakes and great misfortune and famine for all the earth's inhabitants.' Only a return to faith, with prayer and penance, could avert the catastrophe.

The Bishop of Salerno and the parish priest, Don Peppino Amato, gave cautious support, allowing a shrine with a statue of the Madonna to be placed in the castle. The Jesuit mariologist Robert Faricy came to Oliveto in 1987, expecting to find 'a very questionable situation', but was deeply impressed by the visionaries. Besides children, they included adults who were solid, straightforward people – a dentist, a garage owner, a carpenter, a road-mender, a waitress. There had also been numerous cases of healing; physical, mental, moral and spiritual. The resemblance to Medjugorje was striking.

What decided me in favour of Garabandal was being told that it was the link between Fatima and Medjugorje – though I suspect that the real link is Turzovka. I had gone to an English monastery for the annual retreat of the Knights of Malta. There were old friends, Latin Masses and nostalgic hymns. A monk from the community, who knew about the dancing sun, gave me everything he had in print on the subject. He insisted that Garabandal was a vital link and I must go there. In any case a bad period of doubting had set in, and it was high time for me to visit another shrine.

The night before I left England, I found myself unable to sleep. A dog howled, firing my imagination. I thought of wolves, the ultimate predators of European legend, whether as animals or as werewolves. (In today's Russia a story circulates that Lenin howled like a wolf during his last agony because the Devil was at his deathbed.) Yet the only wolf which I have seen at really close quarters – in Montenegro, crossing the Čakor Pass through the snow in the spring of 1986 – looked surprisingly amiable. Our old Catholic liturgy compared the Devil to a lion, not a wolf; *diabolus tamquam leo circuit, quaerens quem devoret*, 'the devil goeth about like a roaring lion, seeking whom he may devour', the Short Lesson warned at Compline. In my favourite abbey they still sing, at that last office of the day, with only a single candle in the darkness, a hymn telling of the dangers of the night and the *noctium phantasmata*.

As I lay awake in my melancholy mood, I wondered why I worry so much about what I and my friends believe. I am a *very* unsatisfactory Christian. There have been totally godless periods in my life when I worshipped money or a woman, even briefly the bottle. It is not from guilt or *angst*. I think that ultimately it must boil down to Pascal's wager; one can't discount the existence of God – I'm more frightened of finding the Christian religion true when I die than of finding it untrue. If I doubt sometimes, I still find arguments for the non-existence of God unconvincing. 'The heart experiences God, not the reason,' Pascal points out, in one of his most quoted passages. (And the most misquoted – the Duchess of Windsor used it as the title for her autobiography. *The Heart has its Reasons*). 'This, then, is faith: God felt by the heart, not by reason,' he explains, adding, 'Is it by reason that you love yourself?'

It was a relief to return to the dancing sun. Activity, mental or physical or both, is the only cure I know for melancholy, even if it doesn't always work. I settled down to read the books and papers about Garabandal lent to me by the monk. I was glad to learn that the shrine was in mountainous country; I knew the Pyrenees a little but not the mountains further west. The more I read, the more intrigued I became. The apparitions here were the most controversial of the present century, more so than those at Medjugorje, which they greatly resembled. While many were convinced that the visions were true, the local hierarchy refused to authenticate them, though Rome had never given an opinion. Indeed the case had recently been reopened by the Vatican. Moreover, there had definitely been solar phenomena, though on nothing like such a scale as those at Medjugorje.

Here is an outline of what took place between 1961 and 1965 at this remote hamlet in the Cantabrian mountains, on the slopes of the Picos de Europa.

About eight o'clock on the evening of 18 June 1961 four little girls were playing happily in the '*calleja*', a sunken path which led up to a clump of pines on a low hill above their village. Their names were Conchita, Mari Lolí, Jacinta and Mari Cruz; their ages ranged from ten to twelve. They were 'Throwing stones at the Devil', a local children's game. There was a sound like thunder and a flash of light. Conchita, then the three others, saw – only briefly – a shining angel. They told their teacher and the parish priest, who advised them to say the Rosary at the Pines. Two days later, after saying it they found their way home barred by blinding light; the angel reappeared. He did so seven times more during June. They realized that he was the Archangel Michael.

Angels are celestial spirits who serve God, beings who are pure intelligence. Many modern Catholics refuse to believe in them, yet the Bible tells us they exist. Since the Renaissance painters and sculptors have given them gentle, feminine faces. In medieval art, however, they are sometimes terrifying. Michael can be a fearsome figure. (I have never been in a more awesome shrine than his cave at Monte Gargano.) This is how the Apocalypse describes his first confrontation with the Devil:

> And there was a great battle in heaven: Michael and his angels fought with the dragon, and the dragon fought, and his

> angels. And they prevailed not: neither was their place found any more in heaven. And that great dragon was cast out, that old serpent, who is called the Devil and Satan, who seduceth the whole world. And he was cast unto the earth: and his angels were thrown down with him.

But Michael was never frightening or warlike at Garabandal.

He bore no resemblance whatever to the statue at the back of the village church at Garabandal, a Baroque paladin with pink cheeks, in silver helmet, silver scaled armour and red robe, who is digging a lance into the eye of a demon beneath his feet. Nor was he Terelya's white eagle or ancient celestial man. In a blue robe instead of armour, he was like no St Michael in religious art. 'His wings were rose-coloured, large and beautiful; his face small, neither fat nor thin,' Conchita recorded in her diary. 'His nose was extremely beautiful; his eyes black and his skin swarthy. His hands were delicately shaped, with carefully tended nails, though one could not see his feet. He appeared to be about nine years old. Though so young, he gave the impression of unconquerable strength.'

If the girls were inventing their story, they would surely have described the statue which they had seen Sunday after Sunday.

On Saturday, 1 July, the crowd, which by now accompanied the girls whenever they went towards the Pines, saw them go into a two-hour trance – the archangel was telling the children that the Virgin would come to them on the next day, the Feast of the Visitation.

On Sunday the four went up the *calleja*. Among the large crowd which followed were a dozen priests and several doctors. Again the little girls fell on their knees in a long trance. Afterwards they said that they had been surrounded by light and that the Virgin had appeared to them, escorted by two angels, one of whom was Michael; the other looked like his twin brother. She herself seemed to be no more than eighteen; she wore a white dress and a blue cloak, and there was a crown of golden stars on her chestnut hair. She spoke to them about everyday things, such as hay-making, in a wonderfully musical voice. She also mentioned a message. This was the first of more than 2000 occasions on which she is said to have appeared to the children until the summer of 1965.

Three days later she gave her first solemn message to the world, though the girls were told not to announce it till October: '"You must make many sacrifices. You must do many penances,"' were her words, as reported by the children. 'We must visit the Blessed Sacrament very often, and above all try to be perfect. If we do not do these things, then we are all going to be punished. The cup is being filled now and if we do not change, then a very great punishment will come upon us.'

At about this time she spoke to Conchita of a great miracle which would occur at Garabandal at some future date. Conchita wrote in her diary that Our Lord would perform the miracle at His Mother's request, to show to the world that her visits really had taken place, and that her message must be heeded. The Pope would see it, and so would Padre Pio, the holy man of the Gargano. (In 1965, according to Conchita, the Virgin added that a warning would precede the miracle, a brief but terrifying warning which would be seen throughout the entire world.)

While living in Puglia I visited San Giovanni Rotondo with an Anglican friend who was writing a book on the region with me. We met the two friars who had nursed Padre Pio during his last illness in 1968 and both of us left San Giovanni Rotondo convinced of the man's holiness. Some of the pilgrims to Garabandal say that among the Pines they have smelt that strange, unmistakable scent, of roses or violets, or of incense, which announced his presence when he was alive.

Some say that Padre Pio saw a vision of the miracle before he died. So apparently did a young Jesuit priest, Luis Andreu, who in August came to pray with the children during the apparitions. Kneeling with them on the hill, he suddenly grew pale and was heard to say 'Miracle! Miracle!' four times. While being driven home the following day he said repeatedly, 'This is the happiest day of my life!' When the car stopped, he was found to be dead. There were solar phenomena. Conchita records:

> During the apparitions Lolí and I were walking down from the pines with a crowd. Suddenly we saw something mysterious in the clouds. It looked like fire. I saw it. Lolí saw it. So did many people with us, even some far off who had stayed in the village. It stopped and the Blessed Virgin appeared to us. We asked her what it was. She told us, 'I came to you in that fire'.

When they were in a trance on the feast of Our Lady of the Pillar. Conchita and Lolí saw 'a red star with a very long tail' beneath the Virgin's feet, as did other people too.

The red star with the tail is the symbol of the chariot of fire in the Fourth Book of Kings: 'Elias and Eliseus were going from Galgal . . . And as they went on walking and talking together, behold a fiery chariot, and fiery horses parted them both asunder: and Elias went up by a whirlwind into heaven.' In the early centuries Eastern Christians confused Elias with Apollo, whose chariot was the sun.

The trances lasted for periods which varied from a few minutes to nine hours. The children claimed that the Virgin sometimes came with the Infant Jesus, even letting them hold him. They also saw the archangel again.

Attempts to wake them with flash-bulbs, by running pins into them or burning them with cigarettes, had no effect. They were oblivious of rain or snow, and in no way depressed by their lack of sleep. They seemed to communicate with each other by telepathy. It was also noticed that when they prayed during the trances, they did so very slowly, pronouncing each word syllable by syllable.

Many doctors examined the children in 1961 and 1962.

Stressing that mental abnormality would have shown earlier symptoms, a psychiatrist declared the four little girls perfectly normal. A neurologist, Dr Ricardo Puncernau, an assistant professor at the Barcelona Medical School, examined them during and after at least twenty trances; he concluded there was no natural or pathological explanation. Hypnosis was ruled out – repeated hypnotic trances lead to exhaustion and the children never needed to replace the hours of sleep lost by visions in the night.

In front of a rapt crowd a Host appeared mysteriously on Conchita's tongue on 19 July 1962, just as she had foretold a fortnight earlier – she said that the Archangel Michael had promised to give her communion that day.

The Virgin also gave messages to the children for especially worried pilgrims to the village, such as priests afflicted by doubts of faith, who were reassured. There were words of comfort for those troubled in other ways. One was a blind New York millionaire, Joey Lomangino, who was told through Conchita that his sight would be restored to him on the day of the great miracle. He has spent nearly thirty years promoting belief in Garabandal.

Conchita was also told by the Virgin that, as a result of the miracle, Russia would convert – an echo of Fatima.

Early in 1965 the Virgin informed Conchita that the Archangel Michael would bring a new message on 18 June. She received it in the midst of a crowd of 2000 pilgrims, from many countries: 'Since my message of 18 October [1961] has not been obeyed or spread abroad, I must tell you that this will be the last message. The cup was filling up; now it overflows. Many priests are on the road to hell, dragging many down with them. The Eucharist grows less and less important. You will have to avert God's anger by your own efforts but, if you ask for forgiveness sincerely, then he will pardon you. I, your mother, because of the Archangel Michael's petition, beg you to change your lives. You are now given the final warning. I love you very much and do not want you condemned. Ask sincerely and we will give to you. Make more sacrifices. Think of the Passion of Jesus.'

A month after this final vision, the Bishop of Santander, Mgr Beita Aldazabal, stated that nothing had taken place which obliged him to affirm its supernatural origin; one must wait for something which might make possible a definitive judgement. Conchita was brought to Rome, questioned by mariologists, and received in audience by Paul VI who seems to have received a favourable impression. However, she was then subjected to lengthy questioning by Beita Aldazabal and broke down, saying she no longer believed in her visions – a statement which she later withdrew. Conchita emigrated to New York where she married. Everyone who meets her is impressed by her sincerity.

Despite the Church's lack of enthusiasm, pilgrims kept on coming. There were reports (unpublished) of solar phenomena, such as that witnessed by an Englishwoman from Ealing on a May evening in 1974:

> The sky was completely overcast but as I stood up to make my way up to the Pines there was a small break in the clouds and the sun then came out. As I glanced at the sun it started spinning and changing into several lovely colours. It then passed behind the clouds.
>
> The clouds then parted to the left and the right, pulled back as if they were curtains. In the sky I saw maps of Russia and mainland Europe. The map of Russia was black, the other maps were white. As I watched something that looked like black smoke or gas started to pour out of Russia and into Eastern Europe. While this was happening I had great difficulty breathing although the smoke or gas did not come near me. All the maps of Europe except Portugal and Spain filled with this smoke. Spain and Portugal remained white . . .

In the sky she saw Padre Pio and a young fair-haired man whom she thought was the archangel:

> I then saw Our Lord in the sky. His face was in a terrible state, swollen, disfigured and covered with blood. There were two babies with Him. It came to me that these were victims of abortion. Near Him I saw a map of the south-east of England. It was black and a feeling of evil came to me from this map. From behind this map a great light rose up in the sky. This was an all-powerful Being and I believe it was the Eternal Father. From this Being there were what looked like rays of light going to the map of England (London). These came to me as rays of terrible anger and it came to me that this city's days were numbered.

Then she saw a white cross above the mountains behind Garabandal. 'Higher in the sky I saw the Eternal Father again, with Our Lord . . .'

Apparently the vision lasted for about half an hour.

Others have simply seen the sun dancing, in the same way that it does at Medjugorje. One woman watched it do so over the Pines. 'It was spinning in a clockwise direction, yet we could look directly at it without even blinking an eye. It looked just like a white disc pulsating . . .'

My first reaction was that what had happened at Garabandal was a hoax, perpetrated by sly little girls who had begun it as a game. The Host on Conchita's tongue reminded me of the 'ectoplasm' which emanated from the mouths of Victorian mediums – sometimes fabricated with white of egg. The 'kissing of holy objects' by the Virgin, which had been such a feature of the trances, especially repelled me. The children asked her to kiss rosaries, crucifixes and holy medals, and then took them to the graveyard for the souls of dead relatives and friends to kiss too.

Although ready enough to believe that the world was

threatened by all sorts of calamities, I knew too many stories of natural disasters – 'Acts of God' – which had *not* been averted by prayer, however fervent and sincere. In particular I recalled the story of Scilla which I had heard in southern Italy. On the morning of 5 February 1783 the town there was almost totally destroyed by an earthquake. More than 1500 survivors took refuge on the beach, which they thought might be safer. The feudal lord of Scilla, the aged Prince Ruffo di Calabria, had been praying in the chapel of his castle, outside the walls, but decided that he must join his people by the sea. Together, throughout the night and for most of the following day, they begged God to have mercy. At dusk another shock split a neighbouring promontory, an entire mountainside falling into the sea. A tidal wave engulfed the beach, sweeping every single soul out to sea, and then a second huge wave swept over the town, hurling their bodies back on to its ruins.

Why then did I go to Garabandal?

Largely because I had heard that Padre Pio, the stigmatic, had met Conchita and undoubtedly believed in her visions, even if he never said so publicly. He told his brethren at San Giovanni Rotondo – and also Joey Lomangino – that they were genuine. I took Padre Pio very seriously indeed; he had healed many people whom I knew, or changed their lives for the better. He was a prophet too, warning Karol Wojtyła that one day he would be Pope, when a Polish pontiff seemed an impossibility.

How could poorly educated young girls like Conchita and her friends have invented all this and kept it up for so long? Those who saw the 'miracle of the Host' (my 'ectoplasm') say that it was entirely credible and very moving. Conchita's diary – a journal rather than a diary – glows with spontaneity and honesty; were it untrue, it would rank with the great forgeries of the century. Her repudiation of the visions followed a long grilling by a team of clerics, who insisted over and over again that these had been hallucinations, a collective dream. Yet even the most hostile Catholic critic has to admit that there was nothing in them which was at variance with the Church's teaching.

Countless men and women of probity and intelligence have accepted that the visions were genuine. In 1983 a Santander psychiatrist, Dr Luis Morales, declared publicly in a series of lectures that he was convinced that the Virgin had appeared to the girls. He argued that 'their functional union with the Virgin was as those described in mystical theology, not in the psychology of spasms, convulsions or hysterical crises'. He himself prayed that he would spend his last years in the shadow of the Virgin of Garabandal. What gives considerable weight to Morales's declaration is that he had been a member of the Bishop of Santander's original inquiry team in 1961, when he tried unsuccessfully to supply a natural explanation based on psychological theory. No one could be better informed about the girls and their visions.

I had not even located Garabandal on a proper map. All I knew was that it was thirty-five miles south-west of Santander. The quickest and cheapest means of reaching the place seemed to be to fly to Bilbao, then go on to Santander and reconnoitre. I would have to rely on bus and rail, and my feet. In the event, it turned out to be the easiest of my pilgrimages.

I do not like flying. Once I was fearful in planes and required whisky. Now that I am older, though I don't relish the possibility of being burnt alive, I even enjoy the actual flight. What I dislike passionately are airports, the large sort, which are true visions of hell. For all my fatalism, I think of death when taking off or landing. In the old days Catholics were encouraged to meditate on death. (I have a minute black prayer book which belonged to my great-grandmother, *Bona Mors or the Art of Dying Happily*.) No doubt I am morbid as well as old fashioned but I still do. I often wonder how I shall die. Will it be a quick and violent death or long and lingering? Tennyson conjures up the latter:

. . . when my light is low,
When the blood creeps, and the nerves prick
and tingle: and the heart is sick.
And all the wheels of Being slow.

. . . when the sinuous frame
is rack'd with pangs that conquer trust;
And Time, a maniac scattering dust,
And Life, a Fury slinging flame.

I know the epitaph which I should like for myself:

RESURGAM

'I shall arise.'

Arriving on a bright April day, after coming down over green sugar-loaf hills, the little airport at Bilbao was very different from the misery of Heathrow. During the Civil War, 'Bilbo' (its Basque name) was the capital of Euzkadi, the Basque Free State, and Republican. However, being staunch Catholics, the Basques did not persecute the Church – unlike other Spanish Republicans who, at a conservative estimate, murdered twelve bishops, 4000 priests, and 2000 monks and nuns.

It was strange to see the bilingual signs. I went through the *Iristeak* (arrivals), not the *Nazio Etorrerrak* (arrivals from elsewhere in Spain), directed by the most complex grammar in Europe. Under General Franco everything had been done to destroy the language. During the 1960s I only just escaped arrest for shouting '*Gora Euzkadi Eskatuta*!' ('Long live the Basque Free State!') in a bar at Zarauz; I could have spent a year in gaol. Euskera is a weird tongue: Basques count in twenties, not tens, while no true Basque word begins with an 'r'.

*

Generally, I find it best not to book hotels in advance. A search with a chance of failure makes one's adrenalin flow, while it is usually much cheaper as well as more interesting. Almost as soon as I had left the bus at Santander I found what I wanted, a modest establishment catering for salesmen and lorry-drivers.

A cheerful city, Santander has known evil times in the present century. It fell to the Nationalists after a ferocious campaign during the autumn of 1937, while four years later a munition ship blew up in the harbour, wrecking the entire city centre. Even so, it retains plenty of character and, since it is the metropolis for Garabandal, I decided to explore it. The cathedral is one of those tunnel-like buildings of the Castilian Romanesque, seemingly designed as a refuge from Moors. The best time for investigating any Latin city is during the hours when the natives take their siesta and I walked for two or three miles along the front in the afternoon sun. I came to the Sardinero quarter, with old-fashioned hotels and opulent villas whose faded elegance appealed to me. At the beginning of the century, in Alfonso XIII's time, this was a fashionable resort, very popular with the Spanish aristocracy. The lizard-like girls on the beaches looked smart enough.

The inhabitants spoke with oddly metallic voices. I gather that the Cantabrian dialect is one of the harshest in Spain – an argument sounds like jack-drills breaking up a road.

I met a man in a bar who spoke good English and who, by some miracle, knew all about Garabandal. 'Most Spaniards have lost interest in that place,' he warned me. 'A few pilgrims keep on coming, mainly from the English-speaking countries – especially from Australia, for some reason. And also from Belgium.' He telephoned a friend. The friend supplied the number of a farmer at Garabandal called Serafin Gonzalez, who let rooms – an amazing piece of luck. He also reminded me that there had been no apparitions there since 1965. I was not discouraged; after all, the Virgin had not appeared at Fatima since 1917.

However, next day a whole morning went by at my hotel while the girl at the reception desk tried to telephone Serafin Gonzalez, apparently in vain. Finally she got through. Yes, there was a room. 'I could kiss you,' I told her. 'Don't bother,' replied that dignified young Spaniard.

Leaving Santander at six p.m. the bus drove through prosperous villages. Many had new houses that were built in a traditional style, though concrete replaced wooden beams. We began to go up into the mountains, the Picos de Europa, and I was staggered by their beauty. It was the most dramatic landscape of my entire pilgrimage, even wilder and more imposing than Herzegovina. I fell in love with it at once. There were great gorges, snow-capped peaks, misty passes, lush slopes, noble woods and foaming torrents. My spirits lifted and lifted; before I had arrived, I was determined to return. For once this was a journey which I was enjoying. Higher and higher went the bus, under a cloudless sky, through green hillsides with white limestone outcrops. About an hour before dark, I was deposited at the village of Cosio. A sign pointing up a steep mountain road said '*San Sebastian de Garabandal 5.8 kilómetros*'.

There was no taxi so I had to yomp, carrying a bag full of books, and, though fit, I am growing a little old for that sort of thing.

The road was a series of hairpin bends, going up and up a steep incline towards a frowning green mountain whose jagged peaks were still covered in snow; a notice warned one to beware of landslides. Goat-bells tinkled on the hillside above me while the Rio Vendul roared below, fed by countless musical streams. At first there was the occasional red-roofed barn or sheepfold in the valley but soon these came to an end, leaving the river banks to the pine trees and the holm-oaks. None of those who had written about Garabandal had bothered to describe the loveliness of its setting.

After I had walked about four kilometres, too happy to be tired despite my bag, a girl driving a car stopped and offered me a lift. The other girl in the car, Mercedes Fatima Gonzalez, turned out to be the niece of Serafin Gonzalez, returning from Santander University where she read physics. It showed how peaceful the region must be for two young girls to stop on a lonely road for a burly, unkempt man, in a donkey jacket.

The 'Meson Serafin' was a pleasant surprise. At best I had expected a rough room with a basin and a cold tap. Instead, I was given a cheerful little white bedroom, scrupulously clean, with a minuscule bathroom next door. Señora Gonzalez – Pacita – was a thick-set woman in her fifties, with grey hair, sharp eyes and a cheerful grin. Fortunately she knew a few English words. 'Supper?' she shouted, in a deep, hoarse voice, producing an enormous salad of white asparagus and Spanish mayonnaise, with a bottle of rough red wine. I thought that was all, but a plate of fried eggs and cold sun-dried ham followed, then fruit. Serafin came in from milking the cows, a bald man with delicate features and a gentle smile. I discovered that he was Conchita's brother, but he spoke no English.

Luckily the only other guest that night was a mine of information. A thin old Frenchman in his seventies, a little frail, he was a retired surgeon from Arles. My father used to say that the older a Frenchman grows, the more likeable he becomes; the doctor was no exception to this rule, if he had a curious look in his eyes. I confided my worries about the Church to him. 'Personally, I'm neither conservative nor progressive,' he replied. (Later I was to find that this was not strictly true.) 'I dislike "isms". God doesn't deal in them, because He's infinite.'

He had been coming to Garabandal since 1967 and knew a great deal about the story. He told me that the children had been persecuted by their own Church; a new parish priest was sent to the village in the mid 1960s with the specific task of discouraging and discrediting them; one method was refusing absolution in Confession. The doctor had known all four girls and was impressed by their spontaneity and sincerity, and by how they withdrew into themselves. He himself believed firmly in the apparitions. In his professional opinion as a doctor there had undoubtedly been cases of healing, in particular cures of sclerosis which were beyond medical help. Dr Morales, the Santander psychiatrist, had informed him in 1991 that cures were still taking place.

The Frenchman had seen the sun dance in Italy, at San Damiano near Piacenza. Here in 1961 the Virgin in the form of a beautiful peasant girl visited a woman dying from an inoperable cancer and cured her. When the woman, Rosa Quattrini, went to the Gargano to see Padre Pio, the same girl greeted her, announcing, 'I am the Madonna of Consolation, of the Afflicted.' She appeared at San Damiano for several years, once over a pear tree which immediately burst into blossom. There were many messages from her. 'The eternal father is tired, very tired', was one of these messages. 'He has freed the demon, who is working havoc and stealing many souls, even the souls of those in high places if they lose their faith and do not love.' People must pray to the Archangel Michael to protect them on the road to heaven. There was the same apocalyptic note. 'A night of great darkness will come, with such darkness that all will tremble . . .' There had been many cures at San Damiano, of the deaf, the blind and the paralytic, frequently after drinking water from a well next to the pear tree over which the Virgin had appeared. Moreover the sun had spun and whirled, emitting multi-coloured rays, without hurting the eyes; sometimes only a glowing ring could be seen, as though an eclipse were happening. Other lights shone in the sky; circles, rays and white crosses.

*

Returning to the subject of Garabandal, he told he how Pepe Diaz (the village stonemason) had described to him the 'miracle of the Host' which he had witnessed. Announced some hours in advance, it took place at one o'clock in the morning. The Host appeared on Conchita's tongue, shining with light, while she kept her mouth open for at least three minutes. It had been an extraordinarily moving spectacle, said Pepe Diaz.

Nevertheless, the bishops had tried to stop people from believing in the apparitions, the Frenchman continued. He had heard that a recent bishop of Santander was convinced they were genuine, but did not have the courage to say so publicly in the face of the rest of the hierarchy's hostility, though he asked his priests to let their flocks know that miraculous cures could sometimes be found at Garabandal.

The doctor related, with a certain relish, how one hostile prelate had been killed in a car accident, when the vehicle in which he was travelling rolled over three times and burst into flames. The man's hands were so charred that it was impossible to insert a rosary between them when his corpse was laid out for burial. Clearly my informant thought it was divine retribution for opposing the children's cause.

After a night of blissful sleep, very rare for an insomniac like me, before breakfast I walked up the *calleja*, a short, steep, stony path like the bed of a dried-up mountain stream, which was bordered by clumps of violets. A one-eyed yellow dog, who had adopted me, gambolled at my side. Almost at the start I came to a drystone cairn on which was a Baroque style portrait of the Archangel Michael in polychrome tiles, by the spot where he had first appeared to the little girls. Fifty yards further on there was another cairn with a similar portrait of the Virgin, where she had first been seen. On that sunny spring morning, as I climbed I heard a cuckoo call; I thought of Sussex, where I live, though I had never heard one in England so early in the year. Another fifty yards and the Stations of the Cross began, cairns decorated with polychrome tiles depicting Christ's Passion. There was a small garden with a tiny chapel, no more than an apse open on one side, with a statue of St Michael over the altar; he was in silver armour and had a feminine face, very different from the archangel which the girls had seen. The chapel was flanked by twelve cherry trees in blossom. Finally I reached the pines.

For some reason, I had never associated pine trees with shrines or holiness. They reminded me too much of suburban villas or cemeteries, not of visions. (There used to be a ghastly advertisement on the railways, 'Sleep midst Surrey pines.') I prefer something more exotic, such as mulberries:

> God in the whizzing of a pleasant wind
> Shall march upon the top of mulberry trees.

Or cypresses or cedars of Lebanon, or even holm-oaks. Yet these pines were clearly very different from the common run of pines, in some indefinable way. Nine grave and stately trees, each with a circle of stones around its foot, they stood in a saucer-shaped depression on a grassy knoll. The tallest had a small statue of the Virgin in its branches, in a little glass-fronted case; the trunk was girdled by bouquets of flowers, and there were more flowers at its foot, together with one or two candles, though there was none of the weird clutter which I had seen at Medjugorje. I said my prayers, made my petition. I felt no sense of response, no sense of rejection; there was, however, a sense of peace but that was inevitable in such a lovely place.

Scrambling down from this miniature 'hill of the apparitions', the dog and I passed the old Frenchman, who was praying – making the Stations of the Cross – and the only pilgrim there on that glorious morning. He bowed, smiling faintly, then went back to his devotions.

*

At breakfast he unfolded a frightful tale, how the Freemasons of the town where he lived in southern France had tried to murder him. A new cook (whom he afterwards discovered to be a qualified chemist) had poisoned his food systematically with lead granules which gradually built up inside his organs. He began to feel iller and iller. Only his natural wariness and medical knowledge saved him from an agonizing death. His suspicions were confirmed when he accused the cook point blank of being a murderess and she went white, 'like a napkin'. The motive had been revenge; he had uncovered a social security fraud in which Freemasons were implicated. Yet the poison had been so cleverly administered, in such minute particles, that it was impossible for him to prove anything. However, he had sacked the cook. '*Monsieur, c'était tout-à-fait un roman de Simenon.*'

In this melancholy mood he spoke sadly of a changing Spain, certainly more prosperous and cleaner, but greedier, with much more crime and vice. Religion was entering a decline; fewer and fewer people went to church. The Spaniards were growing less sane – madness was rampant.

'All has been foretold at Fatima, Amsterdam and Akita,' he confided. Clearly he accepted the gloomiest interpretation of the Third Secret of Fatima – the coming reign of Antichrist. I knew nothing about warnings at Amsterdam (perhaps as well for my peace of mind) but had heard of Akita in Japan. Here, in 1973, a Sister Sasagawa saw sheets of light in her convent chapel. A cross-like wound appeared in the palm of her hand. Then an angel took her into the chapel at night where a statue of the Virgin wept and spoke to her. This was the first of over a hundred visions which continued until 1981, during which the statue wept, sometimes shedding blood. The Virgin warned that if men did not turn to God, there would come a punishment worse than any since the flood: 'A fire will fall from the sky and annihilate large numbers. Neither priests nor the faithful will be spared. The survivors will be in such desolation that they will envy the dead.' I consoled myself with the thought that, like Loreto, weeping statues (an Irish speciality) had always strained my credulity.

We walked to Mass through the village, fifty or sixty red-roofed houses of grey stone, many with long wooden balconies. In the centre, next to the Meson Serafin, a small 'manor house' had been built in the last few years, so skilfully constructed that it looked as if it had been there since the Middle Ages. There was an air of contentment and modest prosperity. Nevertheless most of the villagers were very old or very young. Lowing cattle with bells were being driven through the muddy streets; chickens clucked, a donkey brayed. There was manure everywhere and reassuring farmyard smells.

The church of San Sebastian de Garabandal was a small, well-kept Romanesque building, obviously very old but restored fairly recently with a small, squat red-roofed tower. A statue of St Sebastian stood just over the altar, a statue of the Virgin in blue and white (just as the children saw her) to one side. On top of the Baroque reredos there was that old friend, the gold sunburst. The Mass was short and in Spanish, with no sermon; being a weekday there was no 'kiss-of-peace', which the dignified Spaniards do not enjoy.

I went off down the hill to Cosio where I had noticed a restaurant on my way up. There were primroses, violets, wood anemones and dark purple orchids. Goldfinches and crested tits flitted through the trees at the roadside. I saw my favourite butterfly, the scarce swallow-tail or 'kite', immediately identifiable from its odd, dipping flight. Judging from the arms on a farmhouse and the chapel next to it, Cosio had belonged to the Knights of Calatrava (it had been part of the lands of the great commandery of Puentenansa). I hoped that the villagers had not suffered the same miseries as those of Lope de Vega's play, *Fuente Ovejuna*, where the wicked landlord is a Knight of Calatrava. Outside, the restaurant looked so dirty and unpromising that I nearly went back to Garabandal. Entering, I found a clean, airy dining room where, despite my lack of Spanish, a pleasant young waitress produced a tureen of kidney-bean soup filled with chunks of sausage, and then a white asparagus tortilla, together with excellent wine.

—

When I returned from Cosio, I was disillusioned to find myself turned out of my little white room and put in a kind of annex, hugger-mugger with a group of elderly Spanish pilgrims, as if in a geriatric ward. Señora Gonzalez, who owned three houses in Garabandal, was plainly doing very good business. I would have returned to Santander but there was no bus for two days.

Disconsolately, I watched the pilgrims set out on the Stations of the Cross, an ordeal for elderly people. It was like Medjugorje, if on an infinitely smaller scale. To be fair, the Meson Serafin and its annexes were the only accommodation and there was little sign of commerce; a restrained sign over a single door announced that works of art could be purchased within. The 'Café-Bar Los Pinos', a small, barn-like house, remained firmly shut throughout my visit. Unquestionably, Garabandal is the least spoilt as well as the most beautiful of Marian shrines.

Nor would it be a bad place to live, for someone who needs solitude. I reflected how well it would have suited my friend Karl. He liked being addressed as '*Herr Rittmeister*' (Captain of Horse), since he was one of the last of those cavalry soldiers so detested by Hitler. Werner Bergengruen, a literary idol since my youth – and like Karl a convert from Lutheranism to Catholicism, who had opposed Hitler from the start – wrote a strange semi-autobiographical novel called *Der Letzte Rittmeister*. In it he portrays a White Russian cavalry officer who has taken refuge in a very similar Swiss village; over the door of his tiny cottage he contemplates hanging a sign, on which are the words '*Inveni portum. Spes et fortuna, valete*' – 'Farewell, hope and fortune, I have entered harbour'. Garabandal could be such a haven.

I joined the pilgrims for supper at the Meson Serafin. After two glasses of wine an amiable if badly preserved lady, in a ginger wig and mauve trousers, crashed the language barrier with a mixture of Italian and French. She asked what I was writing in my little blue notebook. 'Did I know,' she inquired, 'that the Virgin of the Escorial has recently been seen several times over Madrid, and that the sun had danced there too?'

My old Frenchman appeared. He had plainly had a good deal more than two glasses of rough red wine. Eyes gleaming, he told me what was really worth seeing in the area; at a church nearby the largest relic of the True Cross to survive, eighty centimetres long and the gift of a Byzantine emperor to a king of Castile – at another church not far away a Baroque statue of Our Lord which had been seen to weep tears by reliable witnesses. We passed to worldly affairs. Was I aware that the Algerians were building an atomic factory outside Algiers with Chinese money, where they were making bombs with which to destroy Paris? That M. le Pen, a devout Catholic, had been traduced? France's sole hope was the restoration of the monarchy – even if the king of Spain was a rabid socialist. I gave him the royalist toast, '*Un roi, pourquoi pas*?' At this he announced in tears that the Sainte Vierge had brought us together, promising to send me a pamphlet he had written about the Freemasons' plot to assassinate him.

I had come across French royalism before. I recall going to a family wedding in Brittany during the 1980s. (French families can be vast; a cousin told me he had counted 600 male relations.) At dinner after the marriage service, a rough-looking man leant over the trestle table and said in a thick Breton accent, '*Monsieur, vous avez l'air d'être un grand buveur et gros mangeur*.' I got up to hit him, but he explained that he merely wanted to know what I was drinking because I was enjoying it so much. 'All Britanny is here tonight,' he continued. 'We like the English but we think they let us down in '93 – if they'd sent us more guns, we might have avoided the Republic.' He was very pleased that I knew all about the 'Catholic and Royal Army of the Vendée', those devout peasants who put the fear of God into the Revolutionaries of north-western France. Called '*Chouans*', from their hooting like owls when signalling to each other in the forest, they armed themselves by ambushing Republican troops, cutting their throats, and then taking their muskets to be blessed by the parish priest. Like many royalists, my Breton at the wedding was an '*Intégriste*', a disciple of the late Archbishop Lefebvre.

While I have some sympathy with the Intégristes and their fidelity to the old religion, I cannot accept their repudiation of the Pope. I went to one of their services in a church at Nantes. The fierce young priest took for his text Pope Urban II's summons to the Crusade, announcing that Islam, not Marxism, was France's real enemy. (This was in the 1980s.) 'We are the Vendéens, the Chouans,' he shouted. 'We have already shown we know how to fight, how to keep the Faith.' I had expected a tiny congregation of aged die-hards; to my astonishment the church was packed with young people. The Intégristes still flourish in France, I gather from my cousins, attracting far more vocations to the priesthood (proportionately) than the mainstream Catholic Church. Their success is due to teaching the catechism indefatigably to any child who goes to their Sunday classes.

Next day I breakfasted with the pilgrims. Although we could not speak to each other, they welcomed me with grave smiles. That sincere, hospitable smile is something very Spanish, a greeting which exists nowhere else in Europe. In Italy they smile as they steal your wallet, said my old Frenchman. (I have ancestors from west of the Shannon who would have smiled as they slit your throat, particularly a Bourke called 'The Devil's Reaping Hook' – son of 'The Blind Abbot'.) I never cease to admire the beautiful manners of the Spaniards – northern European manners are brutish by comparison. Spanish politeness had nothing to do with how to hold a knife and fork – it is a simple but profound respect for other human beings as individuals.

Sunday Mass was not until one o'clock, which was probably just as well. I had used up too much energy in the last two days. So I lay down on my donkey jacket in a flowery meadow just below the village and slept the morning away under the sun, beneath the green and white mountains. I heard strange birds, squalling like cats, and looked up to see a pair of golden orioles.

At Mass, as at Hriushiw, I sat in the gallery – though there was no longer a choir, only piped music. On the way I had passed the freethinking element in Garabandal, elderly sons of the soil with gnarled brown faces beneath their berets, sitting on benches in the sun. Yet the little church was packed; though the congregation must have been swollen by pilgrims, the village was obviously well represented. By the time the service started there was standing room only, even in the gallery. The lessons were read by a boy and girl in jeans, while the bidding prayers included one for '*la marcha de sociedad*'. It must have been altogether different during the years when the girls saw the Lady, with the Latin Mass and a sense of mystery and dignity. However worthy, however friendly, no one could have called the present service mysterious or dignified. But it reduced my friend in the ginger wig to tears. And the priest was unquestionably a fine, sincere, man.

I spent my last afternoon at Garabandal wandering around the valley below, accompanied by the yellow dog with one brown eye. I paid a final visit to the pines. Among the rosaries which had been hung on the biggest tree, I left an aluminium prayer ring which had cost 30p but had sentimental value; at no other shrine have I felt impelled to do such a thing. Again I prayed, again I sensed neither the granting of what I wanted, nor yet a refusal.

Garabandal is a special case among the shrines. Unlike Medjugorje (till recently) the visionaries have left the place of the apparitions. Three are married and in America; the fourth, Mari Cruz, lives elsewhere in Spain. At one point they retracted their stories. Yet the Congregation of the Faith (the former Holy Office) has never issued any formal comment. In 1991 the newly appointed bishop of Santander sent the dossier to Rome, asking for the case to be reopened.

There may well be opposition from among the Spanish hierarchy. During the 1970s *The Tablet* published an article which gives some insight into their minds. A new priest was appointed to a country parish, a village full of devout, Mass-going Catholics; it had been fervently loyal to the faith during the Civil War and several villagers had been martyred for refusing to reveal where their *párocco* was hiding; the church was always packed, even on weekdays. The new priest, young and with a degree in sociology from an American university, at once introduced changes; the communion rails were ripped up, statues were banished from the church, public recitation of the Rosary and Benediction were stopped, devotion to the saints (especially to St Anthony) being discouraged. Even on weekdays there were long sermons on the value of social work. Needless to say, the faithful, being too 'backward', were not consulted, though exhorted to thank God for the changes. A deputation from the village tried to complain to the bishop; he refused to see them. Soon the congregation began to shrink; within a year only a handful went to Mass on weekdays, the church being half-empty on Sundays. Collections fell dramatically, eliciting frantic reproaches from the pulpit, to nó avail – the baby had been thrown out with the bathwater.

Most Spanish bishops would have supported that priest, partly because of the harrowing experience of the Church during the Civil War as an 'enemy of the people'. Whatever happens, they will keep in step with the *marcha de sociedad*. Messages such as that from Medjugorje (that hearing Mass or saying the Rosary take precedence over social work) arouse horror. The hierarchy does not want a Spanish Medjugorje.

I wanted to go back to Santander by bus, to see the country. The alternative was a taxi to Cabezon de la Sal, from where I could take a train – dearer and duller. The bus went at seven a.m. but, as I was spending the next night at Santander and could have a siesta, this did not worry me. I set off from Garabandal at five thirty in pitch darkness, and since it was downhill I had a soothing walk. There was a new moon, with a full display of stars. All I could see was the pale road and sometimes a snowy mountaintop. No car passed me, I met no one. Apart from my own footsteps, wind rustling in the trees and an owl hooting, the only sound was that of water – of the roaring Rio Vendul and streams rushing to join it. I could smell pine needles. No doubt I alarmed nocturnal animals going about their business:

> Night wandering weasels shriek to see him there.

This was a loneliness I could enjoy. I felt as though I were a part of that wonderful valley, sorry that I had not slept rough for the last few nights.

At about six thirty I saw the sky begin to turn a luminous pale peacock blue over the white tops of those dark green mountains, while the birds started an almost deafening chorus:

> *Jam lucis orto sidere*
> *Deum precemur supplices*

(Now that daylight fills the sky, we lift our hearts to God on high.) But it was not truly dawn till well after the bus picked me up at Cosio.

There was an unpleasant moment when I thought I had left my precious blue notebook behind, only to find it in a seldom used pocket. Cantabria's mountains continued to thrill, but I began to doze, and also to reflect. Was I thinking too much about the Virgin, too little about Christ? I am well aware what my Protestant friends would tell me.

'What think ye on Christ?' asks a placard borne by a yellow-faced old maniac outside the supermarket where I do my shopping. 'I know men and I tell you Jesus Christ was not a man' was what Napoleon thought. But as a Catholic I am bound to believe that he was a man, the God-Man. What stranger belief could I hold? Yet I cannot do without it. 'The astonishing thing is that this notion of the necessity of God has been able to get a footing in the head of so wild and vicious an animal as man, so holy and moving and wise is it, and so honouring to the individual,' says Dostoevsky (speaking through Ivan Karamazov). In some moods I find it easy enough to worship Christ; following him is a very different matter.

Over the door of his house Bergengruen's Rittmeister painted a crucifixion on a wooden panel, stiff and rustic but not without warmth which bore the legend:

CREDO O SIGNORE
NEL VOSTRO AMORE

For me the Cross is the supreme symbol of Christ, whether a Catholic crucifix or an Orthodox cross with Adam's skull underneath. I like to have one in every room where I live, to ward off evil. I am deeply moved by the Anglo-Saxon *Dream of the Rood* or by Isaac Watt's *When I survey the Wondrous Cross* – or by the response of old Karl's friend and fellow conspirator, Colonel Marogna-Redwitz, when informed that, for plotting against Hitler, he had been condemned to hang (slowly, by piano-wire) on 14 September. 'What an honour to die on the Feast of the Exaltation of the Holy Cross,' he told the Gestapo.

I fell into bed in my tiny room at the hotel near Santander Cathedral, without bothering to go out for a meal or a drink. Depression had suddenly seized me by the throat. I reached down into my unpacked bag, fishing out my Orthodox prayer book. There I read, 'O my most holy Lady, Mother of God, by thy holy and most powerful prayers, remove from me, thy humble and burdened servant despair . . . from my smitten heart, and from my darkened mind; quench the flames of my passions, for I am poor and lost.' Yet everything had fallen into place. I had arrived at Bilbao, knowing merely that Garabandal was about thirty-five miles south-west of Santander and 'in the mountains'. Some would say I had been guided.

Had *she* come to Garabandal and spoken to Conchita and her three friends? Few shrines make such demands on belief. It is in a kind of limbo, symbolized by the condition of the pines; most are worm-eaten, the work of pine-moth larvae whose obscene cocoons hang from their branches. Nearly thirty years have gone by since the last apparitions; fewer and fewer pilgrims go, and of those who do many are elderly or middle aged. All this would, of course, change should Rome declare the visions 'worthy of credence'.

Meanwhile, because it is so neglected, Garabandal remains the loveliest of the Marian shrines. The mountain setting is magnificent, while the hamlet, the church and the hillock on which stand the pines have a simple, irresistible charm.

The story of '*Las Niñas y la nuestra Señora*' is one of great beauty. The persecution of the little girls, for that is what it was, adds poignancy; the conviction of so many that they were telling the truth makes it heart-breaking. The Church can be very cruel. I myself am almost certain that the sun danced here. I also believe that there is a link with Fatima.

7

Fatima

Mock on, Mock on, Voltaire, Rousseau:
Mock on, Mock on: 'tis all in vain.
You throw the sand against the wind
And the wind blows it back again.

WILLIAM BLAKE, notebook poems

Thus God showed me his grace again, as when the clouds recede and the sun bursts forth . . .

HILDEGARD OF BINGEN, *Epistolae*

The time had come for me to visit Fatima, where the sun first danced. It had done so only once, on a single, extraordinary day. I was going to attend the celebrations commemorating the seventy-fifth anniversary of the apparitions of the Virgin which took place in 1917, hoping that perhaps I might learn something from the prevailing mood among the visionaries.

The recent visions of the Mother of God throughout the world seemed to be connected with what happened at Fatima – all being accompanied by apocalyptic warnings, by calls to prayer and penance, and by solar phenomena. The seers at Medjugorje, Garabandal and Hriushiw had been well aware of this. Even at shrines where she did not appear but where the sun danced, many suspected that there was a link.

I joined a small group on a tour advertised in a conservative

Catholic periodical – a rarity. I wanted to be among fervent believers, people of unquestioning faith; they were most likely to respond to the shrine, while their faith might bolster my own. But although some turned out to be very good company, in the event it made no difference. I might just as well have gone alone.

The group were led by a priest who told me over the telephone that he was 'fairly conservative'. He was a brave man to say so. Nowadays conservatives in the Catholic Church have to put up with unrelenting criticism, constantly charged with not responding to the 'spirit of Vatican 2', which means not being stuck in the 1960s as if in a time warp.

I know a parish where until a few years ago the Latin Mass survived, not the Tridentine but the new rite in accordance with the Council's decrees. However, the local bishop disapproved of Latin Masses. A new priest arrived, a man of the 1960s, and in came an English Mass, interrupted by extempore prayers and prosy reflections. Sometimes sermons were punctuated by shrill cries of 'The past is dead.' During one on-going community event we were bidden to thank God for the changes. Soon familiar faces were missing from the congregation.

I find a poignant resemblance between the plight of today's conservative Catholics and that of Papists in Elizabethan England. For almost everywhere, as at Walsingham after the Reformation, 'Owls do scrike where the sweetest hymns lately were sung.' But this time those who mourn for the old ways have been disowned by their own Church.

One reason for my being traditionalist is that the past is so close to me. Not only was my father quite old when I was born in 1935 but, since his own father died young in 1896, he was largely brought up by grandparents who had married in 1863. His grandfather, 'Andrew Thunder of Boley, Bolinready and Ballycanew in the Co.

Wexford', as he called himself after his little estate near the Gap of Gorey, had been involved in Smith O'Brien's Rising in 1848 but escaped to Paris. (O'Brien was condemned to be hanged, drawn and quartered – a sentence which was commuted to transportation.) Old Andrew's father-in-law had been one of the only two MPs to die of the Famine Fever in 1847. When Andrew died, he was buried in the habit of a Franciscan friar.

My father swam in the 1908 Olympic Games, visited China just after the fall of the Manchu Emperors, was an RFC pilot during the Great War, lived – and I think spied – in Weimar Germany, spent many years in *Sale Époque* Paris, and then became a financial adviser to the oil company Steaua Română at Bucharest, on smuggling assets out of Romania during King Carol's moratorium. He would recount how as a boy he had seen Queen Victoria at Nice, how on the Nile he met an ex-slave of Mehmet Ali who had been born when Napoleon was in Egypt, how he had spoken to the last shôgun's son at Kyoto. He told me what it was like to be shot down without a parachute (terrifying) or being the first man to fly over Masada – 'Had a copy of Josephus in the cockpit' – and described the impression made by T. E. Lawrence when dining in his Mess. There used to be a painting of one of his adventures in the Imperial War Museum, 'The Seward Exploit'.

He watched Field Marshal von Hindenburg driven at breakneck speed into Berlin to avoid Communist marksmen, after being elected President of Germany in 1925, and Major Goering fly down to drop a wreath of flowers on the car; at first everyone thought it was a bomb. During the 1930s a friend in the SS warned him not to visit Germany as he was on a Gestapo black list. More agreeably, he knew and loved Prohibition New York, recalling speakeasies and Eddy Cantor with affection. In my father's company the past was always far more interesting than the present.

For many years a lapsed Catholic, when he began to practise his religion again in late middle life, it was the French Catholicism of his childhood: communion only three times a year, with half an hour's prayer before and after Mass; fasting in Lent; and Easter a more important feast than Christmas.

I accept that too much living in the past can be unhealthy, but I am sure there is nothing wrong with pleasant memories or in seeking inspiration from history. Only the past gives any indication of what is going to happen in the future. As Sir Thomas Browne observed, ''Tis opportune to look back upon old times, and contemplate our Forefathers.' After all, emphasis on the tradition of the Church is what makes Catholicism so different from Protestantism, which relies on Scripture alone, a living developing tradition since Apostolic times; as the present Pope has stressed, the Church brings forth from her storeroom both new and old. I think too that the past often holds the secret of happiness for today and tomorrow. Perhaps this was what Bernanos, another hero of my youth, had in mind when he wrote, 'The mission of the Church is to discover the source of lost joy.'

Fatima is in central Portugal, in the diocese of Leiria, and not far from the great abbeys of Alcobaça and Batalha. At the time of the apparitions, it was a hamlet near the large, straggling village of Aljustrel. Although admittedly more inspiring than the flat fields of Hriushiw, the country round about lacks the dramatic beauty of the mountain settings of Medjugorje, Turzovka or Garabandal; the ground is stony and the soil red, dotted with olive trees and evergreen holm-oaks. About a mile from Fatima there is a saucer-shaped depression called the Cova da Iria – the dell of Iria or Irene. Three peasant children were tending sheep here on 13 May 1917; Lucia dos Santos, aged ten, with her cousins Francisco Marto, eight, and his sister Jacinta, seven. They all lived at Aljustrel, their parents being small farmers.

They were saying the Rosary, as their mothers had told them to, mumbling the prayers so as to finish it quickly. Suddenly there was what seemed to be a flash of lightning and they began to go home, fearing a thunderstorm. There was another flash, then they saw a Lady dressed in white, standing on a small holm-oak. In Lucia's words, 'She was more brilliant than the sun.' 'Where are you from?' asked Lucia. 'Heaven,' was the answer. The Lady told the children that she wanted them to come to the same spot on the thirteenth day of the month for six months, at the same time. In response to further questions, she said that both the girls would go to heaven but Francisco must say many Rosaries before doing so. One of their friends who had just died was already there – another would have to stay in purgatory till the end of the world.

At first the two younger children were unimpressed by the apparition. 'Throw a stone at it,' said Francisco. 'Give her some bread and cheese,' suggested Jacinta. But they changed their minds after she started speaking to Lucia, and knelt down. She opened her hands and light poured into the three. When she left, the intense light streaming from her seemed to open a path in the sky before her as she disappeared into space.

The children agreed to keep the vision a secret, but Jacinta told her mother and soon the story was all over Aljustrel. They were laughed at by their families. Despite the jeering, they sneaked back to the Cova da Iria on 13 June. The Lady came again, preceded by the same flashes of light, repeating her instructions. She also promised to take Jacinta and Francisco to heaven quite soon though Lucia must stay behind.

After this the parish priest suggested to Lucia that the visions came from the Devil. She was so frightened that she wanted to stay away from the Cova but the other children begged her to go with them on 13 July. Her mother and her uncle came too, with a crowd of several thousand. The sun seemed to glow a little less brightly, then Lucia said that the Lady was appearing. This time she told the children to say the Rosary every day, for peace and for an end to the Great War; they must also pray to Our Lord, 'to save us from the fires of hell'. In October she would tell them who she was and what she wanted from them above all. Meanwhile she confided a 'secret'. Lucia was seen to turn pale by those near her. (We now know from Lucia that she was witnessing a terrible vision of hell.)

Lucia pleaded with the Lady to work a miracle, to convince everybody that she really was appearing. The poor girl had good reason to want one; until August her mother beat her black and blue, often with a broomstick, for telling lies. At school Francisco was being scolded by his teacher and bullied by the other boys. The children's parents were alarmed because the authorities were beginning to take an interest.

For, as at Medjugorje, Turzovka and Hriushiw, there was a political dimension. It is important to realize that Portugal was going through a most unhappy period. The monarchy had fallen in 1910, its fall arousing the wildest expectations, but the Republicans' good intentions had resulted in chaos instead of progress and prosperity. There had been countless governments, while crime and corruption were rife, and the country was on the verge of bankruptcy – general strike followed general strike, together with an epidemic of bomb throwing. By 1917 serious inflation had begun and there were food shortages. The misery was made worse by the Great War. In January 25,000 Portuguese troops had sailed for Flanders, and in April they had suffered heavy casualties at the Battle of the Lys during the German spring offensive – the first time for centuries that Portuguese troops had fought abroad. Understandably, the regime lived in fear of the right-wing coup which would eventually take place.

Like most left-wingers in those days, members of the new ruling class tended to be atheists and Freemasons, regarding the Church as an ally of the old order – with some justice, since it had been a prop of the monarchy. Many bishops fled abroad, including the cardinal-patriarch of Lisbon. Those priests who remained in Portugal were forbidden to preach or to wear clerical dress. Foreshadowing Soviet Russia and Tito's Yugoslavia, there was a 'crusade' against religion: a minister of justice declared that Catholicism would be extinct within two generations.

The administrator of the district was the mayor of Vila Nova de Ourém, Arturo de Oliveira Santos. Just over thirty, a metal-worker nicknamed 'The Tinker', he belonged to a type soon to be well known in Russia. (A year later he maimed himself while making a bomb with which to kill someone politically incorrect.) He was convinced that the Lady's 'secret' was the date of a monarchist putsch.

The Tinker summoned Lucia's father to Ourém, ordering him to bring his daughter. She refused to say anything about the secret. On 13 August the Tinker arrived at Fatima and insisted on driving the children to the Cova. Instead, hiding them under rugs, he drove to Ourém.

Meanwhile a crowd gathered at the Cova. A friend of Lucia's parents, Maria Carreira, says that everyone heard a 'thunderclap'; a cloud hovered over the holm-oak. 'What we had seen before – I can't remember when – and would see again in the coming months, took place,' says Maria. 'Our faces reflected the colours of the rainbow – pink, red, blue . . . trees looked as if made of flowers, not leaves, every leaf a flower. The earth wore these colours as did our clothes.'

At Ourém the children were being questioned by the Tinker, who tried bullying to make them reveal the secret, then coaxing – a gold chain each, money. When they refused, they were sent to the city gaol. The convicts were horrified to see children in such a place and tried to comfort them. One played his concertina, dancing the fandango with Jacinta. They even knelt down to say the Rosary with them. A guard took Jacinta away, telling the others she was going to be boiled in oil. A second guard came for Francisco, saying that Jacinta was dead. Then Lucia was called, to be boiled in the same way. She found Francisco and Jacinta alive. Neither had told the secret.

Even the Tinker knew that such treatment of children under the age of eleven was not very impressive, and took them home.

On Sunday, 19 August, herding sheep once more, at a place called Os Valinhos, they saw the Lady. (In Fatima at that very moment Lucia's sister was watching the sun display the same rainbow hues which it had shown at the Cova four days earlier.) Again they were told to say the Rosary and come on the thirteenth day of each month. She would work a miracle in October, though a lesser one than it might have been 'had they not taken you to the town'. St Joseph would come too, with the Holy Child – who would bless the world. Our Lady of Mount Carmel and Our Lady of Sorrows would also come. The children were instructed to use money left by pilgrims for wooden *andores* (litters for statues) and carry them on the feast of the Rosary. Lucia asked her to heal sick neighbours – she promised to cure some.

Despite anarchists trying to start a riot, crowds assembled at Fatima before the next apparition on 13 September. Among them were the diocesan vicar-general, thirty seminarians and priests, and Canon Manuel Formigão, a theologian who came on behalf of the exiled cardinal-patriarch. One priest warned the seminarians that what they hoped to see might not happen or might be Devil's work. What they saw, in a cloudless blue sky, was 'a luminous globe . . . with an extraordinary light' float down on to the holm-oak, disappear, reappear and fly away to the east. Others report seeing a star, 'like a night-time star', come from the east and hover over the little tree.

In addition, Maria dos Anjos, Lucia's sister, speaks of a phenomenon unique to Fatima – the 'rain of flowers'. 'They were very small white flowers, just like those from the olive trees. People with umbrellas tried to catch them as they fell, but they couldn't. Nor could people catch them in their hands. They simply vanished. The air was full of them, all the time. There were so many flowers. I saw the rain of flowers even better than the stars.' Maria adds that this was when she ceased to wonder if Lucia was telling the truth.

Canon Formigão saw neither the globe, the star or the rain of flowers. He only saw the sun grow less bright, which he thought might be due to the Cova's comparatively high altitude. It is unlikely, as some accounts claim, that he was immediately convinced of a miraculous explanation – he could not see what was happening. But he was sufficiently impressed to go to Aljustrel and question the children.

During the apparitions the crowd knelt and prayed. Some shouted at the children, begging them to ask the Lady for favours – 'To cure my son who's blind', 'To heal my son who's deaf', 'To bring my husband home from the war.'

Her message was the same as at Os Valinhos. Our Lord would come in October – they would see him as the Infant Jesus – with St Joseph and the 'forms' of Our Lady of Mount Carmel and Our Lady of Sorrows. Smiling, she told them, 'God is pleased by your sacrifices, but he doesn't want you to sleep in the ropes. Use them only during the daytime.' (Unknown to their parents, ever since that dreadful vision on 13 July the three had been wearing rough ropes round their waists, next to the skin, as a penance to save sinners from hell.) When Lucia asked her to heal people, the Lady, answered, 'I shall cure some but not others. In October I will work a miracle to make everybody believe.'

Canon Formigão returned a fortnight later. A canon lawyer and a professor at the Santarém seminary, he was scarcely gullible. First he questioned Francisco, who told him the Lady always came from where the sun had risen, that though she looked at all of them, she only spoke to Lucia and he could not hear what she was saying. 'More beautiful than anyone I've ever seen', she wore a white veil and a white and gold dress. When Jacinta was asked the most important thing which the lady had told them, she answered, 'We must say the Rosary every day.'

He spoke to Lucia last. Far from being self-conscious or conceited, she looked depressed. (At the prospect of yet more questioning?) She had never seen the Lady until May. Unlike Francisco, she had not noticed where she came from, but 'when she goes away, she goes into the sky to where the sun rises'. She confirmed the white dress mentioned by Francisco and Jacinta: like Francisco, she described the Lady as neither happy nor sad but serious. She admitted having been told a secret which she must not tell anyone.

The canon had friends in the village, a couple called Gonçalves. They assured him that the children's parents were decent folk, well liked, though Lucia's father was a bit too fond of a drink. Manuel Gonçalves also spoke of strange lights. In August the sun had turned blood-red, pink and yellow, making white clouds blood-red and men and women yellow.

Formigão had a second meeting with Lucia, in the presence of four witnesses, just before the October apparition. She told him that the light round the Lady was 'more beautiful than the brightest sunlight'. She said that she could remember her mother reading to her from a book about Our Lady appearing to a girl but had forgotten all about it. (This was the story of La Salette.)

Portugal awaited the miracle of 13 October. People came from all over the country – peasants, fishermen, factory workers – clerks, to form a crowd of 50–70,000. Though it was pouring with rain, many stood throughout the night in the Cova, which was roofed by umbrellas, the ground underfoot a sea of mud.

The children watched in the downpour but she did not come at noon, her normal time. A priest told them they were deluded:

'Run away.' Almost in tears, Lucia insisted on staying. At one p.m. she said to Jacinta, 'Kneel down. The lady's coming. I can see the light.' Some thought the children and the tree became shrouded in mist.

As usual, Lucia asked the Lady what she wanted. 'I want you to tell them to build a chapel here in my honour. I am Our Lady of the Rosary. Go on saying the Rosary every day. The war is coming to an end and the soldiers will soon be home.' Again she said that she would cure some but not others, who must make amends and beg forgiveness. 'Don't let them offend Our Lord any more – already he is deeply offended.' Then she disappeared.

What the children then saw, as Lucia described it that night, puts one in mind of Baroque paintings: 'We saw beside the sun St Joseph with the Child Jesus, and Our Lady in white with a blue mantle. It looked as if St Joseph and the Child Jesus were blessing the world, moving their hands to outline a cross. This vision vanished, and then I saw Our Lord and Our Lady – I think she was Our Lady of Sorrows. It looked as if Our Lord was blessing the world in the way St Joseph had done. This vision vanished too, and I seemed to see Our Lady in the form of Our Lady of Mount Carmel.'

This was the last apparition of Fatima.

Needless to say, none of the spectators witnessed it, though one thought he saw 'a thin column of smoke, scanty and bluish', rise above the children's heads at the moment when the lady was said to have left them. This was reported by Dr Almeida Garret, a professor of Coimbra University.

No solar phenomena at Marian shrines are better documented than those of Fatima. Dr Garret describes the sun as looking like a disc of dull silver with a clearly defined rim, 'like a glazed wheel made of mother of pearl'. It did not hurt his eyes to watch. Then 'the sun spun round on itself in a mad whirl. Suddenly a cry, a shriek of anguish, was heard to burst from the crowd. Whirling as fast as ever, the sun seemed to detach itself from the sky and come towards the earth menacingly, as if to crush us with its huge fiery mass.' There were changes in colour all around him. First he noticed that everything had turned amethyst, including the trees. Then everything went yellow, people taking on the hue of 'old damask'.

Some years later a priest, who at the time was at a school ten kilometres from the scene, recalled that the sun 'zig-zagged'. None of the school thought of Fatima. Terrified, they wondered if it meant the end of the world. The phenomenon was seen over fifty kilometres away.

Curiously, as at other shrines, a few spectators saw nothing.

Some of the best descriptions were in anti-Catholic journals.

> *Ordem*: 'The sun was sometimes surrounded by blood red flames, at others encircled by yellow and soft purple; it seemed to revolve very rapidly, then detach itself from the sky.'
> *O Dia*: 'It began to spin, turning on itself like a giant Catherine wheel, hurling itself at the earth in zigzag fashion. Then it went back to its orbit, only to start the process of descending twice more, appearing to come so close to people's heads that they feared the end of the world had come.'
> *O Seculo*: 'The sun trembled and made sharp, unheard of movements in defiance of all cosmic laws; the sun danced, in the peasants' characteristic expression.'

All these papers stress the crowd's terror.

That evening Canon Formigão questioned the exhausted children. Lucia explained what she meant by seeing the Lady in two forms. One was Our Lady of Sorrows (*Mater Dolorosa*), though without a sword piercing her breasts; the other was Our Lady of Mount Carmel 'with things hanging from her hands . . . like cards' (scapulars). She said that Jesus and St Joseph wore bright red. She did not expect to see the Lady again.

Jacinta too had seen the visions, with the sun going round and round, looking blue, yellow, red and other colours as well. She said that the Lady had told Lucia the war would stop on that day. (Lucia confirmed this.)

Francisco added nothing, but agreed that he had seen St Joseph and the Child thought not the two Virgins, while he remembered the sun spinning and changing colour.

Formigão (later known as 'the fourth seer of Fatima') was convinced that the visions had occurred and were of divine origin. Under the name 'Visconde de Montelo' he published two books: *Os Episodios Maravilhos de Fatima* (1921) and *As Grandes Maravilhas de Fatima* (1927) – the second including a full account of his talk with the children on the night of 13 October. Both are of the utmost importance.

There are certain resemblances to what happened at La Salette in Dauphiné in 1846. Here, on a fine September day, two peasant children herding cattle in the mountains, a girl of fifteen and a boy of eleven, had seen a 'Lady' weeping. She appeared to them near a dried-up stream where they had been resting, in an aureole of dazzling light which spread for several feet around her; they described it as 'incomparably brighter than the sun'. The light which shone from her face was too bright for the boy to bear – he could not see her features – a light even brighter than that enveloping her. She was dressed in white and gold; there was a chaplet of roses round her head on which was a diadem of gold 'as though formed of streams of brilliancy'. She foretold disaster. 'If the people will not submit, then I must let my Son's hand fall upon them.' The potatoes would fail; there was no point in sowing grain. 'There will be a great famine – before the famine comes, children under seven will die in their parents' arms.' Then she glided into the air, fading away with the light.

Almost at once the children's tale was accepted by the clergy, after close questioning. The dried-up stream flowed again, its water healing many, some from supposedly incurable diseases. Pilgrims flocked to the Holy Mountain. In 1851 the Church declared the apparition to be 'worthy of credence' and a basilica was built on the site.

The Lady confided 'secrets' to the children, which they refused to reveal. In the end they agreed to write them down, but in sealed letters for the Pope's eye alone. 'These are the secrets of La Salette,' Pius IX announced in 1851. 'Unless the world repents, it shall perish.' Well informed clergy were convinced that the boy's secret concerned rehabilitation and mercy, but that the girl's foretold 'great chastisements'.

We know that Lucia's mother had read to her the story of La Salette. Was it the inspiration of her own apparitions? Like the critics of Garabandal, one might argue that what occurred at Fatima was a deception by sly children. Could Lucia, a clever ten year old, have dominated the others, who were scarcely more than babies? Only she spoke to the Virgin while Francisco never heard her. Could some form of primitive hypnotism, or even plain bullying, have been used by Lucia to make the other two co-operate in the deception?

Yet, given that the three had tricked the grown-ups with an amazingly elaborate hoax, how did they arrange for the sun to perform so obligingly? At no other shrine had it behaved like this before, however much miraculous light there may have been; nobody was prepared for a 'solar miracle' which must rule out any possibility of auto-suggestion. Mass hypnosis? By Lucia, among that vast crowd? So far, no natural explanation is satisfactory.

I find the Jesuit Fr Martindale the most helpful of the many Catholics who have written about Fatima. (Apart, of course, from

Lucia's account – *Fatima in Lucia's Own Words*, edited by Fr Louis Kondor, Fatima, 1976.) Believing firmly in the apparitions' supernatural origin, Martindale considers the arguments against them. 'No one supposes that the sun was physically shifted from its place,' he concedes. 'That would have meant a world-wide catastrophe.' Although he does not say as much, in the end he obviously concludes that the 'solar miracle' was a mass hallucination of divine inspiration. He also hints at what, for want of a better term, might be called 'supernatural television', stressing Lucia's insistence that the visions near the sun could not be 'drawn', which implies they were variations in the light. So too was the Lady – 'altogether of light', an 'undulating' light.

'Catholics have tried to explain it in their own way, and failed, leaving a trail of enigmas,' Geoffrey Ashe observed of the dancing sun at Fatima in his *Miracles* (1978). 'Even to accept it as Mary's doing is surely to admit that she has an inscrutable and alarming aspect, which does not sit very well with Christian ideas of her.' He was writing before Medjugorje and without kowledge of other Marian shrines with solar phenomena. One can only answer that Catholics have not left 'a trial of enigma'; quite simply, for them it is a miracle. Ultimately it was God, not the Virgin, who worked the miracle, and he is nothing if not inscrutable and alarming.

Some were certain that the apparitions were not divine. Freemasons from the lodge at Santarém with a group from Ourém cut down a holm-oak in the Cova (the wrong one) and destroyed a little wooden altar. There was a protest march through the streets of Santarém, with drums and 'blasphemous litanies', a flood of hostile pamphlets. 'Intensive and tenacious propaganda . . . will raise the mentality of our co-citizens to the realms of Truth, Reason and Science, convincing them that nothing can alter the Laws of Nature and that the pretended miracles are nothing but miserable tricks to abuse the credulity which is the child of ignorance,' says one. It goes on:

> Let us then liberate ourselves and cleanse our minds not only from foolish beliefs in such gross and laughable tricks as Fatima but more especially in any credence in the supernatural and in an alleged God omnipotent, omniscient and omni-everything, instrument of the subtle imagination of rogues who want to capture popular credulity for their purposes. Citizens! Long live the Republic! Down with Reaction! Long live Liberty!

The first chapel on the site was dynamited. Troops were stationed round the shrine but started saying the Rosary.

During October 1918 Francisco and Jacinta caught Spanish flu. The boy died next April, after much suffering. Jacinta followed in February 1920, having contracted tuberculosis. In her final agonized months the little girl was obsessed by the need to save people from damnation. 'So many go to hell. So many burn in hell.' The accounts of the last days in both their lives are genuinely harrowing but also show signs of what has traditionally been called holiness. ('The story of their *spiritualisation*, especially of the boy's, is for me almost proof positive of the authenticity of the apparitions' is Martindale's comment.)

In 1920 the new bishop of Leiria (who believed in the visions) arranged for Lucia to go to a convent school at Oporto. Five years later she entered a house of Dorotheans – a teaching order – at Tuy in Spain, just over the border from Portugal, where she took her final vows in 1934. Her real wish was to join the Carmelites, that strictest of enclosed orders, but she would not succeed in doing so until 1948. She still had much to tell the world.

Meanwhile pilgrims continued to come to the Cova in ever growing numbers, although the place was so remote that in those days the journey involved considerable hardship. A new chapel was built. Very occasionally the sun behaved strangely. The 'rain of flowers' seen by Lucia's sister was repeated on 13 May 1918 and again on 13 May 1924, and perhaps on one or two other days as well. It was not quite the same – a stream of light came out of the sun containing white petals (some described them as 'snow-flakes') which disappeared just above the heads of the pilgrims below.

In December 1925 the Lady came to Lucia on a cloud of light, carrying the Infant Jesus. Both told her to spread the devotion to the immaculate heart of Mary, so that the world would be made aware of her power as intercessor. The Infant appeared to her by himself in February 1926 and the Lady again in June 1929 – on this occasion she instructed Lucia to pray that Russia would be consecrated to the immaculate heart.

By then Fatima was well on the way to becoming a modern Compostella, and the national shrine of Portugal. It symbolized the reawakening of Portuguese Catholicism, after centuries of privileged torpor followed by a decade of persecution during which the Church was purified and gained new strength; from being the religion of the rich and unthinking, or the illiterate and superstitious, it was transformed into a faith for intellectuals. 'For years Our Lady of Fatima has touched the hearts of the Portuguese people, from the humblest to the most cultivated and, in particular it would seem, of the most cultivated,' wrote Antero de Figueirido nearer our own time. The Church recovered its position after the coup of 1926 and has never lost it, despite a brief return of anti-clericalism during the 1974 revolution.

In this new climate the chapel at the Cova grew more and more imposing, the number of pilgrims larger and larger. There were reports of miracles, of many cases of healing. Souvenir shops and guest houses sprang up. Fatima was starting to become a second Lourdes.

For seven years a committee of experts investigated what had happened at the Cova. Some witnesses contradicted certain minor details of Lucia's testimony, while she had obviously been wrong about the date when the Great War would end. However in October 1930 in a pastoral letter Mgr da Silva, Bishop of Leiria, declared the shepherd children's visions 'worthy of credence', and formally authorized the cult of Our Lady of Fatima.

In 1937 her old friend Bishop da Silva instructed Lucia to write a full account of her life and of the visions. She did so, revealing a good deal which had been unknown to Canon Formigão.

An angel had appeared to the children several times before the coming of the Lady. In 1915 Lucia had been herding sheep with some other girls – not with Jacinta or Francisco – when on a hill near the Cova called the Cabeço she had seen 'a figure poised in the air above the trees; it looked like a statue made of snow, rendered almost transparent by the rays of the sun'. Later she said it was like 'a person wrapped in a sheet', meaning that she could not see its features or its hand. She did not know what it signified, and suffered a good deal of teasing.

In the spring of 1916, while herding sheep with Jacinta and Francisco, she was playing with them on the Cabeço. A strong wind began to shake the trees. Looking up, they saw the figure she had seen the previous year, coming towards them above the olive trees. 'It was a young man, about fourteen or fifteen years old, whiter than snow, transparent as crystal when the sun shines through it, and of great beauty.'

'Don't be afraid,' he told them. 'I am the angel of peace. Pray with me.' Prostrating himself, head to the ground, he begged God's forgiveness for those who did not believe or hope, who did not adore or love God. He told the children to pray like this – Christ and the Virgin would listen to them.

In the summer of 1916 they were playing round a well at the bottom of a garden which belonged to Lucia's parents, when they saw the angel again. This time he told them he was Portugal's guardian angel. They must continue to pray, and make a sacrifice of everything they did, so that peace might come to their country. He also said, 'The most holy hearts of Jesus and Mary have designs of mercy on you.'

Later that year they had gone into a hollow in the rocks, to pray as they had been taught, foreheads touching the ground. Then an extraordinary light shone on them. It was the angel, who was holding a chalice with the Host suspended above it. He gave them communion; the Host to Lucia, the blood to Jacinta and Francisco (who had not yet made their first communions). 'Take and drink the body and blood of Jesus Christ, horribly insulted by ungrateful men,' he told them. 'Make reparation for their crimes and console your God.'

In a further memoir Lucia describes the angel as 'looking like a cloud in human form, whiter than snow and almost transparent'.

How can I believe all this? Yet perhaps I can, though I am not bound to do so by my Church. But even those who cannot credit the visions must be struck by the beauty of the scenes and of Lucia's imagery. It is surprising that they have not received more attention from painters – in the age of the Baroque they would have inspired countless artists.

In 1941–2, to borrow a phrase from Martindale, the veils lifted still further. Lucia wrote even more about what had taken place. Part was an account of a terrifying vision of hell given to the children during the apparition of 13 July 1917:

> We saw what looked like a sea of fire; immersed in this fire were demons, black or bronze, and souls like transparent embers, floating in the fire, driven by the flames which came out from them, amid clouds of smoke, falling in every direction like sparks in some great conflagration, without weight or equilibrium, among screams and lamentations of pain and despair. This horrified us, making us tremble with fear. Probably it was

> then that I cried that word 'Woe!' which people say they heard me utter. The demons varied in form, horrible, disgusting, unknown animals, transparent, like black incandescent coals.

She recalled how during the night of 25–26 January 1938, when the sky was lit by a magnificent display of the Northern lights (the *aurora borealis*) she expected a catastrophe to overwhelm the word. It was because of what the Lady had told her during the vision of July 1917:

> When you see a night illuminated by unknown light, know that this is the great sign given to you by God that he is about to punish the world for its grave sins, by war and famine and persecution of the Church and the Pope.

(Lucia writes of Jacinta having other visions on this theme – of the Pope being stoned, of 'roads, paths and fields filled by dead people covered in blood, of many people crying from hunger'.

The Lady had promised to avert punishment if Russia were consecrated to her immaculate heart, dedicated to her special protection. Otherwise, 'Russia will spread her errors all over the world, bringing wars and persecutions of the Church; many faithful will be martyred, the Pope will suffer deeply and some countries will be annihilated.' In 1939 Lucia had written to the bishop of Leiria, warning him war was imminent, that the sins of men would be washed in their own blood, and that nations who had tried to destroy God's kingdom would suffer most. She asked that the Pope and the bishops of the entire world should consecrate Russia on the same day. (She believes that had it been done, the war would not have broken out in 1939. She wrote directly to the Pope, Pius XII, in 1940, asking for the world's consecration 'with special mention of Russia'. On 31 October 1942 Pope Pius did so.

*

Lucia also wrote down the remainder of the secret told to her by the Lady in 1917, which has become known as 'The Third Secret'. It was placed in a sealed envelope and sent to Rome, with the stipulation that it must not be opened until 1950.

Meanwhile Rome and the pontiffs continued to venerate what had happened at Fatima. Pius XII consecrated the world to the Virgin, including 'all the peoples of Russia' on two more occasions. In 1953 the basilica at the Cova was completed. The annual pilgrimage to Fatima is now the most important event in the calendar for Portuguese Catholics.

As John XXIII was known to have a deep devotion to Our Lady of Fatima, it was a surprise – even a shock – when he read The Third Secret in 1960 and decided that it should not be revealed. There were persistent rumours in well-informed Vatican circles that the Pope had emerged white and shaking from the room where he read the Secret. Some suggested that it foretold general apostasy and the reign of Antichrist, as prophesied in the Apocalypse of St John. A less dramatic theory was that it advocated a more radical consecration of Russia, openly branding her Marxist enslavers as tools of Satan, and that this might have seriously hampered the Vatican's plans to establish diplomatic relations with the Soviet bloc. Another plausible guess is that Pope John was affronted by a prophecy that there would be a world-wide loss of faith, in part due to the bishops.

Lucia is still alive at the time of writing while, even more than Pope John, the present pontiff reveres Our Lady of Fatima. Yet Lucia's secret has not been revealed to the faithful. At the end of 1984 Cardinal Ratzinger, who admits that he has read it, told an Italian journalist 'To publish "The Third Secret" would mean exposing the Church to the danger of sensationalism, to its contents being exploited' – a mysterious answer.

Before visiting Fatima, I read *The Cult of the Virgin Mary: psychological origins* (1986) by Michael Carroll, a Canadian social scientist. It is an impressive work, the best of all the attempts (in my opinion hopeless) to find natural causes for the Marian apparitions, which he divides into hallucinations and illusions. 'That hallucinations and illusions often occur to nonpsychotic individuals is well established in the clinical literature,' he concedes.

He suggests, with a wealth of psychological and sociological argument, that Lucia suffered a hallucination; the Virgin of the Cova was really a projection of her beloved elder sister, Maria dos Anjos, a woman of twenty-two who had recently left their home – a 'mother surrogate' who dressed her for her First Communion and took her to grown-up dances. (He also suggests that at Medjugorje Ivanka, the first to see the *Gospa*, suffered a similar hallucination, a projection of her mother who had died two months before.)

Carroll makes no attempt to find a surrogate for the children's vision of hell, which was seen by all of them. Moreover, he resolutely ignores the solar phenomena, for which he does not even try to provide an explanation. Yet the miracle of the sun is an integral part of the Fatima visions, fulfilling a specific promise made by the Virgin.

Another book, which I came upon by accident, was an anthology of the writings of Hildegard of Bingen, a twelfth-century abbess from the Rhineland – the Sybil of the Rhine. Famed for her gifts as doctor, musician and poetess, she was also a mystic who wrote accounts of her visions which have been compared to those of Blake or Dante. What intrigued me was her use of solar imagery; many of her visions are described in terms of light or the sun.' 'Just as the flame contains three essences in one fire, so too there is one God in three persons . . . The flame consists of shining brightness, purple vigour and fiery glow. It has shining brightness so that it may give light; purple vigour so that it may flourish; and a fiery glow so that it may burn.' In the manuscript where this description occurs, there is a miniature of the Trinity as a single, threefold man standing within the sun.

*

There was a nightmare landing at Lisbon, the plane bouncing from one wheel to another. My fatalism was replaced by terror. But soon we were bowling along an unusually pretty motorway, bordered by palms and oleanders. Going north through olive groves, we passed the mountains of Torres Vedras on our left, bleak country compared to Cantabria; stony sierras like carcases with the flesh torn off. We drove up into wooded hills – I was surprised to see so many eucalyptus trees – till we reached Fatima in the Sierra d'Aire, 150 miles from the capital.

Fatima is what Medjugorje aspired to be before the Serbs came, a place of souvenir shops and hotels with such names as 'Verbo Divino', built of white concrete and orange tiling. My hotel was more comfortable than my usual lorry-drivers' shelter, though the drains stank. I had to share a room. It could have been worse as my companion was a fine old Pole, an engineer full of stories such as that of a friend who habitually crossed the Andes with his luggage in two plastic bags; I must have made an odd impression – he asked me if I was a Basque. I was lucky to find a bed at all, even one under the roof, since every hotel was crammed to the attics; enormous crowds were coming for the seventy-fifth anniversary. The foyer and the dining room were a babel of tongues; besides Portuguese I heard Spanish, French, Italian, German, Flemish, English (mostly American or Irish), Polish and what I think was Korean.

Exploring, I found a true pilgrims' town, of greed and shoddy *bondieuserie*, of shops staffed by harridans with cold eyes. Every effort was made to exploit the language gap; ordering white wine, I was brought a glass as a big as a goldfish-bowl. No prices were marked in the bookshops. Fat children begged in the cafés.

My hotel was opposite the Cova. The once lonely Cova da Iria where the children herded sheep had been tarmacked over and partly cobbled. it was dominated by a basilica in pastiche Baroque, flanked by semi-circular arcades. The *Blue Guide*, seemingly written by a Protestant, describes it as 'little less than an intolerable affront to the instinct of veneration'.

For me the basilica had surprisingly little atmosphere, apart from the pilgrims' devotion. I prayed before the graves of Francisco and Jacinta. (There is a gruesome photograph of Jacinta's body when it was exhumed in 1935, fifteen years after her death, and found to be largely incorrupt; it was still partly incorrupt when exhumed a second time in 1951.) I also prayed before the shrine of Our Lady of Fatima, making my petition.

A marble path a kilometre long led across the Cova to the smoked glass 'Chapel of the Apparition' (on the spot where the Virgin appeared) along which kneeling pilgrims edged their way painfully, their penance alleviated by knee-pads. Behind the basilica I found pleasant, slightly unkempt gardens with olive trees, pines, palms and oleanders – a relief after the vast, open expanse of the Cova which catches every ray of the sun. Nearby, troops were erecting tents for the poorer pilgrims.

I had to remind myself that commercialism and undistinguished architecture had nothing to do with whether or not the Virgin appeared and the sun danced in 1917. Unlike the girls of Garabandal, '*os três pastorinhos*' of Fatima have been accepted by the Church, and are as much part of Catholic piety as the Seven Sleepers of Ephesus during the Middle Ages – and with far more reason. For the shepherd children's story is not just a dim legend but a comparatively recent event, well attested; the visionaries were examined by experts who gave convincing endorsements. Above all, the crowd of 13 September 1917 bears witness to the solar miracle.

Admittedly, the danger from Russia and the visits by the angel were not revealed until years later. The warning about Russia came only when Catholics had learnt to fear Soviet ambitions; it would be much more convincing had it been delivered in 1917. The sole contemporary evidence for the angel is Lucia's mother recalling vaguely that in 1915 or 1916 her daughter had said something to her about seeing a form wrapped in a sheet which hid its face.

Critics suggest that in her convent Lucia gave her imagination free rein and dreamt up additions to the story which she had told in 1917. On the other hand, it can be argued that only when a nature adult was she able to see more deeply and understand fully what she had seen as an illiterate child.

We should not be surprised at peasant children using 'medieval' imagery to portray hell, imagery heard in many pulpits until quite recently. Nor would it be astonishing if their imagination contributed something. They had difficulty describing their visions; at most they possessed the vocabulary of their peasant homes, and to a lesser extent of the parish priest – which is why they saw the Virgin in the different 'forms' of the Lady of Mount Carmel, of Sorrows or of the Rosary. They did their best to rationalize what they had seen; one cannot blame them for being selective. They may have misunderstood a good deal, which would explain why Lucia took so long to recognize the threat from Russia.

Just as at Medjugorje, depression struck. I felt like an aged Hamlet, who had 'lost all my mirth'. I tried to comfort myself with the words of an Orthodox *staretz* long ago: 'Keep thy mind in hell but despair not.' No good. I tried to crawl into myself, imagining that I had built an inaccessible lair against gloom. That didn't work either. 'Evil sadness disturbs the soul, leads to disquiet and inordinate fear, breeds distaste for prayer, clouds the mind, undermines the judgement, resolution and courage, and saps our energy,' said Francis of Sales – with uncanny prescience in my case.

For more than a moment I contemplated the possibility of permanent disbelief and not just occasional doubts, of abandoning my faith altogether. At least it would solve the problem of the Bat. But then I realized that this despairing mood was largely induced by melancholia, even by indigestion. Moreover I knew that, however much I might try to be an agonostic, belief would come flooding back, and that even in the intervals without it I should be like some sort of spiritual *Flying Dutchman.*

Next morning I went to see a film on the apparitions. It was dubbed in English, the script containing such lines as 'The sun, rising in the direction of Ourém, transformed each spring into a festival of colour', while the Virgin spoke with a rich Irish brogue – no more incongruous, I suppose, than a plummy English accent. The sheep were shown running in slow motion, presumably to make them more graceful, while the child actors played a little too prettily. However, the film showed the green if stony landscape with its olive groves and holm-oaks, and its red-berried mastic trees.

It also provided some solid information. I learnt that the name Fatima had been given to the area by the Moors who had once inhabited the nearby town of Ourém, and who like many Moslems had a special affection for Fatima, the Prophet's daughter. Paul VI came here on 13 May 1967, the fiftieth anniversary of the first vision at the Cova. The apparitions were formally acknowledged during the Second Vatican Council, the first time in history that a private revelation has been recognized in this way by a council of the Church.

In addition the film recounted how at John Paul II's request the bullet which had nearly killed him in 1980 was set in the crown of the Virgin of Fatima's statue. A year after the assassination attempt, on 12–13 May he came to give thanks for his deliverance, praying at the tombs of Francisco and Jacinta, and concelebrating Mass with a thousand priests and bishops. He also consecrated the world, and in particular Russia, to the Mother of God as Lucia had asked – so that we might be saved from Communism. In 1984 the statue was carried in procession through St Peter's Square, after which John Paul celebrated a further Mass of consecration. (Some think that he has not fully responded to Lucia's request, that the Pope and *all* the bishops should consecrate the world on the same day, so that although Marxism has collapsed, the world is still threatened by other dangers.)

The film showed the eighty-five-year-old Sister Lucia – a tiny, dumpy nun with a strong, amiable, peasant face.

In the afternoon I went on the Stations of the Cross with my party, walking along a *via sacra* paved with white stone. It ran for nearly two kilometres, through country of the sort which the children must have known. The stations were marble carvings of Christ's Passion, vaguely reminiscent of Eric Gill though donated by Hungarians living in America. On that spring day the olive groves were full of mauve and pink rock-roses. The Loca do Cabeço is just off the path, a stony hillock with outcrops of white limestone, crowned by olive trees.

Aljustrel, where the children lived, is a cluster of hamlets not unlike Medjugorje or Hriushiw. The church is undistinguished save for a frieze of *azulejo* tiles round the interior, blue, brown and yellow. Superficially it remains much as it must have been in their time, with small gardens full of roses, lilac and marigolds. The house of Lucia's parents is still there, four tiny whitewashed rooms, one with a large open fireplace where they cooked. So is the house of Francisco and Jacinta 200 yards away, very similar and also with the date '1885' over the door; it has the little bed in which Francisco died.

Not far from the Cova there is a magnificent Byzantine chapel, built to represent the Russian nation and people for whom the Virgin told Lucia to pray in 1929. Consecrated in 1963, it is the only Eastern rite church in Portugal, indistinguishable from any

Orthodox place of worship beneath its onion-domed cupola. Metropolitan Nikodim, of what was then Leningrad, celebrated the Liturgy here in 1975. Two years earlier the 'Holy and Miraculous Icon of Kazan', which had disappeared from its shrine in the Kazan church at St Petersburg in 1929, was installed in a side chapel after many adventures. Another side chapel has a copy of Our Lady of Zarvanystya while a third contains a replica of the Black Virgin of Częstochowa.

The Bolsheviks did everything they could to destroy the memory of Our Lady of Kazan, who is the patron and protectress of Russia. Probably painted at Constantinople in the thirteenth century, it was found 'miraculously' at Kazan in 1579. Before the Revolution eleven icons of the Lady of Kazan were recognized by the Russian Church as 'wonder-working', the original being either that at St Petersburg or that at Moscow. The St Petersburg shrine was turned into a museum of atheism and the Moscow shrine destroyed to 'show that God does not exist and that the "protectress of Russia" cannot even protect her own church' – a urinal was built on the site in Red Square. (Today it is being rebuilt, after a ceremony in which Boris Yeltsin took part.)

In 1991 the Duke of Bragança – Dom Duarte, the man who should be King of Portugal – was officially invited to St Petersburg as the representative of Portugal. In a vast hall dominated by a copy of the icon, he witnessed the mayor return the keys of the cathedral to the Metropolitan. It was explained to the Duke that he had been asked instead of a cleric because of the sensitive relations between Orthodox and Catholics, while his hosts did not want to invite a politician.

It is widely believed that if the Pope is asked to visit Russia he will return the Virgin of Kazan. (When Pius XII consecrated the world to the Mother of God in 1942, he singled out 'that land where the icon of Our Lady lies hidden to await a better day'.)

*

I visited Mafra though it has no connection with Fatima or, so far as I know, with miracles. A monastery palace, a Portuguese Escorial, it dates from the early eighteenth century and is a vast, rather gloomy Baroque pile with a crumbling façade. Here, in the library, the twenty-year-old Dom Manuel spent his final hours in 1910 as the last 'Most Pious King of Portugal'. Its great church is adorned with rich if sober marbles – soft reds, blues, yellows and greys. What is best, however, are the scores of statues in white Carrara marble, of apostles and prophets, of saints and martyrs, with swirling draperies and windswept hair – St Teresa's ecstasy is particularly convincing.

I also found time to visit Lisbon where I was taken to the Jesuit church of São Roque, a Baroque jewel-box; one chapel has an altar of lapis lazuli edged with amethyst. What pleased me most was something less opulent, a monument to a Cornish recusant. It tells how 'Dom Francisco Tregian', persecuted for his religion by Queen Elizabeth of England, had taken refuge in the city, where he died eighteen years later. He was buried upright, perhaps in readiness to return to Cornwall when the Old Religion should be restored. I reflected sadly that today there is no refuge for those who lament the passing of the Old Religion, as there was in Tregian's day.

I saw also the royal tombs at Lisbon cathedral. Dom Manuel, the 'Unfortunate', has been brought home for burial here. He was one of Portugal's five Coburg kings, from the same family which reigns over Britain. Until the end of the monarchy Portuguese sovereigns were embalmed when they died. I was told that when in 1889 embalmers made the first cut to remove the entrails of the supposedly dead King Luis he sat up, screaming 'What agony!', then fell back, killed by the incision. He was Dom Manuel's grandfather and I wondered if they commiserate with each other in heaven.

I admit that it is not easy to believe in life after death. We are so insignificant. During the last fifty years we have learnt that our galaxy is only one of countless galaxies, magnifying the known universe beyond comprehension. As the psalmist asked God, 'What is man that thou art mindful of him?'

Yet there are other ways of contemplating mortality, of daring to hope that we may escape what Sir Thomas Browne calls 'the uncomfortable night of nothing', 'the Land of Moles and Pismires'. Like that saying of the soldiers that there are no atheists in fox-holes. 'One cannot see those ragged and putrid bundles of what once were men without thinking of what they were – their cheerfulness, their courage, their idealism, their love,' General Glubb wrote of the bodies hanging on the barbed wire during my father's war. 'Man is such a marvellous, incredible mixture of soul and nerves and intellect, of bravery, heroism and love – it *cannot* be that it all ends in a bundle of rags covered with flies. These parcels of matter seem to me to be proof of immortality. This cannot be the end of so much.'

However much the galaxies may multiply, even *ad infinitum*, it will not destroy my conviction that we continue – so long as I am able to believe in God. The psalmist answered his own question: 'Thou has made him a little less than the angels.'

Throughout 12 May pilgrims began to arrive in ever-increasing numbers, brought by coaches, lorries and cars, some of great antiquity; others came in carts or on foot, beneath a burning sky. Among them were countless old women in black, with knobbly brown faces and carrying bundles on their heads. Troops ran up still more tents but many pilgrims spread blankets on the ground, preparing for a night in the open and often sleeping like logs after their journey. At a more affluent level, the town was jammed by expensive motor cars. Thousands kept on arriving. There was a feeling of expectancy in the air.

It was very clear indeed that Fatima was a national shrine. The pilgrims came from every walk of life; the faces ranged from the rich and over-fed to the very poor and simple. The latter fascinated me. They had the qualities which, rightly or wrongly, I attribute to medieval pilgrims on 'the green way'; fervent piety and high spirits. This was a holiday as much as pilgrimage. They cooked salt cod over bonfires or grilled sardines over charcoal braziers, swapped bottles of wine, laughed and gossiped.

A surprising number of the men seemed to be wearing scapulars round their necks and under their shirts, small woollen envelopes about the size of a patience card which contain a prayer for the Virgin's protection; their wearers believe that she will make certain they do not go to hell. There were plenty of beggars. They included legless and armless cripples, bent old crones striking dramatic poses – presumably calculated to inspire pity – and a young man with a pathetic new-born baby in a tiny cardboard box. There were gypsies, one of them a very pretty girl with the most horrible goitre I have ever seen; they were pilgrims too. There must have been thieves as well, since I was warned to be on my guard against pickpockets. Yet everyone in sight seemed to be bursting with good nature.

When at about nine thirty p.m. I walked over to the Cova from my hotel I found an amazing spectacle, a vast sea of flickering light shining in the darkness. Over 100,000 men, women and children were there, holding long candles. It was an orderly crowd, with no police and apparently not even stewards to direct it. Fervent worshippers continued to crawl through it on their knees, along the 'path of penance', each bearing a lighted candle.

I was surprised to find the singing, amplified by well-placed loudspeakers, so pleasant – soothing rather than hypnotic – because these gentle people speak the harshest, least musical of Latin languages. Nor did the Fatima hymn have any of the Lourdes tune's banality, though the refrain was just the same – '*Ave, Ave, Maria*'. It was music to move a sceptic. So too was another hymn to the Virgin, '*Ave, O Theotokos, Ave, O Mater Dei*'. That one Greek word '*Theotokos*', Mother of God, appealed to all my Orthodox sympathies.

A procession passed through the candle-lit crowd, led by the flag of Portugal, followed by those of Spain, Italy, Ireland, Austria and the United States, together with many local or sacred flags. Then came the great red and white battle banner of the Order of Malta, escorted by a dozen black-robed knights – one with a face like an eagle. After these came several hundred priests in white, then fifty violet-capped bishops, then three red-capped cardinals (among them Sodano, the papal secretary of state), and then the Cardinal-Patriarch of Lisbon in gleaming gold vestments and carrying a massive crozier. Finally the statue of the Lady of Fatima went by, borne on a litter of white flowers – on her head was a crown like the royal crowns of Portugal.

A great concelebrated Mass began, on a platform in front of the basilica. I was too tired to stay till the end. However, from my bed I could hear singing throughout the night.

Next morning the singing continued unabated. There was another procession and another concelebrated Mass which lasted for two hours, much of it in Latin. It ended at midday with the singing of the *Salve Regina*. Then every woman in the crowd began to flutter a white handkerchief in farewell.

I suspect that the Third Secret of Fatima and the Dancing Sun are very closely linked. Some mariologists are convinced that the Secret is the Apocalypse. One, a Carmelite friar, is certain that evil will be let loose on a global scale against Christ and his Church. 'We are living when the forces of hell are being increasing unleashed', he says. 'Their forthcoming victory, their defeat and the coming of the reign of Christ must be the contents of the Third Secret.' As has been seen, Terelya believed it too.

The Virgin's prophecies of disaster have already come true in what was Yugoslavia. When I heard him at Tihaljin in 1990, Fr Jozo Zovko was only too justified in declaring, 'Fatima is coming true at Medjugorje' – though he may not have realized quite how much until the beginning of 1992. But the secrets of Medjugorje, closely intertwined with those of Fatima, are not restricted to Herzegovina. They concern the whole world.

Each time the sun dances at a shrine, it repeats the solar miracle at Fatima. I am sure that it is a manifestation of the Eternal God. 'Yet burns the sun on high behind the cloud . . . So waits the Lord behind the veil.' Every dance is a warning.

EPILOGUE

The Third Secret?

And there shall be signs in the sun and in the moon and in the stars; and upon the earth distress of nations . . .

The Gospel of St Luke

Fatima was my final pilgrimage. I could not visit every shrine; by now I knew that the sun had danced at over 300 – from Rwanda to Venezuela, from Georgia in the Caucasus to Louisiana. And I accepted that it really had done so. The most plausible natural explanation, auto-suggestion, simply did not stand up; if the sun danced continually at a few shrines, at most it did so only once – confounding the theory that pilgrims had seen it out of wishful thinking. So, what then did the dancing sun mean for the world? What did it mean for me? Had I tamed the Bat?

No one, believer or non-believer, would deny that the world faces problems of a type and on a scale which it has never met before. Civilization cannot reduce the increase in the world's population, while technology is creating more problems than it solves. If the apparitions are of divine origin, then do they announce the end of the world or merely a time of fire?

Regardless of whether one believes in apparitions or not, the problems are indisputable. Since I was born half a century ago the world's population has more than doubled, at the mildest estimate. Because of a gross disparity in standards of living, folk migrations have already begun, from Africa and Asia, from Eastern Europe and Latin America, into the rich and overfed West with its ageing peoples whose growth has been destroyed by birth control or abortion. Even if these migrations can be absorbed, absorption will be only a temporary solution. During the nineteenth century, and until quite recently, Dr Malthus was a figure of some derision for suggesting that population tends to increase to a point beyond which it is unable to feed itself; his ideas do not seem so laughable today when famine on a continental scale is far from inconceivable in the Third World.

Civilization has become too complicated. Natural resources are depleted at a terrifying rate while the environment is being damaged in such a way as to endanger man himself – most notably with the destruction of the ozone layer and the coming climatic changes. The economies of 'advanced' nations have grown so intertwined that the economic collapse of one might mean the collapse of all. They find it more and more difficult to help the Third World. Terrible weapons of war are available to any unprincipled ruler.

> Western civilization is weakened by an ever-increasing confusion of doctrines, customs, classes and peoples; by a species of intellectual and moral anarchy which has generally affected all groups in the community; by the widespread instability of every aspect of society; by a form of all-pervading fever which over-stimulates brains and energies, making men capable of intense endeavours which sadly turn out to be short lived and superficial; by the vulgarization of all spiritual activities and a debasing of the fruits of the earth.

These are the words of Guglielmo Ferrero in *Grandezza e decadenza di Roma*, writing in 1900 about the mortal sickness and death of the Roman Empire. Some might apply them to the modern West, where decay is mistaken for progress.

Even the finest minds have no perception of what will happen in the comparatively near future. Sir Isaiah Berlin, for example, wrote of Marxism in 1939 that it 'remains the most powerful among the intellectual forces which are today *permanently* [italics mine] transforming the ways in which men think and act'. But the dialectic and Messianic Socialism died in 1989. By contrast, to the astonishment of intellectuals, Messianic Christianity is very much alive as we approach the second millennium.

Communism has been overthrown and the Soviet Empire no longer threatens us. At first most people believed that the world would be a better place. Now it looks as though the reverse is true. The message from the Marian shrines is that catastrophe may well overwhelm us. In some of the Gospels' most frightening passages Jesus told the disciples that when they see signs in the sun and moon, with the sea and the waves roaring, and men's hearts failing them for fear, they will see the Son of Man coming on a cloud, for it will be the Last Day.

In *The Lord of the World* that forgotten Edwardian novelist, Robert Hugh Benson, imagines the Apocalypse. He describes how the President of Europe is worshipped as God in London, after the Cardinal-Archbishop of Westminster has been hanged in his own cathedral, and after Rome and the Vatican have been bombed into oblivion. Portraying the Second Coming, Benson pictures solar phenomena which have a startling resemblance to those at modern Marian shrines, though he wrote a good ten years before Fatima:

> Above the hills twenty miles away rested an enormous vault of colour; here there were no graduations from zenith to horizon; all was the one deep crimson smoulder as of the glow of iron. It was such a colour as men have seen at sunsets after rain, while the clouds, more translucent each instant, transmit the glory they cannot contain. Here too was the sun, pale as the Host . . .

No doubt this is a novel which will be in demand again before the end of the present decade.

Like Josyp Terelya, many Christians – Protestant as well as Catholic and Orthodox – may expect the Second Coming to coincide with the second millennium. (Although they will disagree over the exact date, since Christ was born about five years earlier than is generally realized.) For those like myself who do not believe in numerology or astrology, '2000 AD' is a date without significance, no different from any other year. Even so, the message coming from the shrines is clear enough – that the world faces some sort of disaster in the fairly near future because man has turned away from God.

At least one pope predicted the Apocalypse and it did not happen. During the last decade of the sixth century, when Italy was being devastated by Lombard invaders, Gregory the Great announced that it was near, in his first sermon at St Peter's:

> Our Lord forewarns us that nation shall prevail against nation, and kingdom against kingdom, and that earthquakes, famine and pestilence, horrors and signs from heaven are in store for us. We have already been visited by some of these disasters, and of others remain in dread. For that nation rises against nation and subdues the land by fear, our own experience, more forcibly than even Gospel history, might have taught us. We have heard from other quarters that countless cities are destroyed by earthquakes, while we ourselves suffer incessantly from pestilence. True, we do not yet perceive signs in the sun, moon or stars, but changes in the atmosphere lead us to suppose that such signs are at hand . . . The world grows old and hoary, and through a sea of troubles hastens to approaching death.

The world did not die. But in Pope Gregory's time it was underpopulated, while technology had collapsed with the Roman Empire. We, on the other hand, *have* perceived 'signs in the sun'.

*

If one accepts that the sun has danced to proclaim the presence of the Mother of God, and if one compares the messages from the Marian shrines, then it is difficult to avoid the conclusion that Medjugorje must be a continuation of Fatima – that the secrets communicated by the *Gospa* to the visionaries in Herzegovina confirm and develop the Third Secret. Indeed, in August 1991 the *Gospa* was reported to have told one of the Medjugorje seers that with their help she hoped that what she had begun in the Fatima secrets would be fulfilled.

Just as the Vatican declines to disclose the Third Secret, so the Franciscans play down the more sensational aspects of what the *Gospa* has revealed. Yet a good deal can be guessed. The first of the ten secrets is thought to concern Medjugorje's development as a shrine; the second that Medjugorje is the last place where the Virgin will appear on earth (which is why she has gone on appearing here for so long); while the third is a prophecy of Satan leading his army to the very gates of the shrine and then being repulsed – as happened in 1992. Others concern the 'permanent, beautiful and indestructible sign from heaven' on the hillside, together with the future of the shrine and its visionaries – leaving five secrets which are believed to be apocalyptic.

It is far from inconceivable that these last five secrets of Medjugorje, together with the Third Secret of Fatima, concern specific events foretold in the Gospel of St Luke and the Book of Revelation – namely, that the Church will triumph, Satan will be vanquished, and Christ will come in glory. Sister Lucia is reported to have said that the contents of the Third Secret are contained in the Gospel and in chapters 8–13 of the Book of Revelation.

Luke, traditionally writing about AD 57, is the evangelist who warns Christians of the days of vengeance, of signs in the sun and moon, of distress of nations. Men will wither away for fear, in expectation of what will happen to the world. Then they shall see the Son of Man coming in a cloud, with great power and majesty.

The Book of Revelation, or Apocalypse, was written by St John the Divine on the island of Patmos about AD 97. This tells how the future of the world is written in a book with seven seals, which the Lamb – the crucified and risen Christ – will open in succession, each opening bringing a plague upon mankind; when the seventh seal is opened, seven angels will blow trumpet-blasts, one after another, every blast announcing fresh misery and the seventh blast sounding the Last Judgement. The plagues unleashed by the opening of the earlier seals are frightful enough, with sword, famine and death, with earthquakes. There will be solar phenomena, the sun becoming 'black as sackcloth of hair', the moon 'as blood'. When the seventh seal is opened, 'there followed hail and fire, mingled with blood: and it was cast on the earth. And the third part of the earth was burnt up; and all green grass was burnt up ... in those days, men shall seek death and shall not find it. And they shall desire to die, and death shall fly from them.' A great sign will be seen in heaven, 'A woman clothed with the sun, and the moon under her feet, and on her head a crown of twelve stars.' There will be a final confrontation between the forces of good and evil at Armageddon. (Megiddo, a hill which guards a pass through the Carmel Range.) Then the end of the world shall come and with it the Last Judgement.

Many, including no doubt many Christians, dismiss not only the Book of Revelations, with its terrifying visions and catalogue of fantastic beasts, but the warnings in St Luke too, as ravings which only a 'medieval' mind could credit. Nevertheless, they are an integral part of traditional Christian belief. The survivors of Hiroshima and Nagasaki, of Chernobyl, find all too much that is plausible in them.

Meanwhile, religion is increasingly assumed to have no objective reality. Unbelievers are rewriting history; a recent life of Thomas More refused to credit that he was a Christian; a much praised novel about the life of Elgar denied that he could have been a Catholic when he wrote *The Dream of Gerontius*. 'Wherever we look, in all areas of social and personal life, the hold of the past is weakening,' says Sir John Plumb in *The Death of the Past.* 'Rituals, myths, the need for personal roots in time, are so much less strong than they were a mere hundred or even fifty years ago . . . Of course there are areas of resistance, but they are islands of conviction in a surging sea of doubt.' In his view the Christian past has collapsed, and he advises us to clear away the litter.

And yet Marxism, until recently so respectable among the academics, has been consigned to the rubbish bin, while science is increasingly perceived as being unable to explain the mystery of creation, let alone the meaning of our existence.

More than once Cardinal Newman quoted a prophecy by an eighteenth-century Anglican divine, Samuel Horsley:

> The Church of God on earth will be greatly reduced, as we may well imagine, in its present numbers, in the time of Antichrist, by the open desertion of the powers of the world. This desertion will begin in a professed indifference to any particular form of Christianity, under the form of universal toleration . . . from toleration of the most pestilential heresies, they will proceed to the toleration of Mahometanism and Atheism, and at last to positive persecution of the truth of Christianity.

Horsley was reacting against the French Revolution but there is little need to question his analysis; in some London schools religious education now puts Satanism on an equal footing with Christianity. However, Newman anticipated something even more deadly than persecution or Satanism – indifference, the 'general apostasy' which has now taken place.

Everywhere in the West church-going is on the decline. Fewer and fewer hear the call to be priests, or to become monks or nuns. Countless intellectuals and artists have left the Church. (In England they include a former Master of Balliol, once a priest, who 'thought his way out' of belief.) Religious art is dying all over Catholic Europe, which in its time gave birth to the Romanesque, the Gothic and the Baroque. 'But yet the Son of Man, when he cometh, shall he find, think you, faith on earth?'

A fair number of theologians and biblical scholars, especially those who are conservative Catholics or evangelical Anglicans, consider that all the scriptural preconditions now exist for the End Times. It is even rumoured that the Pope thinks so too, and this was why he launched the 'decade of evangelization' in 1990 – that the Gospel might be preached to all nations. Whether or not we shall have to go up to Armageddon, it is clear enough that mankind will undergo torment in the not too distant future. The countries of the former Soviet Union face calamities in abundance, as do those of the Middle East. Already the Balkans are in hideous turmoil. Undeniably, the world has every appearance of growing old and hoary.

While the apparitions of the Virgin have been closely studied by mariologists, very little attempt has been made to explain the solar phenomena, perhaps because they so obviously belong to the paranormal. Some observers at Medjugorje have suggested that the dancing sun may represent the *Gospa* hovering over the world, encased in light reflected by her Son, or that it is the Eucharist in glory. However, even among those who are convinced of the phenomena's divine origin, there is no general agreement on their meaning.

No logical explanation has been found. Is there one within that odd science known as illogical mathematics? G. K. Chesterton laughed that

> There is a place apart
> Beyond the solar ray
> Where parallel lines meet in an unofficial way.

In nineteenth-century Russia a very great mathematician indeed, Nikolai Lobachevsky, argued in all seriousness that two parallel lines may merge and none the less stay parallel. 'Yes, quite conceivable,' a Cambridge wrangler commented, when I asked him for his opinion. 'Like a trumpet.' So, is it possible for the sun to dance while remaining in its place?

I shall never know the answer, not in this world at any rate. As I have said before, I was strongly inclined to believe that – like the apparitions of the Virgin – the solar phenomena were hallucinations, though hallucinations of divine origin. A Catholic friend bluntly dismissed my attitude as 'playing safe', but I could come up with nothing better; I had to agree with Martindale that the sun would not have left its place without disrupting the solar system and destroying the planet earth. Then another friend, someone who had seen the sun dance, asked me an unanswerable question: 'How could over a million pilgrims have gazed into the sun at Medjugorje for fifteen minutes at a time without having burnt out their optic nerves, unless there had been interference with the laws of nature?'

I am convinced, from what I have read and from what I have heard, that somehow the sun did dance and that somehow it still does. I do not expect to see it do so myself; why, I don't know and can't explain – perhaps it is because I am insufficiently spiritual – but that makes no difference. At least I can imagine it when 'Christ's blood streams in the firmament' at sunrise or at sunset. I believe that the Marian shrines are intended to reassure traditionalist Catholics like myself, just as much as they are meant to inspire 'charismatics'. If a dancing sun warns of catastrophes which may or may not be averted, it can also confirm wavering believers in their faith. Those who have seen the dancing sun at last understand that their religion does not need 'relevance'.

Regardless of whether one sees the sun dance or not, the shrines heal, both physically and spiritually. I think that after my pilgrimages I began to find it easier to accept the changes in my religion. Altered emphases within Catholicism are nothing new.

(Especially social emphases; in the 1820s the Archbishop of Paris, Count de Quélen, would tell Charles X's court that not only did Our Lord descend from a very good family on his mother's side but there was reason to think he was rightful Prince of Judah; nowadays we hear a great deal about 'Christ the Worker'.) No doubt modern Catholicism may look a very different religion from the one I learnt at Ampleforth forty years ago, yet I know that underneath it is just the same. I also realize that to be a conservative who is not wholly in tune with the prevailing spirit of the age does not necessarily mean being out of tune with God.

Whatever the stern witness at Turzovka may say, I do need a crutch for my lame religion. My conviction that the sun really has danced is a wonderful support in the struggle to keep it. Although I could never feel at home with the new rites, I can at least tolerate them, while there are a few rare oases where one may still hear the Mass celebrated with beauty. I see also that my conservatism has been a peg on which to hang far deeper and more fundamental doubts (neatly arranged by the Devil), but I see too that a faith which does not question can only be a dead faith. And if the dancing sun means what I think it does, then I am going to need all the faith I can muster.

Somehow, like Pascal, I remain sceptical about scepticism. Once more, like Newman, I even start to find the probabilities adding up to certitude again – almost. I shall always have doubts, but that is part of the Cross. So I begin to hope that my unhappiness with the new ways need not trouble my faith or my membership of the Church. Anyone, everyone, troubled by a Bat, should go to a Marian shrine such as Medjugorje and pray for reassurance to the Mother of God.

I remain profoundly grateful for that education for death by the monks on the moors so long ago. Although not a man of sombre temperament, I cannot help ending on a gloomy note. I am quite certain that the dancing sun really does mean global disaster, a warning which will surely be confirmed by the Third Secret.